Steppes of• Faith

Discovering God's Goodness in Ukraine

Janice Lemke

Purpose Press

ISBN: 978-0-9845949-2-4
Library of Congress Number: 2010908227

Printed in the United States of America.

Dedication

Cory, I appreciate our friendship.
Thanks for all the walks and for sharing your life with me.

Janelle and Alicia, you have added joy to the journey.
I am glad we are family.

I value our friends and co-workers in Ukraine.
Their stories and commitment have inspired me.

I appreciate all who prayed and supported the ministry in Ukraine.
Their partnership has made a difference.

Most of all, thanks to our Lord,
the Author and Perfecter of our faith.

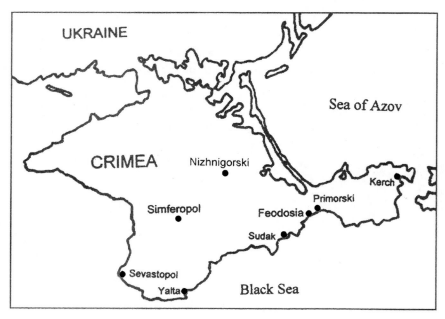

Ukraine and Crimea

Contents

Acknowledgments

I appreciate the help of others in making this book possible.

Thanks to Gail Heffron for the cover picture. More of her art can be viewed at: www.artistgailheffron.com

Thanks to my family for their patience and support while I was distracted.

Thanks to Joyelle Schwarz, Kathy Harless, and Betty Coleman at CMF for their valuable assistance with the book.

Thanks to Angie Bartel for her technical assistance.

I appreciate all who read and commented on this manuscript. Awards for finding mistakes go to: Barbara Loser, Linda Hartwig, Pauline Conrad, and Britta Minkler.

The grand prize goes to Denise Nash, who found bloopers such as: "Even with stretch plants under my long skirt, several layers on top, a heavy coat, boots, and hat, I still got chilled." She wanted to know, "Poison oak? Sweet potato vines? What kind of stretch plants were you growing?"

Observant readers are invited to submit any errors they spot to purposepress@gmail.com in order to improve future editions of this book.

Preface

We live in an age of uncertainty. Many people fear economic collapse and political disaster.

In Ukraine, I lived among people who experienced war, famine, social upheaval, and persecution. We tasted a little turmoil ourselves. Their testimonies and our own experience with God's faithfulness bolster my trust in God's ability to provide, whatever the future might hold.

Even though this story took place in Ukraine, I sometimes refer to the local people as Russians. We lived in a part of Ukraine where most people spoke Russian and identified themselves as Russians.

I changed the names of the local people to reduce possible risk to them and to reduce confusion for the reader, as many of the characters have the same first name.

Most conversations took place in Russian. While trying to preserve accuracy in content, quotes are paraphrased for readability.

I added approximate dates to chapter titles to help readers who want some sense of the timeline.

Space would not permit me to write about all the teams and visitors who served in some way, but we are still grateful for their contribution.

Some readers from Ukraine felt offended by references in my first book, *Five Loaves and Two Bowls of Borscht*, to conditions I found difficult. My goal was and is to show how God helped us. If all were pleasant or easy, we would not need God's help. Russian and Ukrainian immigrants to the West find other things difficult, but God is still sufficient to meet all needs.

"The Lord will give strength to His people; The Lord will bless His people with peace" (Psalm 29:11).

Janice Lemke

1

God Is Never Dull

July 2000

"How do you feel about going back to Ukraine?" our host asked, passing the barbecued chicken to my husband, Cory. Though we expected to leave in less than a month, the final stress of packing had not yet hit. We felt relaxed enough for a backyard barbecue with friends in Oregon.

Cory took some chicken. "Working in Ukraine is the hardest thing I've ever done," he began.

I could agree with that. Before I ever set foot on Ukrainian soil, some people had warned me, "Life in Ukraine is hard on women." I shrugged off their words, thinking those other women must be wimps. I had grown up on a farm. I liked adventure and liked camping. When still single, I had done mission work in Kenya. I looked forward to the next challenge and went with confidence when we moved in 1995 to Crimea, the southernmost part of Ukraine.

As it turned out, life in Ukraine was much harder than I had expected. Unlike my experience in Kenya, where I was single and could get by with English, I now had two toddlers and a language barrier. We landed in the middle of the economic, social, and political upheaval of *perestroika* not long after the Soviet Union fell apart. We endured regular outages of power and water, and had little or no heat in the winter. I hated the dirt and sense of isolation. We lived in a busy part of town and desperate passersby used the entrance to our apartment building as a toilet. I developed back problems packing food from the market, washing clothes in a tub, and sleeping in a bad bed.

Cory felt uncomfortable hearing stories of mafia crime. A man is supposed to protect his family, but much felt out of his control. When he left the apartment, he often noticed he was being followed. Officials treated him harshly, like an unwelcome character. We heard that our phone calls were recorded. Our ministry plan was not working out so well either.

We had come as part of the package when an American church set up a partnership with a congregation in Feodosia. We liked the idea of helping the existing church instead of trying to start an American version. After all, God was already working in the country before we got there. Instead of starting from scratch, we could tap into the existing network of relationships and help the church become more effective in their outreach.

In the beginning, Cory helped carry bricks and mortar for church construction. The physical labor gave him a way to build relationships while learning the language and culture. He hoped to eventually train leaders for evangelism and church planting. He began to realize, however, the pastor we came to help did not share our broader goals and seemed threatened by our presence.

We never expected immediate results, but this was like banging our heads against a wall; putting out much effort and feeling great discomfort without any benefit. Growing up in the United States, I had often heard, "If you follow God, He will bless you." I can't say I went into missions for what I could get out of it, but it felt as though God was not holding up His side of the bargain.

I looked forward to the end of our four-year term so we could leave without losing face—leave and never look back. Missionaries go as change agents, but not everyone welcomes change. Furthermore, our goals seemed lofty and unrealistic. We could not even keep the bathroom sink attached to the wall.

We were too proud to quit early and tell people we could not handle it, but I figured if we made it through four years we would not have to apologize to anyone—not to our supporters nor mission agency, not even to God. It seemed a little un-Christian to leave God out of the decision entirely, so I changed it to: *If God gives me the desire to come back, I will consider it.* I thought that was safe enough since I could not imagine ever wanting to return.

We had lived in Ukraine about two-and-a-half years when I visited an old friend in Kiev. I complained freely and concluded, "I am able to live here, but I don't like living here."

"Is there something else you believe God is calling you to do?" she asked.

"No, I just want a nicer house and an easier lifestyle. It's hard being so far from my family, especially with children who grow up quickly without getting to see grandparents and cousins."

"Does Cory like it here?"

"No. It's hard for him too."

"On the one hand," she said, "I know God is a Shepherd who takes care of His sheep. But I don't think you can make a decision based on whether or not something is hard. God sometimes asks us to do difficult things. He knows how much you can handle, and He can make up for the difference."

I went home and read Galatians 6:9: "Let us not become weary in doing good, for at the proper time we will reap a harvest if we do not give up." Those who give up too soon miss out on seeing the results of their labor.

Moses, the Apostle Paul, Jesus, and others did not persevere because it was "fun," but because they had a task to fulfill. The effects of sin around us made us uncomfortable, but if everyone already possessed the qualities I valued—integrity, kindness, and hope—our presence as missionaries would not be necessary.

My reluctance slowly changed to renewed trust in God's ability to provide. As a child I had sung "Jesus Loves Me," but as an adult, I had to trust that love in the hard places. I had felt called to missions in my early twenties, but that early commitment to Him would not carry me through new challenges unless I leaned on His commitment to me.

When I stopped fighting with God and fearing the future, life in Ukraine became more enjoyable. Our water continued to go off for half the day and the entry to our apartment building still smelled like an outhouse, but I stopped looking for things to justify my discontent. God does bless those who follow Him, but His definition of blessing is sometimes different than mine.

In spite of a rough beginning, ministry opportunities improved. The time Cory spent carrying bricks and attending every single church service resulted in relationships with men who shared his goals. Cory joined forces with them and several pastors; together they started a leadership training program.

Eleven men from five churches in Eastern Crimea joined the Training Center's first two-year course. Every other week they came for five days of teaching. During their week at home, they shared the Gospel in villages lacking a church and started groups attended by those wanting to know more about Christ. The second year the church planters came less often for training, but the leaders visited them on-site.

Without giving all this background, Cory took another bite of chicken and continued, "Even though it was hard, I can't think of anything else I'd rather do than to be involved in leadership development and church planting. The Training Center is meeting a need, and we are seeing fruit. We went to Ukraine planning to help the Feodosia church, but it didn't work out there. God had bigger plans than we did. We are working in a broader area now than we ever expected."

As Cory talked, the wife kept glancing at me. She finally asked, "What about you, Janice? I know it hasn't been easy for you in Ukraine."

"Life was harder there than we expected," I said, "but God used us in ways we never imagined. The hardships helped us understand how small we are, so when we saw results, we couldn't take the credit. All we can say is 'Look what God did.' He was strong in our weakness."

"How do you feel about going back?"

"I'm ready to go, at least I will be when I get packed," I replied. "But, I feel like I'm in the middle of a novel. I wonder what will happen in the next chapter, except I'm a character in the story. What will the author do with me now?"

That night, I dreamed of a horse harnessed to some contraption that kept the animal walking in circles. I thought the horse might like to run, so I unhooked it and hopped on bareback. While growing up on our family farm, I always rode bareback. I loved the feeling of intense power under my bare calves when the horse ran. Before climbing on, I'd roll up my pant legs so I could grip the sweaty sides better and feel an exhilarating sense of oneness with the horse. The steed in my dream was faster, more powerful, and more uncontrollable than any I had ever ridden. All I could do was hang on for the ride. Then I woke up.

I lay in bed thinking, *It is safer to try to keep God hooked up to our merry-go-round and quite another thing to hop on for a ride out of our control.*

In C. S. Lewis' novel, *The Lion, the Witch and the Wardrobe*, Lucy hears about Aslan, the awe-inspiring lion ruler, and asks, "Is he safe?" Mr. Beaver answers, "He's the king. 'Course he isn't safe. But he's good."

Some people think God is boring and look to other things for excitement. When I follow God on His terms instead of my own, God is never dull. I just need to get beyond the terror of "What did I get myself into?" and enjoy the exhilarating ride and oneness with the One who carries me.

Where would the ride take us next? We did not know what lay ahead, but hearing about continued progress helped us look forward to going back. Andre, the Training Center director, wrote that all eleven men who went through the first two-year program had started at least one group.

He described how the Training Center leaders met to evaluate strengths and weaknesses of the program and discuss how to improve it. They realized the evangelists who struggled most had weak ties to established churches. For better results, they hoped congregations would take more ownership of the church-planting vision. They also hoped churches in other parts of Crimea would participate, not just those in Eastern Crimea.

Since Andre belonged to the leadership council for the Evangelical Christian Baptist Union (ECB), he got a speaking slot the next time Crimean pastors gathered. He told these men, "The Lord gave us the command to tell everyone about Christ. You put people in charge of children's work, women's ministry, and helping the poor. According to Scripture, the church needs to concern itself with evangelism." He encouraged them to choose someone to be in charge of outreach and described our training program as a way to equip them. He believed the best way for people to know Christ was to plant new churches—one for every village of Crimea.

During the Soviet period, authorities tried to wipe out Christianity. Even now, after ten years of religious freedom, most towns and villages still had no church of any kind. The ECB Union was the strongest evangelical denomination in Ukraine. Nevertheless, the Crimean peninsula, with 1200 towns and villages and 3.5 million people, had just 40 ECB churches.

Not everyone agreed with Andre. Some said too many new groups would dilute the purity of the existing church. Andre replied, "If the church wants to live, it needs to grow. It is a principle of life. If something does not grow, it begins to die. The Apostle Paul said he would rather perish for the sake of his countrymen, so they may be saved. Do we have the same attitude toward our countrymen?"

Others said they felt stretched already, and there was no need for so many churches. Andre told them, "We feel intimidated by the goal because we look at the obstacles and our weak resources, but our own resources are just the tip of the iceberg. We need to look at what we have available to us in Christ, the one who gave us the command to tell everyone everywhere. He promised to be with us. We have more than the original eleven disciples. They did not sit down and analyze; they simply obeyed and trusted God and saw the victory."

At the next meeting, Andre asked the pastors to cite obstacles to church planting, reasons they had not been involved. They mentioned barriers such as: they did not see it was important, did not think it was scriptural, lacked personnel, lacked funds, lacked concern for the lost. At subsequent meetings Andre and other Training Center leaders used this list when choosing topics for teaching.

Many pastors agreed with the goal and sent men for training. Thirty-five came. Not knowing who was gifted and motivated for church planting, Training Center leaders decided to take these men through a three-month evangelism course first.

The course began in February. They met four days every other week, covering key points of Scripture and practical tips for evangelism. By the end of three months, twenty-five proved they were serious and were working to start cell-groups. They got the blessing and prayer support of their home church, as well as some financial support, typically the cost of transportation. Five more men would sit in on the lectures but not receive a stipend.

In May these thirty men began their two-year training as church planters. Much had happened during our nine-month absence, and Cory looked forward to meeting the new trainees. I looked forward to getting settled after months of travel. Our daughters, Janelle, now eight years old, and Alicia, almost seven, looked forward to seeing their friends.

As we prepared to depart in July, June Johnson, our nurse teammate in Feodosia, wrote, "Crimea is running on 30% electricity. The electricity goes off at 6:00 or 7:00 a.m. It comes on for a couple hours in the afternoon and goes off again in the evening from 6:00 until 11:00 p.m. From what everyone says, this pattern isn't going to change. I don't mean to depress you, just prepare you. It's a bit frustrating to try and get stuff done."

The Lemke family during our first term in Ukraine.

2

The Land of Miracles

Flying over the Atlantic, I watched *The Tigger Movie* with Janelle and Alicia and found it oddly moving. Winnie the Pooh's friend, Tigger, realizes he is different from the other animals and wants to find his family. He thinks they will be just like him. In the end he discovers the odd bunch around him *is* his family. Though different, each one loves him. I blinked back tears. We may have left blood relatives behind, but another family waited our arrival.

Stefan welcomed us warmly at the airport before grabbing our luggage cart and wheeling it out. He was like a guardian angel to us, our go-between with government officials, and knew just what to do if something needed to be fixed. He hoisted our suitcases onto the train, rented our bedding, and helped make the bunk beds in our compartment. We soon fell asleep as the train clattered south over the flat steppe of Ukraine.

Andre, the Training Center director, met us at the train station. Driving to Feodosia, he said, "My family and I pray for you every day, morning and evening." His words brought tears to my eyes. As Jesus promised, when you leave family for the sake of the Kingdom, He gives more fathers, mothers, brothers, and sisters. Sure, they spoke a different language, but they showed commitment to us.

June and Stefan had searched long and hard to find us a new apartment. As we climbed the stairs to the third-floor, I saw the graffiti and peeling paint but decided not to judge the book by its cover. Stefan unlocked a metal security door, then a second door, and we stepped into our new home. Right away it looked so much better than our first apartment.

"The entry is bigger!" I exclaimed. We could easily set down all of our luggage in the foyer. From this small room, doors led to the bathroom, two bedrooms, the living room, and the kitchen. I wanted to see the most important room first, the kitchen. It was big enough for a little table! I would not have to carry all our meals to the living room—and this kitchen came with cupboards and cabinets, unlike our first rental.

I turned on the faucet. Water blasted out instead of a faint dribble. We could get a water heater and a washing machine. We had gone without both during our first four years. In the beginning they were not available, but our electric wiring and water pressure could not have handled them anyway. I opened the refrigerator; June had already stocked it with basic food items. What an angel! What a wonderful welcome!

When expecting June's arrival during our third year in Ukraine, we arranged for her to stay with an older woman. Our task had been easy compared to the hours she had spent seeking for and then cleaning this apartment. She bug-bombed for cockroaches, installed screens on the windows, and got our furniture moved. She had some help, but went the extra mile to leave a bouquet of flowers on the table.

"Christopher's here!" Janelle exclaimed from the living room. She greeted our parakeet, and he chattered back.

Stefan informed us, "You don't have a telephone yet, but I will work on getting a connection for you." He headed for the door. "I'll let you rest and unpack. The owner of the apartment, Galina, is coming tomorrow morning at 10:00. I'll come back then."

Janelle and Alicia exclaimed as they pulled treasures from their cardboard toy box, excited to see these old friends. "Here's my rabbit, Peter," said Janelle, "and my wooden dog!"

Alicia pulled out a white cat with matted fur. "Here's Mary!"

Two mattresses lay on the floor of their room. "If we get a bookcase and dresser," I noted, "I don't think we can fit two beds in here."

"We can probably find a bunk bed or get one made," Cory said.

We needed a bed for us too. During our first term, we slept on a fold-out couch, the only double-wide bed we could find. I think it contributed to my back problems, so we brought an airbed with us this time. Cory worked to assemble it, but I was ready for a walk and wanted to explore the neighborhood.

Our five-story apartment building stretched for a whole city block. The apartment entrances lay around back on the quiet side, but stores took up the first floor, facing the street. I checked a furniture store but saw no bunk beds or bed frames. The next store sold fabric and dishes. At the end of the building and across the street, I found the open-air market.

"Close to a market" had topped my list of priorities for a new apartment, and we lived just five minutes away. Under a high canopy, vendors stood behind long concrete tables tending to customers and guarding produce. Women waved leafy twigs over fresh fish to keep flies away. Shoppers chose from colorful piles of tomatoes, potatoes, cucumbers, cabbages, and carrots along with the fruits of July: apricots, peaches, melons, plums, and raspberries.

Next, I wandered through the maze of booths, each with its own specialty: cleaning products, clothing, cookies. Those selling flour, sugar, and rice weighed out the desired amount from large gunnysacks. I stepped briefly into the meat building where chunks of pork and beef hung and other portions lay on the counter.

When our landlady came the next day, she gave us permission to make improvements and assured us, "You can live here as long as you want." We could not have hoped for a better arrangement. With Feodosia located on the Black Sea, many apartment owners wanted the much higher rates of the summer tourist season over a lower year-round rent.

Before we returned to Ukraine, Cory had said, "I'd like to spend the first few weeks not doing much, just take time to get settled." When we arrived, however, Andre invited him to go car shopping west of Kiev. Andre sought a van and wanted to go that week, before the next Training Center seminar. The drive would take about fourteen hours one way, on 600 miles of bad roads. Nevertheless, Cory needed a car and good imported vehicles were more common in Western Ukraine, closer to the border.

Cory returned home three days later with a Volkswagen Passat. He looked tired but satisfied. "We got a good deal," he said.

Andre tried for two days to get the car registered without success. Cory explained to me, "The number on the engine does not match the number on the body, and that's a problem. They won't register it." The car apparently had a new engine, which meant it probably came through customs on a bribe.

Cory continued, "We have two options. We can sue the government for letting the car in the country, which is what many people are doing. Or else we can take the car back to Western Ukraine and try to get our money back. Andre thinks we have a better chance of success with the latter option."

"That's a long way to go," I said. He still looked tired from the first trip.

"We can't keep the car and drive it without registration. They could confiscate it, and then we would have nothing."

"Do you really think they will give you your money back?"

"All we can do is try. I call Ukraine 'the Wild East,' but Andre calls it 'the Land of Miracles.' He says, 'That's because anything can happen—good or bad.'" We hoped our "anything" would be good.

Before his next trip, Cory got a plumber to install our water heater and put in extra pipes near the kitchen sink for our washing machine. Those two appliances made my life so much easier! I no longer had to heat water on the stove. The washing machine washed, rinsed, and spun out all by itself.

Cory left, but I happily stayed home. It felt good to settle in after the travel and demands of furlough. I made curtains and put our house in order. The power occasionally went off for a couple hours in the evening, but we escaped the more severe problems that June wrote about earlier.

The girls and I explored the neighborhood looking for a good place to play. One slide near our apartment had portions missing. The other slide looked whole, so Alicia climbed up and slid down to an abrupt landing. "Ouch! That hurt," she exclaimed, rubbing her back. Janelle decided not to try it.

Next door I saw playground equipment by an old two-story building. A neighbor later told me it used to be the best kindergarten in the whole city. It now stood abandoned with broken windows and whitewash turned gray with black streaks. "Let's look over here," I said. I saw no one and climbed through the broken-down fence.

"Are you sure it's okay to go in there?" Janelle asked.

"Sure it is. Come on!" I urged. We tramped through tall weeds and stepped over chunks of concrete. The playground equipment may have been nice at one time, but it no longer looked child-friendly. The swing-set had no swings. The monkey bars and a slide remained, but with so much broken glass and used syringes lying around, we soon left.

Janelle prayed at dinner, "Thank you for giving us a better apartment, even though it doesn't have a good playground."

Hoping to meet our neighbors, I baked cookies and took them around. Though missionaries moving to some countries are immediately surrounded by curious children and other onlookers, the people of Ukraine are much more reserved. In my attempt to deliver cookies, either no one was home, or no one would answer the door. A week later I met one neighbor when a repairman left a door open. I met another when I needed a missing part to our meat grinder.

I took cookies with my request and rang the doorbell of the apartment above us.

"*Kto tam?*" a voice called. "Who's there?"

"A neighbor," I replied in Russian.

The door opened, and I saw a stout woman with gray hair pulled into a small bun. She wore a faded housedress. I showed her my meat grinder and explained my need.

"Come in, come in," she urged. Her smile revealed several gold teeth. "Are you the ones who moved downstairs? What brings you here? Oh, my name is Valentina. My husband lives here too, but he's at our garden outside town." I had noticed a box of produce in the entryway.

"We came to help the church," I replied simply. "We have two daughters, seven and eight years old. We used to live in the city center. We lived there four years. We moved to this region and I like it better."

"It is a good building. It was built for the military—my husband was in the military, of course—but all kinds of people live here now. So many have sold

18

or rented out their apartments." She chatted some more, excused herself, and soon brought back her meat grinder and a long orange squash. "I'm happy to have good neighbors," she said. "Let me know if you need anything else."

With a little exploration, we found the quickest route to the Black Sea. We lived just ten minutes away on foot. I doubted it was very clean, but the girls liked to play in the water on hot days. A ten-minute walk in another direction brought us to Stefan's house, where I could visit his wife while Janelle and Alicia played with ten-year-old Lilya.

While on furlough in Oregon, Janelle and Alicia spent much time outdoors, but here, they seemed reluctant. "Why don't you take these meat scraps outside to feed the cats?" I asked. With a little more prodding, they went out but soon came back.

They preferred to stay inside and entertain each other. They created caves with chair cushions in the living room and played "Noah's Ark" with stuffed animals. They found directions for making origami frogs and created a whole frog family with folded paper.

I overheard Janelle and Alicia discussing how long they had lived in Ukraine. "I was three and you were two when we first moved here," said Janelle. "We've lived in Ukraine more than America!"

I asked them, "Where does it feel more like home, here or United States?" Almost in unison they replied, "Here."

That surprised me. They had often talked about wanting to go home to the U.S. during our first term.

Janelle said, "We don't have as much stuff here, but we don't need it. We have friends, and we know what to do when the electricity goes out."

Where was home to me? Before we returned to Ukraine, someone told me, "You are probably eager to get back. It probably feels like home over there." It was a normal comment—why else would missionaries keep going back? But inside I thought, *This person has no clue how hard it is to live over there. I doubt I will ever feel at home in Ukraine.*

Somehow though, I did feel at home. I knew how to ride the bus and get around town. I knew the language and had friends. I had become more patient, more tolerant of the differences. Standing in line at a shop for a loaf of bread, I watched the cashier find each item for every customer from the stock behind the counter. It seemed inefficient, but it effectively prevented shoplifting.

In some ways the quality of life had improved. New conveniences, like garbage bags, made my life easier. Several stores now offered water heaters, microwaves, and automatic washing machines. We saw large and fancy houses going up. Most people struggled financially since wages had not kept pace with inflation, but salaries and pensions usually came on time instead of six months late.

Early in our first term, I often felt: "Nothing works right here!" To be more precise, I had to adjust to a new normal. If something didn't work, we learned we could often find someone to fix it. When our toilet tank took a long time to fill up, a plumber cleaned dirt and gravel from the inlet pipes. "We live near the sea," he explained. "You need to expect pebbles in the water."

Service wasn't necessarily immediate. We still did not have a phone or beds but expected them eventually. We did not mind sleeping on mattresses on the floor while waiting for the beds we ordered from the furniture factory.

One day I smelled something like burning paint and followed my nose to the hall closet. I saw black spots and bubbles on the wall. Parts of the wall were too hot to touch. Fortunately, the building was made of limestone and concrete, not wood. With Cory still gone, I called Stefan, who notified the housing department. Someone came and fixed a faulty wire. At least I thought they fixed the problem.

Various stores used the first floor of our five-story apartment building.

3
A Car Is Like a Wife

August 2000

Cory came home four days after he left. The fellow who had sold him the Volkswagen willingly returned his money since he thought he could now sell it for an even higher price. "If I had known there was a problem, I would have fixed it," he said. He offered to put the right number on the engine, but Andre knew they could not take the same car back to the registration office. They looked for a different car there and in Kiev. Cory did not find anything he wanted, so they went home.

Two weeks after our arrival in Ukraine, Cory got his first chance to meet the thirty men now receiving training as church planters. With Andre, he traveled a little over an hour north to Nizhnigorski, where they held sessions. The men stayed in an old dorm, once used to house temporary workers. Cory described it to me later: "The beds sag, the water is turned off most of the time, and the bathrooms are really bad. But the building has a lecture hall, and rent is reasonable."

Andre and four others taught. All the Training Center leaders served as pastors in outreach-oriented churches. Cory said, "They have really grown in their teaching ability." With this as their second time through the course, they refined the material and their presentation.

Each afternoon the trainees spent time evangelizing in villages around Nizhnigorski. They came back and enthusiastically told about conversations with various people, even with the Muslim Tatar. Each evening they reported on their efforts to start churches and prayed for one another.

Mikhail told how work with children had provided an open door for his ministry. That summer, church members helped him hold a Bible club outdoors. During one meeting a police car drove up. Officers rounded up the leaders and said, "You did not get permission from town authorities for this gathering."

One leader asked, "Is it illegal?"

The officer replied, "You are leading these children down a wrong path, and the parents do not approve."

About then, some parents stepped up and voiced their support for the Bible stories. "What do you have to give us that is any better?" they asked.

Mikhail went to see the town official who had sent the policemen. He learned that the school principal, an atheist, had sparked the incident. The town official was friendly and proved helpful in the future, but the principal began going out of her way to avoid Mikhail when she saw him coming.

By deciding to work with churches in the Evangelical Christian Baptist Union, we could partner with mature believers ready to serve Christ. At meetings for ECB pastors, Andre and the other Training Center leaders tried to promote evangelistic outreach. Several pastors stood and enthusiastically told of their efforts and progress in starting groups in neighboring villages.

Not everyone embraced this new direction, however. One elderly leader, Feodorovich, told the group of pastors, "We cannot move too fast here. A car needs brakes. I am the brakes." As the designated head over ECB churches in Crimea, he believed he should protect the flock from worldly influences. New churches, if hastily formed, might not follow honored traditions.

Our first four years we had attended the type of church Feodorovich supported. Spirituality was measured by conformity to a conservative dress code: no makeup, jewelry, or pants on women. Those who stepped out of line risked rebuke. Married women, if dressed properly, wore a head covering. I copied the younger ladies who rolled their scarves into thin headbands. The head covering symbolized submission to one's husband. Once I heard, "Those who cover their heads fully are fully submitted; those with a partially covered head are partially submitted." I laughed but wondered how many people believed it. I hoped they would not judge me too harshly.

Occasional sermons against makeup and jewelry stressed the importance of modesty and striving to please God instead of looking like the world. But what pleases God? I felt torn between my desire to show respect for the values of the local believers and my desire to help visitors feel more comfortable. I did not want them to equate holiness with homeliness. I settled on wearing just a little makeup with my skirt and scarf. I noticed even the men tried to look their best for church services.

Certainly not all pastors loved traditions more than people. After our furlough, we began attending the church, or house of prayer, in the neighboring town of Primorski. We liked the pastor, Piotr, and June worked with the church clinic there. The dress code seemed a little more relaxed and the atmosphere, more loving.

Since each service included three sermons, Cory usually went prepared to preach. All men with some spiritual maturity gathered before the service in the "brothers' room," where the pastor decided who would speak and when. We let Janelle and Alicia go outside after the first sermon and play with other children who also lacked endurance for a two-hour service.

One Sunday Piotr told about a camp held the previous week. Though many of the children came from rough homes, an atmosphere of peace still reigned. Some, just ten years old, brought their cigarettes. The leaders told them, "This is a Christian camp. No smoking." They obeyed, but one boy went to a leader later in the week and asked her to pray for him since he really wanted to smoke.

Another boy, twelve years old, disappeared while they played at the beach. Piotr reported, "When I heard that, the first thing that came to mind was that I would end up in jail, but then God gave me peace." The other children prayed for the boy. The next day Piotr drove to the home of the missing child in a distant village and found him there. The parents explained, "He always does what he wants." They were surprised the church cared enough to look for him.

Piotr said, "On the last day, the children cried since they had such a good experience and did not want to go home. They had seen what the Christian life is like and compared it to the life they had seen before. They saw that the Christian life is better."

Cory still needed a car. Andre heard about a suitable van west of Kiev and wanted to go and buy it. "Let's see if we can find you a car this time," he told Cory. Stefan also planned to go.

Cory did not want to make the long journey again and suggested, "Why don't you and Stefan just get one for me? You know what I'm looking for."

Andre disagreed. "A car is like a wife," he said. "A man has to choose his own, and he doesn't share her with anyone." Cory decided he could use the trip as a time for fellowship and to discuss ministry. He left at 5:00 a.m. for his third attempt.

The next day I smelled burning paint again and checked the hall closet. I touched the wall, avoiding the black circles. It was hot. I didn't know who to call or what to tell them. With Stefan and Cory gone, I asked Valentina, the woman upstairs, to look at it. She notified *Zhek*, the housing department, but when workmen came, the wall was no longer hot. They saw the burnt paint and offered to come again later if I had any more problems.

The doorbell rang; it was Valentina. "Is everything okay?" she asked. "It seemed too quiet down here so I thought I'd check. Did *Zhek* come and fix the problem in your wall?"

I invited her in. "We're fine. They came but didn't fix anything since the wall wasn't hot, but thank you for your help."

"It's wonderful to have good neighbors," she said. "I knew you were a good person when you first visited me. I felt such peace. The dog didn't even bark; he just lay down."

I was also glad for a good neighbor. She told about her work at a boarding school for needy children, the *internat*. I understood Russian better than I spoke it, but she had enough words for both of us.

"I know you are believers," she continued. "I think there is a God, too. When I was in school, teachers made fun of children who said they believed in God. I never said I believed, but I always thought there must be something else."

She told of the day her television stopped working; while inspecting it, she got electrically shocked. "I could not let go, and I thought I was going to die. Finally, I cried out, 'Oh, God!' and I saw a form in front of me—a face with kind eyes. At that moment, I got free. I was afraid to tell anyone about it because I worked in a school, and I did not want to lose my job. But I started going to the Orthodox Church."

I continued to nod and insert an occasional "hmm" as she talked.

"Are you part of that Orthodox group that brought literature to the boarding school?" she asked. "If you are, do you have any more?"

I shook my head. "We didn't go. I don't know what they gave you, but I have something else." I gave her a copy of *Our Daily Bread*, in Russian.

She thumbed through it and nodded. "I need something like this."

W hen the doorbell rang again, I looked through the peep-hole of the metal security door and saw a man in uniform.

"*Kto tam?*" I called, as I had been taught. "Who's there?"

"The police."

I opened the door. He asked for my passport. I left him standing outside, found the document, and handed it to him. He thumbed through it and said that something was wrong. I didn't understand what.

"Where is your husband's passport?" he asked.

"He's gone," I told him.

"When will he be back?

"In two days."

"You have to come with me," he said.

That seemed like a big hassle. I thought about the girls and did not feel comfortable going without Stefan and Cory.

"It would be better to wait until my husband comes," I said.

"You must come with me," he repeated.

"It is better to wait, then we won't need to go twice."

He finally returned my passport and said, "Come see me at the police station when your husband gets back." He wrote his name on a scrap of paper and left. I felt relieved but wondered what could be wrong.

Janelle and Alicia continued to play, oblivious to my ordeal. I later overheard one of them say, "I wonder what age we will be in heaven."

"I think we will all be children."

"It would be fun to see Mommy and Daddy as children." They laughed.

Jesus once said, "Unless you become like little children..." Children take each day as it comes. They don't worry about how things will turn out.

When the doorbell rang at 3:30 a.m., it was Cory, four days after he left. "Well, I got a car this time," he said. I was ready to go back to bed, but he needed to unwind. "I spent more money than I'd planned, but I got a really good car for the price—an Audi wagon. It's eight years old but has low miles. I saw a lot of pieces of junk and then I saw this one. There was nothing in the middle. I was tired of looking, and I didn't want to go through this again, so I bought it. I think it will serve us well."

Officially the car belonged to Stefan. Foreign owners were required to get a bright yellow license plate, but Cory did not want to stand out as a target. Besides, we had to renew our visa every six months and didn't know how long we could stay in Ukraine. If we had to leave, Stefan could sell it for us.

Cory had parked the car in a garage he had rented. Though it took fifteen minutes to walk there, he could not leave the car near our apartment since unattended cars left outside overnight became a source of spare parts.

The next day I told Cory and Stefan about the visitor from the police station. Stefan looked upset. "Do not open the door for anyone you don't know," he scolded. "Anyone can dress up in uniform and say he is a policeman. If anyone like that comes again, you tell him to go talk to me."

Stefan took our passports to the police station. Everything was in order, although the registration stamp was in the back—not where one might expect. The person who left his name was not working that day. The police chief said he had sent no one to our house, and the person who left his name with me was not on duty the day he came. Stefan told the officer, "Tell your people to leave this family alone. If you have any questions, you call me."

Even though eight years had passed since Ukraine became an independent country, many policies from Soviet times remained. Crimea seemed especially slow to make changes, since most people identified themselves as Russians and still mourned the break-up of the Soviet Union. One old policy was that a citizen must assume responsibility as the guardian for a foreign visitor. If the foreigner messed up, authorities would expel him, but the guardian might face harsher consequences such as fines or a jail sentence. Not all would accept such a risk, and we hoped Stefan would not suffer on our account.

We lived a five-minute walk from the open-air market.

Fish at the market.

4
Your God Did This

We knew this was not the first time Stefan stood up to local authorities. I had heard bits of his story before and asked him for more details.

"The problems started with our wedding," he said. Since he and Nadia had once lived in Kiev, they invited a group of young people from there to their wedding in Feodosia in November 1978.

The group came one day for the ceremony and festivities. They planned to return the next morning but wanted to see the Black Sea first. After the wedding, a group of twenty-five or thirty followed Stefan and Nadia down the hill to the waterfront. During the thirty-minute walk a few started to sing, and soon all were singing Christian songs as they went.

Stefan understood the risk they were taking. He grew up attending schools where teachers mocked Christianity, saying that only foolish old women believed in God. Laws restricted religious freedom. Christians could not receive higher education or good jobs. President Khrushchev had promised to show on television the last Christian in Russia by 1980. This group of singing youth proved Christianity would not die out with the elderly.

As they passed the theater, people poured out after watching a movie. Seeing the wedding party, the moviegoers followed them, intrigued by this new entertainment. When Stefan looked back and saw a huge crowd behind him, he knew this would certainly attract attention of the authorities. His friends seemed oblivious to the risk and continued to sing as they passed the statue of Lenin and the train station, heading to the waterfront.

Reaching the sea, their audience had grown even larger, and the youth decided to use the situation as an evangelistic opportunity. They sang more songs, recited poems, and gave testimonies, telling how they had hope through Jesus Christ. Stefan said, "I don't remember how long they shared, maybe thirty minutes, maybe an hour." It was long enough for the police to gather in force. Over fifty policemen came by car and truck. Instead of making a scene in front of the large crowd, they waited by the road. When the wedding party left the waterfront, the police met and surrounded them. The rest of the crowd saw trouble and watched from a distance.

An officer demanded, "Who gave you permission for this assembly?"

"This is a wedding," Stefan said. He showed them his marriage license. He knew other wedding parties walked in the streets, but they were often drunk and rowdy. "We have not been drinking," he continued. "We are not disturbing anyone."

The officer told Stefan and Nadia to get in the police car, and he took them home. The police told everyone else to leave in groups no larger than two or three.

News traveled quickly around the city about how the Christians held a parade, sang, and preached in public. Early the next morning, Stefan's supervisor drove up to Stefan's house. "Come with me," he said. He had already heard about the incident and knew there would be trouble.

Arriving at the optics factory, he told Stefan to finish his project, and he locked Stefan's door. When Stefan completed his job, the supervisor sent him home early and told him, "Stay home for seven days." Maybe things would cool down by then.

They did not cool down, however. The KGB summoned Stefan for interrogation at their office. They used a mixture of threats and kindness. Because of his connections to the church, he would make a good informant. They offered him a good position with plenty of money and benefits if he would work for them. If he did not cooperate, they said he would never see his wife again. He left the meeting shaken, not knowing what would happen to him or his wife.

The pressure continued. After his daughter was born, they called him in again and said if he didn't comply, he would never see her again. He had heard unpleasant stories of what happened to those who did not submit to KGB demands. Many simply disappeared. Sometimes their children were used for medical experiments.

One pastor, a relative, set out to build a house of prayer for his congregation. Authorities tried to stop him, but he would not listen. Medical officials came and took his three small children, saying they needed some tests. Two days later, someone from the hospital called and said they should come and get their children. "You must quickly take them to the sea to rest, or they might develop problems with their legs," they said. The children soon complained of severe leg pain, and before long none of them could walk. Two died and one remained crippled. The father continued building the house of prayer and eventually had twelve children.

Stefan had seen the struggles of his own parents. His father served as a pastor, so authorities often raided their home, looking for Bibles and Christian literature. They paid fines and faced threat of prison for breaking a law forbidding children in church.

When he left home at the age of seventeen to study in Kiev, young Stefan decided he would live his own way—it was simply too difficult to live the Christian life. Lacking much money, however, he returned to his parents' rural home occasionally for food. His parents always asked, "What house of prayer do you attend? Tell us about the service." Knowing how much his parents loved him and sacrificed for him, he did not want to disappoint them. He attended Sunday services and gave his report but did not live as a Christian.

Stefan recalled, "God brought me through some difficult times and situations where I could have lost my life. After one close call, I realized that if I had died, I would not have gone to heaven. I went to my dormitory, fell to my knees, and repented. I decided to live for Him no matter what might come."

Stefan knew he must remain faithful to God despite the risk. "I will not work for you," he told the KGB officials.

Since Stefan worked around top-secret technology but did not agree with Communist ideology, they told him he could not be trusted. They assigned someone to sit with him at work, though he was the most skilled and diligent worker in his division.

The young KGB agent who sat next to him seemed pleasant enough. He asked detailed questions about Stefan's church attendance: "Who was there? What did they talk about?" Stefan did not name names but described the sermons in detail.

"You are missing out on so much in life," the young man told Stefan. "Come to the disco with me, or to the movies. I'll pay."

"I'm too busy," Stefan replied.

Four others who worked in that room heard every conversation. They knew Stefan had not requested this companion, but they still resented it and complained to him. With a KGB agent present, they could not steal or slack off on the job.

After one year the KGB agent died suddenly. He was not very old—in his late thirties. This alarmed his co-workers and others who worked with the KGB. They told Stefan, "You prayed to your God and He did this."

Stefan replied, "I did not pray for this, but God controls life and death."

Stefan's supervisor, a Jew, respected Stefan and told him, "If everyone were as conscientious as you, I would not even have to come to work in the morning, and the job would still get done." He once asked Stefan for a copy of the whole Bible, so he could read the Torah. "Please wrap it up, though, and give it to me in private."

One morning this supervisor stopped by his workstation and seemed upset or nervous. "Don't go anywhere," he said. Stefan could tell something was wrong.

Soon two men approached him and demanded, "You must come with us."

"Who are you?" he asked them. He had a good idea, but he was stalling for time.

They showed him identification—they worked with the KGB.

He told them, "I am not allowed to leave work without permission."

"We will get permission," the leader said. They headed to the office.

When Stefan went to the KGB office before, he had received a written summons. He could tell his family and ask believers to pray. This time was different.

He had heard stories about Christians who simply disappeared, and he understood they had come for him this time. He had already had two narrow misses when a KGB car almost hit him on his motorcycle. An agent once invited him to go hunting, but he politely declined, expecting a set-up for an "accident."

He wanted desperately to let his wife know what happened to him. Company rules prohibited employees from leaving the building during work hours, but he asked his supervisor anyway. Permission granted, he stepped out, hoping to see someone—anyone he knew.

At that moment, a man from the church walked by. Stefan quickly explained, "The KGB has come for me. Tell Nadia and ask people to pray for me."

The KGB agents found Stefan standing alone outside and took him to their office. They led him to a small room and locked the door. The interrogation covered the same topics he had heard before but with greater force this time. They offered him a job working with them. Since the church met at his house, he would be an ideal informant. They offered him many rewards. They would send him to a special seminary. They would give him a car, a nice house, a good salary—everything he wanted. They pointed to agreement papers on the table and said, "Just sign here."

Stefan told them, "I will never work for you. A man cannot serve two masters. I must serve God."

"You will be sorry. Think about your wife. You will never see your family again."

Nadia was expecting their second child. He worried about them. How would they get along without him? Suddenly he understood God loved them more than he did, and he felt a great peace. God would take care of them. "Even if you beat me or kill me, I will never work for you," he declared.

"No one knows where you are," the leader said.

"Yes, they do."

"How can that be?"

"I went outside while you were in the office and saw someone from the church. Right now, Christians are praying for me."

The two men stood still, one on either side. They looked at each other for a long minute in complete silence. Then the leader slammed his fist on the table and began shouting threats at Stefan. "You'll be sorry!"

When Stefan saw their reaction, he felt such peace and joy he wanted to laugh. He said nothing. Finally they unlocked the door, opened it, and told him, "Get out of here."

When he arrived home, Nadia was surprised and relieved to see him. They held each other and cried. Stefan learned that three groups had gathered to pray for him during the interrogation.

When Stefan went to work the next day, his supervisor looked at him with wide eyes, shocked to see him again. "What happened?" he asked.

"They let me go."

The KGB stopped calling him to their office but began applying pressure through his living situation. When Stefan had first moved to Feodosia early in 1978, the church had no building of their own. They met in private homes but needed more room. They pooled their money and asked Stefan to buy a house they could remodel and use as a church. The plan included risks, but Stefan was young, unmarried at the time, and willing to help.

Church members worked together on the reconstruction. They knocked out walls, replaced the roof, and leveled ground for a courtyard. Even the old women helped. Meanwhile, Stefan lived in a shed on the property. Later, church members helped him build a house on the same piece of land for his growing family.

In 1982 authorities came and informed Stefan that they were confiscating his home. They pointed to a law which said that a family could not own more than one house. They told him he had to live in the original house, where the church met.

The same week, he lost his job. "They were trying to break me," Stefan explained. By this time, he and Nadia had three children, and she was expecting their fourth. "I know in America people often lose their jobs or get fired, but it almost never happened in the USSR. The law required everyone to work, and the penalty for not working was to go to jail." Even those who came to work drunk or did not work well still kept their jobs.

"When the authorities confiscated my house," he recalled, "some in the congregation said it was my own fault, and I should not have given the house to the church. So I felt pressure not only from outside the church but from inside it, too."

Stefan went without employment for one month. It gave him time to work on construction. Then one day, a man from whom he bought building materials offered him a job working for him in a different department of the optics factory. This job provided a higher wage, and after completing his quota for the week, Stefan was free to go home and work on his house. God provided. Not long afterward, the section Stefan used to work in closed and those workers lost their jobs.

The congregation decided to fight against the move to close down the church. They wrote many letters to various officials, including one to President Gorbachov. After six months they received word that they had the right to continue meeting in the building, and Stefan could continue living in that house until the factory provided him with an apartment.

"What they meant for evil, God used for good," he explained. "Because of how many children we had, they were required to not only give us an apartment but also put us at the top of the waiting list." They could now look forward to indoor plumbing, running water, and a more convenient location.

Ten more years passed before they got an apartment, but Stefan could still look back on this difficult period and say, "I saw God provide for me and my family. When I consider uncertainties of the future, when I wonder how I can afford a good education for my children or how they will find good jobs, I remember God's faithfulness. He helped us before, and He promised to be with us always."

Lenin's statue still stands near the train station.

5

Deeper Roots

August 2000

Stefan occasionally saw those who once worked for the KGB, but they looked more humble. Some apologized to him saying, "I was just doing my job."

Even though Ukraine now had freedom of religion, we still saw leftovers from the Soviet period: suspicion, jealousy, authoritarian attitudes, and fear. Those who stood out or showed initiative became a target.

Our former language tutor, Tatiana, came to visit us with her three-year-old daughter. "It's great to see you," I said. "How's it going at the art gallery?" She had taken a three-year maternity leave, the maximum allowed, and had worked the last two as a translator for June Johnson, our teammate.

"They inspect everything I wear and ask, 'Is this American? I've never seen anything like it here.'" She laughed. "I wore this outfit yesterday. It does no good to tell them I bought the top at a second-hand shop and I made the skirt. They believe what they want to. I just try to do my job and keep a right attitude."

The Communist ideal—no one should have more than anyone else—resulted in a big problem of jealousy. Those who thought someone had something better usually condemned that person instead of trying to work harder to improve their own state.

"Fortunately," she said, "there is another woman at work who earns money selling her paintings, so I am not the only object of envy. I don't tell them I still take private students, but Feodosia is a small town and they will find out." Tatiana earned less than $20 each month as a department supervisor at the gallery. Her husband earned a similar wage as a security guard at a military base, so they needed the extra income from her English students.

"I have a question that will surprise you," she added. "Do you have a devotional guide I can read with the Bible?"

Though not surprised, I was pleased. I had never made it my goal to try to convert her but treated her as a friend, not hiding God's role in my life.

She told how her boss often criticized her or put her down in front of others. "There is a rumor I will replace her as director, so I think she feels threatened. Maybe she hopes I will quit. I just try to do my work quietly. I know I cannot change her, but I can try to change my own attitude."

Before she left, I gave her a devotional booklet and prayed God would give her peace and the ability to persevere.

Maybe it was a changed attitude that made life now seem easier for us in Ukraine. Cory and I talked about it during our walk to the Black Sea one morning. Our daily route gave us forty-five minutes to talk and pray, along with fresh air, exercise, and a view of the changing mood of the sea.

As we headed up the beach road, Cory said, "You know how they say new missionaries pass through different phases. They start with, 'I love everything,' and move to 'I hate everything,' and finally learn to live with the good and the bad. We never had a honeymoon stage, but maybe we've finally reached middle ground."

We had been back in Ukraine only six weeks, but it already seemed easier than our first term. Maybe it came from putting into practice the phrase I had heard, "In acceptance there is peace." Of course, having a water heater and washing machine helped, too.

Cory continued, "Things don't seem to bug me like they used to. I don't know why. Even during all the problems we had getting a car, I could take all the hassles in stride."

In my next newsletter home, I wrote: "When people used to ask, 'What do you like best about Ukraine?' I couldn't think of anything. All I could think of was the dirt and difficulties. Now, what do I like about Ukraine? I like lace curtains and tea sets. I like the abundant fruit of summer. I like bobbing in the Black Sea with Janelle and Alicia. I value the precious old women who tell us, 'I pray for you and your family.' I like being part of a God-sized project and seeing how many are finding hope through Christ. We learned much about perseverance, about hanging in there when our work was not fun or fulfilling. Life includes such times, but it's nice when joy comes again."

When Cory reviewed my letter, he thought my report on our sense of joy was risky, as though inviting the troubles of Job. I wondered the same, since feelings of satisfaction can be fickle.

In mid-August I attended a farewell tea for June Johnson. She planned to return in the spring after spending the fall and winter in Oregon, but I knew many loved her and would miss her. When we attended the Primorski church, I noted how old women greeted her warmly and covered her face with kisses.

Several stood at the reception to express their appreciation. The head doctor of the church clinic said, "In university we learned medical skills, but June taught us how to love. She gets down on her knees in front of patients and touches them with the compassion of Christ."

Another said, "Nonbelievers see Christ in her. After June treats them, they say, 'I've been touched by an angel.'"

June did not feel saintly or even adequate for the task but simply did what she could. She once joked, "I think you have to be at least five feet tall for this job. At four-foot ten, I feel a little stretched!"

After she left, Cory and I went downtown to clean her apartment and collect the items she left behind. The four years we had lived there, used needles littered the stairwell, but a security door now kept out drug addicts. Our old neighbor greeted us warmly, but once inside the apartment, I told Cory, "I'm sure glad we don't live here anymore." I could smell exhaust fumes and hear the noise of traffic on the busy street outside.

Still, the place had been an answer to prayer and the only apartment we could find at the time. It was a step up from our first residence, Stefan's old house on the outskirts of town with no indoor plumbing. The apartment brought us close to the market and near Anya, a church member who became a good friend. When we left for furlough, June moved in. It seemed bare now, without our furniture, but still looked better than it did when we first got it.

Cory said, "I'm just glad we won't have to deal with the landlord anymore." At every opportunity, he had tried to wring more money out of us. When cleaning the apartment, we decided to leave behind light fixtures where bare wires had been, cupboards in the kitchen, and linoleum covering rough boards in the hall. We thought these improvements should appease any imagined offense.

We were wrong. After Stefan gave him the keys, he called us and claimed that June had not paid him all the rent she owed. "If you don't pay," he said, "I will call the police." Stefan found documents proving that she had paid. Two weeks later the man called again and said we owed a huge phone bill. He brought a computer print-out he got from the phone company showing several months worth of phone calls, totaling a couple hundred dollars. We asked our friend Anya to look into it. She went to the phone company also and brought back proof of payment. Finally realizing his American milk cow had dried up, the man asked, "Do you know anyone else who would like to rent the apartment?"

Those previous feelings of satisfaction disappeared under new opportunities for delayed gratification. We visited the furniture factory to see if the beds we ordered a month earlier were ready. They said they did not have the materials and did not know when they would get them. We told them we'd look somewhere else.

Cory discovered our new car needed some repairs. Labor was inexpensive, but parts were not, and we would have to wait for them.

I forgot to unplug the water heater while using the electric stove and the power went out. Since we could not find a breaker switch, I figured I had burned out the wiring somewhere. We went three days without electricity on half the house until an electrician pointed out our breaker switch.

On the positive side, we finally had phone service, thanks to Stefan's perseverance, and the housing department fixed the problem of hot spots in our closet wall. They beat holes in the concrete to break the metal reinforcements. Apparently, someone in the building was trying to use the metal rods in the wall as an electrical ground instead of using the water pipes like they were supposed to.

Our problems could not compare to Job's, but my joyful sense that "life is SO much easier now that I have a washing machine" faded. Nevertheless, I did not want to be an emotional hypochondriac, checking for symptoms every hour. Am I happy today?

I wrote in my journal: "A tree planted by waters keeps green leaves even through the drought. Dry spells simply force the roots deeper. God is still on His throne. He cares for birds and flowers, and He says we are more important than these. He carries us through."

While getting his car fixed, Cory got to know the mechanic, a Christian named Nikita, who lived not far from our apartment. Nikita told Cory how his uncle, a believer, had influenced him.

During World War II, his uncle refused to carry a weapon. As a result, he was sent to prison for fifteen years along with five other Christians. One day the prison guards took the six Christians to a field and told them to dig six holes. "If you do not renounce your beliefs, your bodies will go in these holes," barked an officer.

Four of the men gave in. Nikita's uncle kept the faith and gained the respect of his guards. The guards led the two faithful men back to prison and shot the rest. By doing hard labor, the uncle got his prison sentence cut in half.

The example of his uncle made a lasting impression on Nikita, but he said the prayers of his mother finally brought him to Christ. During the chaos that accompanied the break-up of the Soviet Union, he joined others in illegal activities that brought wealth but no peace.

Nikita recalled, "When I visited home, my mother often tried to tell me something from the Bible, but I always forgot it as soon as I left. When I picked up hitchhikers, I often ended up with a believer in the car who wanted to talk about God. They invited me to church, but I never went."

After his youngest daughter was born, she suffered constant health problems. Almost every month, they had to take her to the hospital for treatment.

Nikita said, "I got out of bed one night when she was sick and stood by the window. I looked out and began to pray. It seemed as if God was punishing my daughter for my sins. I was the one who should be punished. I prayed and cried and asked God for forgiveness. Then I felt like someone was standing next to me, hearing and forgiving me. That happened in 1996, but even now when I talk about it, it gives me goose bumps." His daughter's health problems improved.

Since Nikita's uncle had been an evangelical Christian, he looked for a church like that. He knew a former mafia member who attended the Evangelical Christian Baptist House of Prayer and asked if he could visit.

He recalled that first meeting: "I did not understand anything at all from the sermon, but when people prayed, I saw they had the same questions and needs I had." During parts of the service dedicated to congregational prayer, believers poured out their concerns for family members and other loved ones.

I understood Nikita's love for family. My own children added a spark of life and joy to our home. Simple antics made me laugh.

I had brought to Ukraine a big bottle of flavored vitamins for the girls. Janelle liked the taste, but Alicia ate hers with a theatrical shudder and grimace. She began poking her vitamin into various food items to help disguise the taste. One day she tried to dissolve her vitamin in milk. I put her cup in the refrigerator after breakfast and brought it out again for the next meal. She drank it all with just a little prodding.

"Bleck!" she said, with a bigger grimace than usual. "I'll never do that again. It tasted awful, and I could feel all the vitamin lumps going down my throat. Oh, Mommy! That's a good way to punish us. If we do something bad you can make us drink milk with vitamins in it."

I got different vitamins for her instead.

Janelle and Alicia looked forward to helping celebrate Anya's birthday. When we had lived downtown, she often took them for walks to the beach. We had met her the first day we moved into that apartment and she came to help us clean it. She lived on the same block, so we saw her several times a week, and we walked to church together. When we knew little Russian, she chose simple words. If we still did not understand, she acted out her message. Perhaps her giftedness with children helped her stoop to our level.

The girls eagerly prepared for her birthday in late August. They made a card, decorated her cake, and decided to dress as "upside-down" clowns. When she arrived, they greeted her wearing socks on their hands, shirts on their legs, and skirts over their shoulders. Anya laughed.

As we ate, she told us about her week spent leading a day camp for village children, "I'm tired, but it was a great week," she said. "The children were wonderful. I thank God for this ministry with children and for the peace I now have." She paused and looked at me. Tears filled her eyes. "Thank you for standing with me in my time of difficulty and correcting me when I needed it. I would not be in church now if it weren't for you."

I remembered well her time of difficulty. She loved children and served as a Sunday school teacher at the Feodosia church. When she refused to stop wearing makeup, the pastor told her she could not teach Sunday school. She saw nothing in the Bible forbidding makeup and left the church feeling hurt and bitter over the incident. I don't remember correcting her particularly. I had listened to her and finally told her, "It is better to keep looking to God and what He wants you to do instead of thinking about how other people should change."

"God showed me I was being stubborn," she said. She decided to return to church without makeup and apologize. Stefan invited her to develop a Sunday school program for the new congregation he led in the village of Batalnaya.

"I am surprised how God has used me in Batalnaya," she said. "It is such a blessing to see fruit." Besides teaching children, she mentored several teenage girls who helped her teach in Sunday school and camp. Around forty children came to the day camp for younger children and another forty during the week for older kids.

I also felt grateful that God used me in some small way and felt blessed to see Anya thrive in ministry. She was gifted in ways I was not. If I had refused to come back, I would have missed seeing this fruit.

6
Look for Beauty

September 2000

With September and the beginning of school approaching, I pulled out a new batch of books. Janelle and Alicia eagerly sorted them. Looking through picture books on Greek and Roman history, they asked for sheets to play dress up. I loved watching their excitement for learning.

When they were younger, people expected me to put them in daycare. I saw no reason to do so. I enjoyed my children, at least most of the time. Our language helper, Tatiana, explained, "It is commonly thought that parents do not know how to raise their children properly."

As they reached school age, the sense of surprise increased. "How can you teach them yourself? Are you a trained teacher?"

"No, but I have a good program and good books."

"It must be so difficult to teach them."

"I have only two students. It is much easier than teaching twenty or thirty." Questions ended when I said, "They will take exams in America."

I had heard so much about unheated schools, health epidemics, and harsh teachers, I did not want to subject Janelle and Alicia to that. My sister, a trained teacher, gave advice. With Janelle in second grade and Alicia in first, I could easily combine most school subjects but gave them separate math books.

Still, I could not teach Russian as well as Anya. She agreed to come four afternoons a week and made her lessons fun for the girls. Anticipating her afternoon with Anya, Alicia prayed at lunch one day, "Thank you we can learn to read and write Russian."

They sang vowel sounds. Anya used flash cards and taught them poems. Sometimes, I heard so much giggling it sounded like a party, not Russian lessons. After an hour of instruction, she took them to the beach.

Adult attention was fine, but I hoped to find something like gymnastics, where the girls could mingle with other children. Asking around, I heard about a "Center for Creativity for Children" not far from our apartment. They offered courses like gymnastics, drawing, computer, and English. Anya helped me find the place, where we learned they had not yet started fall classes. It was an answer to prayer. I signed the girls up for gymnastics and a craft-sewing class.

Cory had his own educational focus and prepared lectures for the next training session with church planters. The thirty men were already four months into the two-year program. He had visited the group during their last session, two weeks earlier, but he still did not know many of them and felt he had some catching up to do.

Before starting his lesson, he told the group, "Some say I'm a missionary, but I prefer to be called 'a helper.'" He told them he would have a different perspective since he came from a different culture. "If you don't agree with something I say, I hope you will come and talk to me."

During his lecture on evangelism, he told the group how he became a Christian. He did not grow up going to church but felt attracted to Christians he met as a child. A teacher said she prayed for him. A neighbor made him feel welcome. He attended church occasionally when Christian friends invited him. At the age of twenty-one, he wanted a fresh start on life and moved to a different town with his job for an electric company. There, he met some Christians at the office and some more on the basketball court. He accepted an invitation to church, felt welcomed, and soon gave his life to Christ.

Four years into his Christian walk, he quit his job and went to Bible college. There he understood God's heart for the peoples of the world and prepared for cross-cultural service. We met after I returned from five years in Kenya. Our common interest in missions drew us together. We added two children to our family, considered options for mission work, and felt attracted to Ukraine.

Some of the Training Center students expressed surprise when they learned that Cory actually lived in Ukraine with his family. They thought he simply came over to teach.

We thought it better to live in Ukraine than to try to commute. Though much of my time centered on Janelle and Alicia's education, my routine included sights and sounds unique to Ukraine. I bought milk every morning shortly after 7:00 a.m. I learned by trial and error that was the best time to catch the women who brought dairy products to the courtyard outside our apartment. We could buy boxed milk at the grocery store, but it was more expensive, and we did not like the taste.

In September, the morning air felt crisp on my milk run. An old woman swept trash and fallen leaves using a bundle of twigs strapped to a long pole. A thin man wearing dirty clothes poked through the garbage bins. I often saw him with his stick and two dirty sacks.

During the day, boys played soccer on the asphalt-covered area in our courtyard. Each morning, however, several women waited there with milk in three-liter jars and tin milk cans. Some sold homemade cottage cheese and thick sour cream, brought to market in enamel-covered pots. I handed an empty three-liter jar to the woman with the purple jacket, and she gave me a jar of milk so fresh it was still warm. I took it home and pasteurized it by heating it on the stove.

When Janelle and Alicia's gymnastics class began, they said they liked it even though the floor was hard, and they did not have any gymnastics equipment. Children practiced somersaults and cartwheels on a large, thin carpet instead of padded mats. The teacher drilled them in various exercises for an hour and a half.

I stood near the open door with other mothers and watched the children. Some mothers complained, "Twice a week is not often enough," but the schedule worked well for us.

In their sewing class, Janelle and Alicia made soft toys by hand. For their first project, they sewed white mice with the help of two older students. They proudly brought home their handiwork, lined up their stuffed cats in the living room, and introduced the new mice. Janelle told the cats, "You be nice to them."

Janelle and Alicia found a friendly gray kitty outside and reported, "She likes to be held." A neighbor told us she was a house cat, but her owners had moved and left her. With a parakeet we did not need a cat, but the girls sped through their schoolwork so they could take her food. They often sat in a tree holding her, adopting the lifestyle of their new friend.

When Anya came for their Russian lesson, the girls told her about the kitty. Cory added, "She's a good cat and needs a home. Why don't you take her?"

"Oh, no," she replied, "I've had three. No more. When Tisha never came home, I decided the *bumzhi* probably ate her—you know, those homeless men that sleep in abandoned buildings and basements. Someone told me they eat cats." She paused. "I've also heard some people make hats out of cat fur. At the market in the back, I saw a fur hat that looked just like my Tisha. I asked how much it cost; it was really cheap. I was too embarrassed to ask where they got the fur."

I did not doubt her story. I had seen a skin in the weeds near our apartment and hoped the gray kitty would survive.

Every day after lunch, the girls lay on our bed with me while I read aloud. The book *Red Sails to Capri* provided new perspective. An artist asks the boy to take him to the most beautiful place on the island. The boy complies, but to get there, they must climb long, steep steps of which the boy says, "I hate them. I think they are ugly...like a scar on the landscape."

They finally reach the most beautiful spot on the island with a grand view of sea, sky, and cliffs. The artist paints all day. When he shows his work, the boy sees not the lovely view but those hated steps. The stone stair is beautiful, however, with colors he had never noticed before. The artist notes his surprise and says, "I look for beauty no matter where I go."

My daily view included gray concrete buildings, peeling paint, potholes, and scattered trash. The story challenged me to look for beauty. I found well-trimmed shrubs, children playing, and a cat peeking between lace curtains. The market included colorful displays, such as red and green peppers carefully stacked on a table. Some historic buildings downtown got a facelift, with bright Easter-egg colors replacing dingy gray.

Perhaps humans are bent toward complaint in general, but it seemed epidemic in Ukraine. I used to be surprised when I asked, "How are you?" and got a long list of aches, pains, and other complaints. The most positive answer was "nechevo," meaning "nothing" or "I have nothing to complain about." A Christian might say, "Nothing, praise God."

For a long time, I found all this negative talk depressing. I eventually adjusted, maybe even adapted too well. When people asked, "Life in America is much better, isn't it?" I replied, "There are problems everywhere."

In church one Sunday, a man said, "I was in an office to get some documents. While I waited, I listened to other people complain about how hard life is and how much better it was under Communism. I asked them, 'Is there anyone here who had nothing to eat for breakfast?' There was no one. I asked, 'Is there anyone who will go without dinner?' There was no one. I asked, 'Did any of you thank God for your bread, or for the feet that brought you here, or the eyes God gave you?' There was no one. No matter how hard life is, we can still thank God for His goodness."

I could be grateful for beds, which we finally got two months after our arrival. Cory had found someone willing to make us a double bed with storage underneath. I did not mind sleeping on a mattress on the floor, but locals who heard about it always said we would get cold and get sick. Stefan gave us their bunk bed for the girls, saying they no longer needed it. Adequate furniture helped us feel more settled.

The Training Center leaders continued to meet with pastors to promote evangelism and church planting. Some had claimed they had no money for outreach, so Andre talked about giving at the September meeting.

"A couple of churches give twenty-five percent of their income toward evangelistic outreach," he said. "That's great. If your church can give only ten percent, that's also good; but some give nothing. You need to encourage your people to give. If your congregation knows about the need, they are more likely to help."

One pastor stood up and said, "This is crazy. The members of our church do not give, and I do not expect them to."

Andre asked him, "Do you preach about love?"

"Yes."

"Forgiveness?"

"Yes."

"You need to preach about giving too. It also is in the Bible."

Another man stood and told how God had blessed his congregation since they started to give. They used the offering of the last Sunday of each month toward evangelistic efforts. The giving on that Sunday was always much higher and donations on other Sundays increased as well.

No one had to convince Pavel to care about those without Christ. As a former alcoholic and mafia member, he knew what it was like to live without hope. Several years after becoming a Christian, he went through the Training Center's first course and turned into a prolific church planter. The first church he organized was now three years old. He started groups in two more villages and baptized sixty-five people.

I liked Pavel and his wife, Vera, so I looked forward to visiting their village church. Cory parked the car near the hall they rented. When Pavel saw us, his wide smile revealed several gold teeth. He shook my hand firmly but greeted Cory with a kiss.

He and other believers took seriously the Biblical admonition to "greet one another with a holy kiss." This meant women kissed women, and men kissed men. Though most Christians gave a simple peck on the cheek, Pavel and many others kissed on the lips. We learned to adapt.

I found Vera with their little girl, now two-and-a-half years old. The first time I met Pavel, Vera was in the hospital, having just given birth. Doctors and nurses had advised her to abort this child, saying she was too old at forty-two to have more children. Their daughter now gave them great joy.

I sat next to Vera in the crowded hall. Today it was decorated with produce for *Zhatva*, or Harvest Celebration. Unlike American Thanksgiving, Ukrainian churches chose different Sundays in the fall to celebrate *Zhatva*, so guests could help with sermons and special music.

When Cory preached, he spoke on gratitude for God's goodness, the traditional accent of American Thanksgiving services. Other sermons, songs, and poems focused on the more common theme of Harvest Sunday in Ukraine: "You will reap what you sow." "Be prepared for the final harvest at the end of life." Pavel stressed the gift of salvation available to all through the sacrifice of Jesus.

Afterward, we followed Pavel's car to a nearby school for the special meal. The rough floorboards of the hall reminded me of a barn, with holes patched by sheets of plywood. Nevertheless, murals brightened the room: a forest scene painted on one wall and cartoon characters on another. Geese and goats grazed in the school yard.

Pavel said, "Our church has grown so much, it's not so easy to hold our harvest meal. The last two years, we met in homes, but we are too big now. Praise God for that."

I helped the women make open-faced sandwiches with kielbasa sausage and small, salty fish. We set these out on long tables, along with plates piled with chunks of cucumber and tomato. Finally lunch was ready. During dessert of cake, tea, and watermelon, church members took turns sharing songs or poetry. Some sang quite off-key, but no one seemed to mind. Janelle and Alicia escaped outside and threw leaves at each other until Alicia tangled with a cow pie.

Pavel sent us home with extra watermelon and loaded us down with more grapes than we could ever eat. I took them all with gratitude, wanting to can grape juice. When we got home, the girls put on a story tape and set to work plucking grapes from stems, already knowing the routine.

Our kitchen was big enough for the whole family.

7

Still Dying of Starvation

October – November 2000

Tatiana called me and asked, "May I visit you? I have some time at my disposal tomorrow, and I could not think of any more pleasant pastime than to call on you." She spoke in a formal manner, like a duchess. I enjoyed visits with Tatiana—she gave me something to think about besides homeschool and housework.

"This week I learned I might be related to nobility," she told me over tea. Then she began at the beginning. Many years ago, when she lived at home, they had a big garden and fruit trees. Their peach tree produced an abundant crop every year, enough to can some, give some to neighbors, and sell some at the market.

Their aunt and uncle visited from Moscow one summer during peach season and looked forward to taking some peaches home. However, young soldiers working on a building project nearby discovered their garden and stripped the tree one night. The family found the tree empty when they left for work the next morning. The aunt and uncle woke later and thought the family had taken all the fruit to the market. They packed up and went home, offended that the family had not shared their peaches.

They had no contact for many years, with each side waiting for the other to apologize. Tatiana said, "Then in May of this year, when I was watching the Moscow May Day parade on television, I started to cry. I am not one to cry easily, but I felt alone and sorry that I did not have any family. My mother is gone now—she died of cancer—so I decided to call my aunt. No one answered, and I later learned that was the day of her funeral. My uncle called me this week and said I may be related to nobility. He's a writer and has access to KGB documents and all sorts of information."

She explained it was now popular in Moscow to prove relation to nobility. Her uncle found several documents where a great-aunt repeatedly denied she was related to her family. As a member of the Communist Party, she could not afford any association with nobility.

"I never knew my family was affected by the Communist revolution, but I realize now it was. My grandmother and grandfather used to move a lot. Even though they were both teachers, they moved often, even before the end of a school year. I realize now, they must have been afraid."

The grandmother and grandfather eventually had eleven children, but nine of them died during World War II from hunger and sickness. Grandpa also died during the war from a heart attack, since there were no medicines to treat him. Of the eleven children, only Tatiana's mother and aunt survived.

"Nine out of eleven children died during the war?" I repeated, just to make sure I heard correctly.

"Oh, yes. That's not unusual. I have heard of many families with a similar story. In my stepfather's family, there were ten children, but six of them died. They had it easier since they lived in Crimea instead of Russia. There was more food here, yet they still died of hunger. My stepfather was half German since his mother was German. He looked just like a German boy, with curly blond hair and two dimples. He used to go into the Nazi camps and sing in German, and the soldiers gave him food. It helped him survive."

A few days after this conversation, Janelle asked me, "Why are all the grandmas fat? Not all of them, but most of them." When one has been close to starvation, a few extra pounds probably seems like good health insurance. After Tatiana's story, I understood better why old women nagged me and told me I was too thin.

One large woman, a former neighbor, saw me and exclaimed, "You've gained weight! You look better now. I used to think your husband didn't have anything to look at."

Hearing stories of the past helped me understand who the people had become. I enjoyed listening to Vladimir, age 65, and Ivan, 76, reminisce about village life when they grew up in Russia. Ivan said they had no shoes, not even in the winter. He recalled running to the river in the snow to check the fishing line he had set out. When his feet got cold, he squatted on them to warm them. He got his fish and ran home again. He and the other children played barefoot in the snow, taking frequent time-outs to warm themselves on the Russian oven in the nearest house.

He and Vladimir praised the virtues of the Russian oven, the central feature in a village home. The large brick oven also served as a family bed. The warm bricks cured bad backs and winter flu. Housewives used it to simmer soup and bake bread.

"We have lived so long because going barefoot in the snow made us hardy," Vladimir said with a smile.

"And we had the Russian oven," Ivan added.

"The air was clean back then," Vladimir continued. "The water was clean. Our food was pure."

Still, they knew hardship. Collective farm villages lacked electricity or running water. Residents could not get a passport, an identification document, so they could not leave the village. "We were slaves," Vladimir remarked, "but it got even worse." He told how they lost everything during World War II through various raids. The end of the war brought no relief since drought came the next year. "Our food was gone. We had nothing to put between our teeth. Mama took a piece of leather and baked it in our Russian oven. She cut it into squares like pieces of chocolate. The only thing that saved us from starvation was when the collective farm gave us a head of sunflower seeds."

The war killed over 20 million people, but Stalin's policies led to more suffering. Instead of using food supplies to feed citizens during the famine, the USSR continued to export grain, especially to the newly obtained countries of Eastern Europe where they sought to establish control after the war.

Cory occasionally went to the village of Batalnaya to help Stefan with the church he led. Batalnaya was named after the battalion stationed there during World War II. Like much of Ukraine, hard times had hit this village since the break-up of the Soviet Union. Young people moved away hoping to find better jobs in bigger towns.

People got little pay, if any, from the collective farm and survived by growing their own produce and meat. Even that was not easy since those who left cows or goats outside after dark found nothing more than a head and skin in the morning. A main road passed through the village, so thieving strangers took what they could—but villagers also stole from one another.

At one Bible study, a man in his sixties got up and spoke. "Many people say life is hard now," he said, "but this is nothing compared with how life was after the war. Our life is much easier now. I never saw electricity until 1956. We had no bread for many years. Everyone was hungry. Children died of starvation. We had no communication with the outside world."

The older folk in the audience nodded, also recalling those difficult times. "Now we have radio," he continued. "We have television. We have bread, but people are still dying of starvation. I am not talking about physical starvation but spiritual starvation." He referred to several in the village who hung themselves. "People have no hope and see no other way out."

He said that when he talks to people now, he tries to tell them of God's love and the hope that comes from Him. A woman came to the house of prayer while he was cleaning it and said, "I have food, but I am empty inside."

He explained how God loved her, and he invited her to church services.
"Maybe I will come," she said, but so far she had not.
"People are afraid," Stefan told me later.
"Why?" I asked.
"They are afraid people will laugh at them—people who have no peace in their hearts and yet mock others who seek God."

The Training Center continued to train men to meet these spiritual needs. At the next session, Cory taught on the cell-group model of church planting, the idea of forming fellowship groups that meet in homes and would multiply. Other teachers discussed the doctrine of salvation, Christian character, and the role of the Holy Spirit. Every afternoon they went for evangelism in neighboring villages.

We felt good about the church planters' progress, but not everyone did. Cory told me, "Andre says Feodorovich is now criticizing us because some of the church planters have been divorced." The elderly church leader had never supported the Training Center's vision to equip people for outreach.

Cory explained to me, "Feodorovich won't even baptize someone who has been divorced. He says that anyone who got remarried is living in adultery, even if it happened a long time before coming to Christ. He says they must divorce the new spouse and return to the former."

Cory pointed out to Andre that divorce is not the unforgivable sin. If the Bible says God hates divorce, how can the church encourage anyone to get a divorce? Andre came to the same conclusion. When the leaders met to discuss what position they should take, Andre pointed out the passage in 1 Corinthians 6:9-11, which says that even though some had been adulterers and other types of sinners, they had been washed, sanctified, and justified.

Feodorovich called another meeting to hash out the issue. A broader question was the standing of divorced believers. Could they be involved in ministry?

Andre told the council that Jesus commanded all believers to be witnesses. He pointed out the overseer's inconsistencies since he had given some divorced people ministry positions and performed the marriage ceremony for some. "If you don't like someone, you bring up divorce as an issue. If you do like someone, you ignore it. You are being a hypocrite."

Others gave similar criticism; in fact, he found no support for his ultra-conservative position. One leader said he found it hard to believe the old pastor would not baptize someone who had been divorced. "Being divorced or not has nothing at all to do with salvation," he said. "If a divorced person cannot be saved, then when we evangelize, we need to ask, 'Have you been divorced?' If they have, then we say, 'There's no hope for you.' The Gospel is no longer good news if that's how we base our salvation."

Someone from the housing department came to the door and demanded that we pay for heat and for three years' worth of overdue heating bills. Cory explained that it was not our apartment; we rented and had only recently moved in.

When he phoned our landlady, she replied, "That building has not had heat for three years, so why should we pay? It was so cold, my daughter was sick most the time. They called me and said they would sue me for back payment, but I told them I would sue them for the doctor bills, and it would be more. Of course if they provide heat, then we will pay for it." She promised to come by that week and bring us our record book for paying for electricity.

Cory was not yet home when she arrived, but I invited her in for tea. "I have some questions about your faith," she said. "I did not feel free to ask you the first time I met you, but now we know each other. Are you Jehovah Witnesses?"

I explained that we worked with the local Evangelical Christian Baptist Church. In spite of the propaganda during Soviet times, they were not a cult, but Protestant, like the Protestant churches of Europe and the United States. "They are good people and believe the Bible."

"How are they different from the Orthodox?" she asked. "You don't have icons?"

"No. I understand that icons began as a way to show the stories of the Bible in picture form for people who could not read. After a while people started bowing before the pictures and praying to them, but how can a picture help? People think God is too distant and they hope Mother Mary or a saint will pray for them. The Bible tells us we can pray directly to God, because of Jesus."

Cory arrived, and she showed him the record book for paying the electric bill. She explained that he should read the meter each month and take payment to a certain office. Someone from the electric company would come occasionally to see if the number on the meter matched the number in the book.

"If you have used a lot," she said, "you can still write down 100 kilowatts. I can get someone to come and turn your meter back. Everyone does it."

She looked surprised when Cory said, "We will pay the full amount."

A few years earlier, Cory rented a garage next to a man named Grisha. He worked as a mechanic in the winter and changed money on the street in the summer. Money-changing was illegal, but he knew where to go and whom to pay off. Wanting to practice his English, he made an effort to get to know Cory. We had him over for dinner a few times, and he consulted with Cory on some computer questions. He boasted about his ability to steal electricity and hack computers but seemed to respect what we did.

Cory asked him to do some work on our car. As Cory watched him work, they talked about many topics. Out of the blue Grisha said, "I don't know where I'm going...heaven or hell." Cory explained how it's possible to know.

We knew several people like Grisha, our landlady, and Tatiana who seemed open to spiritual things, but we did not want to invite them to the church in Feodosia. We no longer attended there but heard the pastor continued to wound people in his campaign to cleanse the church of evils like cosmetics and jewelry.

When Anya came for Janelle and Alicia's Monday afternoon Russian lesson, she said, "When I went to the house of prayer last night, Igor told me to leave since I was wearing earrings." She shook her head. "Cory, you need to start a new church in Feodosia."

"I can't do that," Cory said. "You don't need an American church." Since Ukraine already had a viable church presence, Cory believed he should focus on equipping local believers for leadership.

"I told Stefan he should start a church," Anya continued, "but he says he is already busy with Batalnaya. Andre also says he has his own ministry. I think they are scared of Igor."

Cory, Stefan, and Andre had often talked about the need for a new church in Feodosia, but they understood it could easily turn into a messy church split if not handled correctly. None of them knew quite what to do.

Cory told Anya, "You just need to pray."

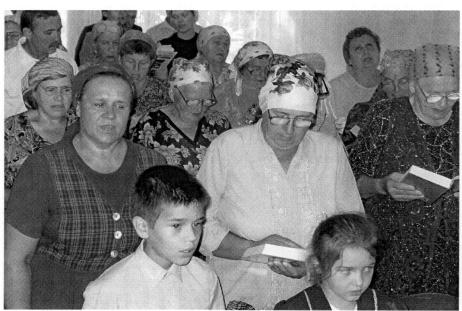

A new village church

8

God Is Capable Enough

November 2000

The next time I saw Anya, she was in the hospital. Over the past few years, she had visited doctors off and on for heart problems. Her diet probably did not help much since she once told me she loved slices of raw pork fat, *salo*, on bread with garlic cloves on the side, washed down with sips of pickle juice. Apparently, the health benefits of garlic could not counteract all that fat and salt.

After a recent minor heart attack, she visited the doctor again. They decided it was serious enough for a two-week treatment in the hospital. They told her to go to various offices for different tests and take the results to the hospital. Anya hustled from one office to another and checked into the hospital a week later when a bed became available.

The girls and I went to visit her one day. I stepped tentatively into the dark entryway at the hospital and waited for my eyes to adjust. It smelled of disinfectant. I asked a nurse for directions; she pointed out where we should go. Metal beds with thin, stained mattresses lined the halls. I eventually found Room #8 and looked in. Eight beds filled the room. Some women sat up reading; others lay down.

Anya's face lit up when she saw us. "Oh, Janice! Girls! Come in. Sit down!" She moved over and offered a seat on her bed.

I showed her the food I brought from home, knowing the hospital gave little. "How's the food?" I asked.

"Not bad," she said, and chuckled. "We get buckwheat for breakfast, bread and soup without meat for lunch, and then buckwheat again for dinner. When the nurse brought us our buckwheat for dinner, she joked, 'This is the first course; I'll be back with the meat.' Everyone laughed, knowing there would be no meat."

Anya said she went home once to get some butter and sugar to add to her mush and bought some cheese and kolbasa sausage. "So I'm eating well. People from the church visit me and bring food too." She told about her treatment; she thought the shots she got twice a day helped stabilize her heart.

The girls sat as patiently as possible. Alicia tapped her foot on the floor. A woman across the room snapped, "Stop that noise!"

I suggested we go outside. Anya wore her bathrobe and slippers as we walked into the courtyard and off the hospital grounds. We stood and talked near an old abandoned church, built in the fifteenth century. It was my favorite part of town, near the ruins of fourteenth century fortress walls. The girls ran up and down a small hill, much happier to be out in the open.

Cory drove us to the hospital again on Sunday since Anya's stay had been extended. She was not there. We eventually found her at home—she had gone home to bathe and do some laundry. The hospital had no hot water, and patients had to bring their own bedding and clothes from home.

Cory started having heart problems too. "Listen to my chest," he said one evening. "My heartbeat. Does it seem strange to you?" I put my ear to his chest. *Ba-bum. Ba-bum. Ba-ba-bum.*

"It seems a little irregular. How do you feel?"

"Sometimes I have some chest pain. It's about like it was when I had those heart problems three years ago." At that time, a doctor thought his irregular heartbeat was related to stress.

Compared with our first term, much had improved, but Cory still found it difficult to live and work in Ukraine. He lacked the relaxing outlets he enjoyed in Oregon. Even though the Training Center seemed like a good idea, it still faced opposition. It bugged him every time he heard of problems in the Feodosia church.

I had often seen him upset about attitudes or events he encountered, but one day he came home acting so strangely agitated, I knew something else was up. Finally he told me in a hushed tone, "Someone we know is being threatened, but I can't say anything else. I know too much."

I did not press for details, but about a week later, he told me a little more. A family in the church applied for passports to emigrate to the U.S. The passport official said his daughter had already applied for a passport. The father insisted that could not be.

The official showed him the application. The picture was right, but the signature was not his daughter's. The daughter had been hanging out with bad company. Apparently, she had gotten mixed up in a trafficking ring and narrowly escaped being taken out of the country to serve as a prostitute.

Before long a visitor came to their home and gruffly warned the father not to tell anyone about this. If he did, he and anyone who knew about it would have serious problems. Someone close to us had helped sort out the mess, so the threat applied to him too. "I know too much," Cory repeated.

Not long after we first moved to Ukraine, someone was shot right outside our apartment, so the mafia threat seemed very real. Hearing about corruption in law enforcement added to a sense of vulnerability.

During our first term, a doctor suggested that Cory walk or run every day to help his heart. We now walked together every morning, but Cory decided to start running too, at a track not far from our apartment.

When the girls heard about his heart problem, Janelle asked, "What will happen to Daddy?"

"I don't know," I said, "but you can pray for him."

"What causes it?"

"Stress."

Alicia told him, "Daddy, you don't need to worry. God is on your side."

Cory prepared a sermon on the topic of worry. "The remedy," he said the next Sunday, "is to trust that God is capable and cares enough to handle the details of our lives." He admitted, "I am preaching to myself as well."

With ongoing opposition to the Training Center, Cory's co-workers also felt pressure—especially Andre. Some church leaders criticized him for trying to promote evangelism and church planting. He believed, however, that Christ died for the whole world and that those outside the church must hear this good news too.

Andre grew up in a non-Christian home and never heard about God except when teachers said that only foolish, uneducated people believed in God. His grandparents were Christians, but his parents forbade them to talk to the children about Christ.

At age seventeen, Andre went to Moscow to study in a geological institute. Along with classes teaching evolution, he was required to take a class called "The Science of Atheism." Professors said the rich invented religion as a way to oppress the poor. During school holidays, he visited his grandparents and had long discussions with his grandfather.

When Grandpa tried to talk about God, Andre explained that everything came about by evolution. Grandpa listened patiently. Finally, he pointed to a chair and asked, "Do you think that chair just appeared or that someone made it?"

"Of course someone made it."

"Well, I think it just appeared. After all, I did not see anyone make it. I believe it made itself."

"You are stupid if you think that," Andre countered. "Why do I even talk to you?"

Grandpa persisted. "You cannot believe that small chair made itself, but you believe this big world just made itself? Who is more stupid?"

Andre married a fellow student from a Muslim family and worked for a while in Uzbekistan as a paleontologist. In 1985, at the age of twenty-six, he quit his job and moved back to his hometown of Feodosia.

Needing some money, he called on his grandfather for a loan. Grandpa also gave him a New Testament and the address of a church in Feodosia. Out of respect, he read the Bible and visited the church. Out of interest, he continued. Before long he gave his life to Christ and was baptized in 1987. His wife followed one year later.

One Sunday morning, Andre joined us on our visit to a village church. While Cory drove, I asked Andre, "How did you get interested in church planting?"

"To be honest," he said, "I did not have the desire to start new churches, but I came to understand this was God's desire. It's like when God called Moses to go to Egypt. It was not his desire but God's desire. I understood there would be many problems."

He first heard the challenge to plant churches in 1992 through a series of seminars by the Association for Spiritual Renewal in Moscow. With so many towns lacking a body of believers, he saw church planting as important in evangelism.

He thought the most valuable part of the training, however, was greater insight into God's grace. He recalled, "When I understood what Christ did for me, I felt such joy inside, and everything else fell into place. Strategy and all the rest are not the most important. It's like the branch and the vine. When we understand God's grace and love and believe it, we will produce fruit. You can't just tell people, 'Go and evangelize.' If I do not understand God's grace, that command fills me with fear and I just can't do it. But when I understand God's love, I want to tell others."

He later worked with Cory to start the leadership training program in Crimea. Cory had already told me a lot about the process and challenges involved, but I wanted to hear Andre's perspective.

"How do you try to build vision for evangelism in local churches?" I asked.

"If you have a relationship with the leaders," he said, "you can start to work with the church. If there is no relationship, they will work against you. Other than working with the leaders, I don't know of a different way to bring about change...and for change to take place, it is important to speak gently, not rebuke, since repentance takes place in an atmosphere of love."

Many pastors initially resisted his invitation to work together toward evangelistic goals. He explained, "They said, 'We think you are working toward your own aims. You just want to use our churches, take our best brothers and leave the church weak.' I wanted to show that we sincerely wished to help them, not just get something from them. We asked them to list their needs and tried to respond to those needs. Now, most understand that the men who study with us remain in the church. We only teach them, and then they return to their churches. They are able to give back to the churches and strengthen them."

Nevertheless, not all church leaders agreed with this goal. Andre added, "God gave authority to the church to do His work on this earth. If Satan tries to hinder, that's a small problem; but if the church tries to hinder, that's a big problem. When the brothers criticize or don't want to be involved, my desire fades. Then I have to go back to the fact that it is God's desire."

With Thanksgiving approaching, I still had not found turkey at the market. I saw an occasional plucked goose or skinned rabbits with fuzzy feet but no turkey. Chicken would be the closest substitute.

On the day before Thanksgiving, I wandered around the back of the market, where people sold potatoes and onions from the trunks of cars. There I spied two plucked birds displayed on a piece of plastic covering a wooden box. Too big for chicken, they must be turkeys.

They bore little resemblance to the plump fowl I remembered from my youth. These looked like they had been on an exercise program or special diet. The breastbone poked in the air like Mount Everest. Bits of dark feather remained in the skin, like so many blackheads. Nevertheless, I was thrilled. We would have turkey after all!

"Fresh turkey," the woman said, noticing my interest. "Mamma butchered them yesterday after lunch. They're young. See? The feathers are still soft."

I grabbed a scrawny leg and hoisted it in the air so I could inspect the back side. I grabbed the other turkey and compared them. "How much?" I asked.

"Thirty hryvnia. Ten hryvnia a kilogram." That was the same price as boneless beef. I would get more bones than anything, but I didn't care. She weighed it for me. Sure enough, it was three kilograms—about six-and-a-half pounds.

I took my anorexic turkey home and was greeted by cheers when Janelle and Alicia learned of my successful hunt. Then came cries of, "Oh, gross!" when they got a closer look.

Our teammates, Jonathan and Heather Powell, drove down from Melitopol to join us for Thanksgiving. They had just finished one year of language learning and planned to move to Berdyansk when repairs to their new apartment were complete. Ministry possibilities looked good with their new host church.

I had hoped someone would fix the oven on our gas stove before Thanksgiving, but another call or two brought no results. The repairman was too busy. By chopping off the legs and tail, I could squeeze the bird into a pan that fit into our little electric oven. Despite its doubtful appearance, the turkey provided tasty meat—enough for our meal and leftovers too.

Thanksgiving produced many scraps for the little gray kitty, but we had not seen her for over a week. The girls finally stopped looking. "Someone probably adopted her," I told them.

We still had our parakeet, Christopher, but Alicia thought we needed another pet. Cory had described how someone caught two sparrows using a box, a stick, and sunflower seeds, and then kept them in a cage. Alicia tried to catch one too. "Christopher needs some company," she said.

Christopher seemed content enough with his human companions. He followed the girls around the house, usually walking instead of flying. He boxed with the balls on Janelle's slipper. He sometimes meowed like a cat, imitating the girls' conversations with their pack of stuffed cats.

Instead of confining a wild bird, I told the girls we could get another parakeet. They skipped and chattered all the way to the market, where they chose a young female with purple feathers. They walked home carefully, taking turns holding the small box. The young parakeet flew wildly around our apartment before Cory caught her and put her in the cage with Christopher.

Even if Alicia thought Christopher needed company, he did not agree. The female fluttered toward him, seeking comfort after her traumatic experience. She had lived in a small cage with many birds, but he was a confirmed bachelor. He tried to get away from the intruder, who kept chasing him. Eventually they settled down on separate limbs. The girls named her Violet.

When Cory came home from his next session with church planters, he told me about Vanya, a cheerful man with a vibrant faith working in northwest Crimea. Vanya told how he once accepted Christ and then fell back into a worldly lifestyle. While playing volleyball one day, he hit the ball and broke his arm. A doctor set it, but a couple weeks later, his fingers started turning blue. They decided the bone was infected. One test showed cancerous cells, so they cut off his arm. This served as a wake-up call, and he turned back to Christ.

Vanya was now twenty-eight years old, married, and had a six-year-old son. Before he signed up as a church planter, he had earned 1000 hryvnia each month. Though just $182, it was five times the typical salary. The stipend he received from the Training Center was a fraction of his former income, but he wanted to focus his efforts on reaching others for Christ.

He had started groups in three villages. Through his influence many had come to Christ, including some from a Muslim people-group, the Tatar. He worked on learning their language.

Tensions usually existed between the Tatar and Russians of Crimea. When Stalin deported the Crimean Tatar to Central Asia after World War II, about half of them died on the way or soon after. As the Soviet Union broke up, many returned to their homeland. They now made up about twelve percent of

Crimea's population. Most Tatar firmly identified themselves as Muslim, even if they did not practice the faith.

A Tatar woman who came to Christ through Vanya's ministry boldly shared her newfound joy with others. She worked for the director of the local House of Culture, a building for cultural events where people once listened to speeches promoting Communism.

One day Vanya went to visit the Tatar woman at work. The director saw him and said, "You have come to see me. Step into my office." He had not gone to see her but followed her anyway.

"My name is Vanya," he began.

"I know who you are. My worker told me all about you. I have refused every other religious group wanting to use our auditorium, but I am giving you permission."

He had not asked. He had not even thought much about where his growing groups should meet. He now led two groups in this village, in houses on opposite ends of town.

"It's wonderful that my worker became a Christian," the woman continued, "but I'm not ready yet." He had not said a word to her about Christ. She continued, "Go to the mayor tomorrow to complete the paperwork."

The next morning, he arrived early at the mayor's office. He watched as someone else approached the mayor, who gruffly turned him away saying, "I'm too busy to see you."

Vanya figured he had wasted his time in coming but prayed, "Lord, I didn't initiate this. If it is your will, you will have to work it out."

The mayor greeted him warmly and invited him into his office. He said, "The director of the House of Culture has already talked to me and signed the papers."

We saw it as a modern-day miracle. We knew how bureaucrats could adeptly build blockades with red tape. Nevertheless, God can part red tape as easily as he parted the Red Sea.

One part of Feodosia.

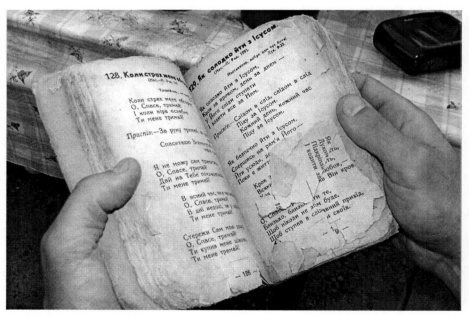

A well-loved hymn book.

9
My Reward

December 2000

We saw a notice on the door to our apartment building that said the people of Feodosia owed the equivalent of over $80,000 for electricity, and unless debtors paid up, the city would start turning off the electricity. We had lived in Ukraine long enough to know the lights would go off for everyone, not just the debtors.

Cory had paid our electric bill. When he filled out the paperwork reporting 433 kilowatts for the month, the cashier exclaimed, "There's no way that can be correct. That's way too much!" With a microwave, washing machine, and water heater, we used more electricity than most, and many people did not report all they used. Cory felt embarrassed by her loud outburst, but insisted on paying for the full amount.

As promised, the electricity began going out, sometimes for just half an hour, sometimes for over seven. Cold weather hit and we appreciated long underwear. Our propane heater warmed the living room a little, but other rooms remained a chilly 60 degrees.

Winter, especially winter in these conditions, was a good time to get away. We had long looked forward to attending a large missions conference in Israel at the end of December, but fighting broke out there. Should we still try to go? Unrest in Israel was common, but this time, the fighting seemed more widespread, serious, and prolonged.

Cory said, "I think we should go anyway. I just need to get out of here for a while."

Since he was usually cautious about matters of security, I knew he must really need a break. I wanted a vacation too. I had looked forward to this conference for a whole year. It even included a full program for children.

During our last furlough, I had told my sister, "At least if we go back to Ukraine, we'll get to go to Israel. It's so close."

We agonized over the question for weeks, hoping the fighting would calm down. Especially now, in the dreary days of winter, I wanted to get away. Nevertheless, tensions continued to escalate. We had already paid the required fees but decided to cancel.

My head knew we should not go, but I still felt disappointed and depressed. When Cory and I prayed before sleeping, I prayed with tears through the Twenty-third Psalm, acknowledging the Lord as a good shepherd who supplies all I need. He restores my soul...leads in right paths...makes my cup overflow...prepares banquets for me.

Cory admitted, "I feel like I'm being held captive." The next morning, he said, "I'm reading in the book of Daniel. Daniel was in captivity, but he made the best of it."

Janelle and Alicia took the change of plans in stride. "That's okay. We'll have a family Christmas and go for a walk."

The conference organizers soon canceled the event and refunded our money, but I still mourned the loss of this expected perk of mission life: a vacation in an interesting place. Then a phrase from the Bible came to mind: "I am your very great reward."

I looked and found it in Genesis 15:1, as God's words to Abraham. The King James Version reads: "I am your shield and exceedingly great reward." The Amplified Bible adds, "...your abundant compensation." Abraham had obediently moved from his homeland and lived as a foreigner without security or stability. How did God repay him? "I am your reward."

God gives good blessings, but most precious is His presence. Paul says everything else is like "rubbish" compared with knowing Jesus. He sustains us.

Stress and disappointment are facts of life. During the Christmas season, I often feel life should be easier or better than it is. Christ came as Emmanuel, "God with us." He walked dirty streets and experienced the same kinds of difficulties we do. He understands and enables us to run the race with perseverance as we keep our eyes on Him. According to the psalmist, fullness of joy comes from God's presence, not the existence of ideal conditions.

Our building finally got heat and the radiators brought the temperature in our apartment up to 65 or so. Cory's heartbeat evened out, but Anya spent a week in the Simferopol hospital getting tests and treatment for her heart. She told us they recommended an operation in Kiev to fix a faulty valve, but it was too expensive and lacked any guarantee. She decided against it. "I will live as long as God wants me to," she said simply.

When she got home from Simferopol, she found her apartment had been ransacked, with clothes and papers thrown everywhere. Since she lived on the ground floor, she thought the robber gained access through a small window. "He even took apart my table," she said. "He was probably looking for money."

She called the police but did not expect to recover anything. The little money she had was gone, along with about $200-worth of goods, including clothes, sheets, and towels. She suspected the drug-addict son of a church member, since he sometimes came asking her for food and knew she would be gone.

The horrible shock did not help her heart condition any. "The worst thing was that he took my tape player," she said. "I need it for the children's Christmas program in Batalnaya." We gave her one.

A few days later, she called and said, "I'm in the hospital again." From the quiver in her voice, I knew she felt discouraged. She explained, "I didn't feel well yesterday, so I went to the doctor. They did a cardiogram and told me to go immediately to the hospital. I forgot to bring toilet paper. Would you bring me some? And I don't have enough money. If you can help me, I will pay you back."

Stefan drove me to the hospital to visit her. She cried when she saw us. I brought out gifts of fruit, toilet paper, money, and pictures from Janelle and Alicia. We could not stay long, but I asked, "Do you have a Bible?" She nodded. "Read all of 2 Corinthians. It's my favorite when I'm having a hard time." God gives comfort and hope in difficulty. We are afflicted but not crushed. We do not lose heart. God's grace is sufficient.

Children in Ukraine look forward to New Year's Eve, celebrated with a decorated tree, gifts, and a feast. Christians honor Christ's birth on January 7, using the Julian calendar. Though out-of-step with everyone else, we still observed Christmas on December 25.

Janelle and Alicia excitedly opened gifts sent by a church and passed out those they had prepared. Alicia made Cory a family of clothespins: "So you can take us with you when you're gone. That's Mommy, there's Sissy, and me, and that's you with the mustache."

Cory had brought home a frozen goose from his last seminar, the gift of a church planter. It was the first year I ever had Christmas goose and probably the last. I served it for dinner, but we did not eat much. The bird was tough, with dark meat. Cory said people in villages served him goose soup, so I decided to stew the rest and put the broth in the freezer for later.

Goose stewing would have to wait though, since the girls and I had a party to attend. Valentina, our neighbor upstairs, worked at a residential school for children and invited me to bring the girls to a "New Year's" party on December 25. She worked as a housemother to around fifteen students in the sixth grade. Around 240 children of all ten grades lived at the school. They came from homes with poor or negligent parents, such as alcoholics, drug addicts, and prisoners.

The girls and I met her at the school, and she took us to her small office on the third floor. As we neared her room, the smell of an outhouse grew stronger. "The toilets are not working," she said and closed the bathroom door. Her office contained a narrow bed, a small table, and a cabinet with soap. Her children crowded into the room and eagerly chose costumes for the party. Most girls became "Snow Maiden" with white dresses trimmed with tinsel. Several boys wore beards and red outfits as "Grandfather Frost."

Janelle and Alicia brought the snowflake outfits they had made for their gymnastics class and went with the other girls to a dorm room to change. The room contained five single beds, a small cupboard for clothes, and little room to walk. Valentina scowled and barked out orders to several squabbling children.

I had wondered if I really wanted to spend my Christmas afternoon away from home when I had company coming for supper. I had wondered if I had done enough to make the day happy and memorable for Janelle and Alicia. Sitting in that shabby room, I realized it was the best thing I could have done for myself and the girls. By sharing our day with those less fortunate, I saw how blessed we were.

We moved to their classroom and the party began. Children sang and danced in a circle around the New Year tree. They recited poems; Janelle and Alicia did too. Then Valentina passed out the small gifts we brought.

The next day the girls and I visited Anya in the hospital and took her some Christmas goose. We found her in pain. "My leg hurts," she cried, rubbing it, "and it's cold."

She cheered up when the girls gave her the music box they bought for her. "Oh! It's beautiful," she exclaimed. "I love you. I miss you so much!" They recited the poem she taught them and sang a Russian song about "kind grandma."

"Anya is like our second grandma," Janelle said when we left. Anya was old enough to be a grandmother; in fact, her son in Siberia had a daughter.

"I'm glad Anya isn't like the other grandmas here," Alicia said. "She doesn't dress like them or wear a scarf. She's nice to us. She smiles a lot, and it's easy to make her laugh."

That evening I looked in our medical book to see how leg pain could be related to heart problems. Poor circulation. I wondered if Anya was dying. I knew she had a bad heart valve, but I wasn't ready for her to die. She was a one-of-a-kind friend and teacher for Janelle and Alicia. Her Sunday school class in Batalnaya had blossomed under her care. She still had so much to give.

When we went to visit Anya two days later, the white-coated woman behind a desk said, "She went home for the night." I felt relieved; she wasn't on her deathbed after all. The next day I found out she had not gone home at all.

I checked Anya's room and she still wasn't there. I asked the white-coated woman again. She snapped back, "How should I know? Go look in all the rooms." I started looking, but after peeking in some rooms with men by mistake and not finding her in the rooms for women, I asked another lady in a white jacket. Anya had moved to the surgery building.

When I found her, she looked much better. She explained that her leg pain came from a blood-clot. Two young surgeons from Simferopol had come to operate on her but decided to try treating her medicinally first, using blood thinners. "It's good you brought me money," she said. "If you don't have money, they won't treat you. I heard another woman crying and crying, but they would not help her because she did not have money."

The blood thinners seemed to do the job, but they kept her in the hospital for almost two weeks. Anya said, "They want to make sure I don't cut myself or something. A lot of people from church have come to visit, and my daughter sent a long letter. She wrote, 'I love you and I can't live without you.' She also asked my forgiveness and sent money."

Men being trained as church planters look to God as their source of power.

This 90-year-old woman prayed for a church for her village.

Believers in this village gathered to worship in a former kindergarten building.

10
Caught in the Current

January 2001

When Cory's co-worker, Andre, had been a Christian only two years, the Feodosia church council decided he was ready to lead a small church in Sudak. Sudak was over an hour from his home, but no one else wanted to go. Andre often hitchhiked to get there. "I felt so inadequate," Andre recalled. "I didn't know what I was doing, and I didn't feel gifted to be a pastor."

Sixteen-year-old Romon soon joined the church, became the pastor four years later, and now also served as a teacher with the Training Center. Wanting to hear the story from Romon's perspective, I asked how he became a Christian and got involved in ministry.

"I went to Leningrad, now St. Petersburg, to study when I was fifteen," he said. "One day I saw a Christian library, just a small bookstand, downstairs in the metro. They had a Bible there, and I asked to borrow it. I was excited since I had never seen one before. I thought of the Bible as some kind of mystical book. I started at Genesis and soon got bored. A month later, I returned it and asked, 'Don't you have any books about Jesus?'" He chuckled. "I'm sure they knew I had not read it, but they gave me something like a comic book about the life of Jesus."

In the books he borrowed, he found an address. He figured it must be the address of the main library, and they would have a bigger selection. He showed up at the hour listed and discovered it was an Evangelical Christian Baptist House of Prayer. He liked the sermon and the people he met.

"I was always something of an idealist," he said. "When I was twelve, my family moved from Uzbekistan to Sudak. In Uzbekistan many kids in my school swore, drank, and did bad things. I looked forward to moving since I thought the people must be better in Crimea. It was closer to Moscow, so I thought they would be more cultured. I was naive. Instead, the kids at school were even worse.

"When I visited that house of prayer in Leningrad, I found the kind of people I wanted to be around and be like; but I also heard about Jesus, who gives peace. It was like I had been at the edge of a cliff and could have gone over, but God preserved me."

He lived in Leningrad a little over a year when his mother became ill, and he returned to Sudak in December 1990. He hoped to find a similar church, but the Christians in Leningrad did not know of any. While riding a city bus not long after his arrival, he saw a sign, "Christian Book Library," and thought, *Those must be my people!* He got off at the next stop and ran back.

At the bookstand he met Andre, who traveled from Feodosia for evangelism and led services for a small flock of fifteen members. Romon attended their meeting that night, December 31. When the Black Sea warmed up that summer, he was baptized at the age of seventeen.

Andre soon asked him to preach. Romon recalled, "I started tending the book stand after work. People came every day to get books and ask questions. I invited them to the house of prayer and the church grew. Lena, my wife, and her mother started coming to church because of that library."

He got married and was ordained as a deacon at the age of twenty. Andre began coming less often and then stopped coming at all. Responsibility for the church rested on Romon.

Andre had not forgotten him, though, and invited Romon to be part of the leadership team for the Training Center when it started. Romon was then twenty-three.

He later told Cory, "When I joined the Training Center, I did not really understand what I had joined. It was like...you know the movie, *Finding Nemo?* I felt like Nemo's father when he got caught in the Eastern Australian Current. He felt out of control, but he knew if he got out of the current, he would be lost.

"This vision for evangelism has given me and our church a greater sense of purpose. Without vision, I'd be like a computer without an operating system. You turn it on and it's blank."

Romon invited us to their Christmas service on January 7, followed by dinner in his home. About a hundred people gathered for the program, held at the city's cultural hall. I noticed that many women did not wear a head covering, and I liked the apparent lack of legalism.

Janelle and Alicia preferred the party for children after the service. After a retelling of the Christmas story, a tall young man came in wearing a silky lavender bathrobe and a turban. As he passed out gifts, I realized he must be one of the magi.

Clutching their bags with candy and mandarins, the girls squeezed into the backseat of our car with Romon, his wife Lena, their three-year-old daughter, and a baby girl. Their apartment seemed small and shabby, but Lena said, "It's much better than living with my mother-in-law in her tiny apartment."

She ushered us into their small living room. "We don't have any heat," she said, "but this room gets warm from the kitchen." She pulled back a curtain, revealing several shelves. The bottom two held various toys. "We give toys to the poor, but we still have too many." I thought about our own abundance.

During dinner, we learned that their baby had emergency surgery for a blocked colon just two weeks earlier. She had been in pain for two days. They finally took her to the doctor, discovered she needed surgery, and drove four hours to Simferopol. "They operated from midnight until 3:00 a.m.," Lena said. "The believers here were praying for us. They prayed all night until 3:00 a.m. It was like God told them everything was fine then, and they could go to bed."

Romon added, "It's a miracle she's still alive. God gave her to us twice, once when she was born and then again with her operation."

I heard about a public service announcement on Ukrainian television encouraging people to conserve electricity. A cartoon figure sat in a corner reading, with a bare light bulb shining overhead. He turned on a reading lamp and the whole city went dark outside his window. He turned off his lamp, moved his chair under the bare bulb, and the city had light once again.

Apparently Feodosia's residents used too many reading lamps since our power continued to go out—not every day but several times a week. It usually went off in the evening, during the hours people used more electricity for cooking and heating.

Our first winter in Ukraine, we used candles and sat in semi-darkness. Many nights, Cory made shadow figures on the wall to entertain Janelle and Alicia, while I tried to stifle a growing sense of irritation as the evening passed without enough light to do what I wanted. The next year we got a kerosene lamp. We eventually found lamps with rechargeable batteries and bought two, one for the kitchen and one for the living room. Cory also got a rechargeable car battery that put out power when the lamp batteries failed. Thus equipped, life went on for us, even when the electricity did not.

People usually took the blackouts in stride. Students in the girls' gymnastics class continued to exercise by the light of a candle. Store clerks ignored fancy new cash registers and went back to using the abacus. During our first four years, all shops used this square contraption with rows of beads for adding up purchases and calculating change.

Often we had no electricity four hours in the morning and another four in the evening. Less often it was off all day but came back on at bedtime, to cool the contents of our refrigerator and recharge our computer battery.

A notice appeared on each entrance door of our apartment building. It said the electricity would be turned off because the following apartments had not paid their bills. Of the 176 apartments in our building, it listed ten numbers, a lower percentage than I expected.

The next day the electricity went off at 6:00 a.m. and did not come back on until 10:00 that night. Every time I went outside, I passed clusters, usually of women, clucking loudly about the lack of electricity. Janelle said, "They sound like hens."

Alicia asked, "Mommy, what did you do when you were a little girl and the lights went off?" I could not think of any time the lights went off. If they did, it was the exciting result of a storm, not an "oh, no, not again" affair.

During our brief tour through Greek history, we read about the Stoics, who believed happiness comes by taking an "it doesn't matter" attitude about everything, either good or bad. The Apostle Paul took a little different approach and said he learned to be content in everything, either good or bad. Some things matter in life, but electricity is not a prerequisite for joy. While washing dishes by flickering candlelight—since our rechargeable battery lamp had not recharged—I could be grateful for eyesight, thinking of those who lived in complete darkness their whole lives.

With a propane tank for our gas stove, I could continue to cook. I pulled a jar of stewed goose broth from the freezer, our leftovers from Christmas, and made some goose noodle soup.

Several years earlier, Cory began a contest with the girls to see who could be the first to say, "Thank you for the good food." Hardly a meal went by that I did not hear, "Thank you for the good food."

The goose noodle soup brought on one of the variations: "Thank you for this nutritious food."

I tried goose borscht next, thinking the strong flavors of bay leaves, garlic, onion, and cabbage would cover up the goose taste.

In response to my efforts, I got a halfhearted "Thank you for this, uh, colorful food."

"Colorful food?" I asked.

They complained, "There's too much meat in it!" They preferred the watery, meatless borscht served in Russian homes.

"People who eat out of garbage cans would be happy to have that borscht," I lectured. Other mothers talk about starving children in Africa, but I did not have to go that far.

I got a call from Yeva. "I don't have any money," she said, "and I don't have any food. I won't have money until Wednesday." She had joined the church several years earlier, but she still heard "voices" that frightened her. She once told me, "The devil sits right there," and pointed to the back of her neck. I had talked and prayed with her. Many others had too, both local believers and visitors, but she never seemed to get better. Anya told me, "She grew up in an orphanage and likes to be dependent."

Yeva earned some money as a street sweeper, but it was never enough. She called on church members with a merciful bent, seeking food or money, but had worn out her welcome with most. Her husband had returned to their shack from prison and added an extra drain on finances with his thirst for alcohol.

I thought of Christ's words, "Give to those who ask of you," but I wondered what I could give that would truly help her. I did not want to encourage dependence and feared her leach-like tendency—but she probably really was hungry. I doubted she weighed even one hundred pounds. For now, a jar of meaty goose borscht would help. I invited her over for a bag of food.

Cory met twice a week with Andre and Stefan. They prayed for the men receiving training as church planters and talked about how to help ordinary Christians become more effective in evangelism. The Bible shows that all believers are to share their faith, not just the "professionals."

Andre said, "Americans come all the way to Ukraine for outreach. People in our churches should be able to evangelize too."

They discussed the idea with the other Training Center leaders and decided to challenge believers to give one week of their summer vacation for evangelism, since most people got a month off every year. Each church could decide how to use those who participated, either to build up their own congregation or to help form a new church plant.

They planned to hold seminars once a month, from February until June, to help Christians feel more prepared to share their faith. Andre pointed out, "Effective evangelism is not a program to add to other programs in the church. It must flow out of a vital relationship with Christ. Many believers don't understand salvation is based on what Christ did for us." They wanted to use the seminars to give a better understanding of the Gospel.

After their planning meeting, Cory told me, "I can't believe how long it took to write the proposal today. They wanted to make sure they got it worded just right. They included lots of Scripture so they won't be accused of heresy."

Even if the groundwork took time, it helped to partner with local leaders who understood the culture and knew better than we did how to pass along the vision.

The next Saturday, Cory attended the meeting in Simferopol for church leaders from all over Crimea. Andre presented the plan for a summer evangelism focus and encouraged the pastors to promote it in their churches. "We often think of evangelism last, but we need to make it a priority," he said.

Some nodded, but Feodorovich stood up and said that people could not do evangelism unless they were spiritual, and they could not be spiritual unless they got rid of their televisions. Furthermore, pastors should be a good example and get rid of their televisions first.

He went on to blast Americans for being liberal and directed several questions at Cory, expecting confirmation. Wasn't it true that American women wore pants and makeup to church, but no head covering? And

Americans didn't show respect for God by standing or kneeling when they pray? Cory felt uncomfortable and decided not to say anything.

Then another pastor jumped in. He told of an American missionary who was shocked by the immodest swimsuits worn on Crimean beaches, even by believers. She had said, "We would never dress like that!" So in some ways, Americans were more conservative. He gave a long speech defining spirituality as having one's heart right with God.

Even at the market, I realized outward appearance does not guarantee quality. I went through two coffee makers in two weeks before buying a more expensive model from Germany. I bought Janelle a jacket labeled "Made in Germany," but doubted it really was. Sure enough, the zipper soon broke. Anya said she once bought ground meat that quickly turned black—she thought they probably added ground potatoes to the mixture.

I had never seen any decaffeinated coffee at the market, so I inquired one day. The woman recommended a jar of "Neeckafe." The label looked almost identical to the name brand in color, picture, and lettering. It read: "100% coffee. A drink for connoisseurs from the best plantations of Central America." I bought it and took it home.

The contents smelled and tasted like a cereal-based coffee substitute. I got something decaf, but I thought this "coffee" was like some people. It might say all the right things, but inside it was not the real thing. Still, the presence of a poor imitation does not mean the genuine does not exist.

11

Without Ruts,You Need More Faith

February 2001

The building they had used in Nizhnigorski lacked heat, so the Training Center leaders moved their sessions for church planters to the Primorski House of Prayer. Cory came home each night, figuring he would get more sleep in his own bed. In spite of his early departure and late arrival each day, I got a brief update and could follow the ups and downs of his week.

"My lecture was horrible," he said on his first night. "They couldn't seem to get it. I know my Russian stinks, but it doesn't help when they laugh at me. I still don't have my endings right." I understood that difficulty very well. Russian words have six possible endings, which change according to how the word is used in a sentence.

"I wonder why some of the guys are even in the program," he continued. "They ask these questions, like they just want to argue or show how smart they are, not because they want to learn. Sometimes I wonder, what are we doing here? Let's just go home."

Tuesday was better. He thought his lesson on how to lead a Bible study discussion group went well. One student asked, "Why should I ask questions when I'm the leader, and I should already know the answer?" The men had few examples to follow, since teachers usually lectured without encouraging discussion. Cory explained that through discussion they could build relationships, teach group members to think, and hold Scripture as the final authority instead of the leader.

Wednesday he told me about the church planters' ministry reports and how they had used the Christmas season to make contacts. One said he focused on the five-story apartment buildings in his region and went door to door wishing people a Merry Christmas. If they did not slam the door in his face, he asked them if they knew Jesus and offered them a tract or booklet.

As a whole, the students saw fruit from their efforts. The 28 men now worked with 41 groups, attended by a total of about 500 people. This included groups for children, but we felt encouraged.

On Thursday Cory said, "Sergei did a great job teaching about discipleship. The teachers have really improved. It's encouraging to watch them take ownership of these topics." Cory had taught on discipleship when Sergei was a student in the previous course. Sergei took the information and made it even more applicable to the local culture.

While Cory struggled with Russian grammar, I battled the phone system. The phones had always presented a challenge. If we dialed too fast, we got a wrong number; we sometimes got a wrong number anyway. When checking e-mail with our dial-up service, I sometimes heard, "Hello?" instead of the buzz of a successful connection. If we talked too long, we lost our connection. Someone told us, "You get cut off after an hour because their tapes are only sixty minutes long."

Whether or not that was true, this week I could not get through to any number. An occasional dial tone encouraged me to try e-mail one more time, but I could never connect. The aggravation brought the what-are-we-doing-here feelings to the surface for me too. The Apostle Paul called trials "momentary, light afflictions," but he never dealt with computers or Russian telephones. This no longer seemed light nor momentary.

At last I went to our neighbor upstairs to call the phone company. I did not have all my Russian endings in place either but wanted service. I felt less confident on the phone than in person, since I could not use hand motions or facial expression to help get my point across. Not all strangers were as patient as our friends.

Valentina led me to their telephone in the kitchen. There I found the source of the sour smell that met me at the door—great pots of fermenting cabbage for homemade sauerkraut. I successfully made my phone call, and she urged me to sit for a bit. No, she commanded me to sit. It is useless to argue with a Russian grandma.

"Do you have something you want to tell me?" she asked.

I could not think of anything special. I shrugged. "The children are fine. The oldest daughter has a cough, but it's the season for it."

It soon became clear she had questions about my faith. She said, "I go to the Orthodox Church sometimes, but I am never sure where I should stand—you know they do not allow you to sit. And I cannot understand anything there since they use the old Slavic language." She told how she went to the Pentecostal Church for a while. "I can sit down there, and I understand the music and preaching; but someone told me to throw away my icons, so I left. What do you think about icons?"

As I had told our landlady, I explained that icons began as a way to help illiterate people remember important parts of the Bible. People started praying to these paintings, but only God can answer prayer.

She seemed satisfied by my answer. "Do you have any prayers I can read?" she asked.

"Written prayers can help focus our thoughts," I said. "There's the Lord's Prayer, for example. But God wants to have a relationship with us and wants us to go to Him with our concerns. God is like a good father. My children don't read from a paper when they want to talk to me." She nodded and looked thoughtful.

My what-are-we-doing-here thoughts disappeared, but I felt renewed regret over the lack of good church options for people like Valentina. I continued to hear stories of people getting wounded by the local pastor's harsh manner. I did not want to encourage anyone to go there, lest they become embittered toward Christianity.

We had met Andre and Stefan at the Feodosia House of Prayer, where we regularly attended our first four years in Ukraine. Although we now worshiped elsewhere, they felt compelled to stay. They saw the negative effect of Igor's leadership on the church but did not know what to do about it. They told Cory about long and frustrating council meetings. The brothers tried to correct Igor, but he simply turned on them. He criticized each of them, both in their meetings and in public. One brother gave a woman a ride in his car. Another one's daughter started wearing makeup and got her ears pierced.

Since each service contained three sermons, Igor often used his position as the final speaker to discredit what others had said before him. For example, when Andre taught on forgiveness and how our willingness to forgive relates to the quality of our relationship with God, Igor used his follow-up sermon to rip Andre's sermon apart.

When we had attended there, I saw how he used the Bible to tear down and discredit others. It seemed evil to me. Nevertheless, I knew "our battle is not against flesh and blood" but against a greater enemy. I could pray.

I decided to attend church in Feodosia the next Sunday. Cory told me, "Go ahead, but I'm not going. The girls and I will go to Primorski."

"I don't have very high expectations," I replied, "but I can use the time to pray." I went early so I could visit a bit.

Many people greeted me warmly; men shook my hand and women kissed my cheek. Igor scolded the women talking to me: "Sisters! Go sit down!" We obeyed, even though fifteen minutes remained until time for the service.

I thought the service was fine until Igor started speaking. He said that some people might be starting new churches, starting small groups, and doing evangelism. But these activities were not as important as worshiping God in

73

spirit and in truth. "These people are like Pharisees who want to be seen for their good works. Jesus said we are to pray in our closet. Martha was busy, but Mary had it right."

It looked to me like an attack on those in ministry outside his control, like Stefan, Andre, and us; and a warning to church members not to get involved. It wasn't the first time I had seen Igor try to undermine the influence of others. I had gone prepared to pray, and I did, but his sermon disturbed me so deeply I felt wiped out the rest of the day.

I told Cory, "I've been a lot happier this year than in the past. Maybe it's because we haven't been attending at Feodosia. I feel sorry for the people who have to listen to him all the time. They want to hear some fresh teaching. A lot of them told me they miss you and want you to come and preach."

"Even if I went there, I wouldn't be allowed to preach," Cory replied. "If I did preach, he would rip it apart afterward. I don't need that."

The church council finally complained about Igor to Feodorovich, the overseer of churches in Crimea. He agreed to meet with them and Igor. In a long, tense meeting, he supported Igor and rebuked the brothers. The meeting ended at midnight, but neither Stefan nor Andre slept much afterward.

Cory and I renewed our prayers for a healthy church body in Feodosia, a channel of healing and life to people who needed hope. We prayed Igor would repent or be removed, or that God would bring in someone who could set up an alternative. Cory, Stefan, and Andre still thought it would cause too many problems if they tried to form another church.

In spite of this discouragement, we saw godly pastors who sought to equip Christians to bless their communities. Sergei was one of these. He led a growing congregation in Nizhnigorski, oversaw church plants in the surrounding region, and served as one of the leaders for the Training Center.

Sergei grew up not far from Chernobyl in Ukraine. He was twelve when the Chernobyl nuclear power plant blew up in 1986, and his parents sent him to Crimea to live with his older sister. He began attending church with her. At the age of eighteen, he gave his life to Christ and looked for ways to serve.

He joined our first church planters' training program when he was twenty-five. Soon afterward, the pastor of his church in Nizhnigorski moved away, and he agreed to take on that role. Fortunately, it was a healthy flock, teachable and mainly made up of newer believers. Under his leadership, the church continued to grow. In three years, church leaders baptized 120 people and started fourteen church plants in the surrounding region. All members of the church council helped with evangelism and worked to start new groups.

I visited the Training Center one day and sat with Sergei at lunch. I wanted to hear his philosophy of ministry and get clues to the church's success. He could not be personally responsible for all those additions.

In his gentle, soft-spoken manner, Sergei said, "It is hard for me to take the role of a leader. I prefer to simply help someone else, so I try to help the brothers and help the church reach her potential. The church is a body, and when all members work together, it is healthy and can accomplish something."

I asked him, "How do you encourage people in your congregation to reach out?"

"Christians need to understand that the church exists to serve the world, not itself," he replied. "They also need to understand the grace of God. Some people think of God as a God who wants this, this, this, and this. They don't see God as One who gives to us. If I understand God's love, then I want to serve others."

I recalled how Andre had also said knowing God's grace had motivated him for evangelism, so he included that focus in his teaching.

"The church can get so concerned about things God is not concerned with," Sergei continued. "Some people stay in ruts, like we have in our dirt roads. They don't even think about where they should go; they just follow the ruts. When you don't have ruts to follow, it can be frightening—it takes more faith in God."

"Many older churches have a hard time reaching out to new people," I noted. "Is that because of persecution during the Soviet Era? Are they afraid of outsiders?"

"No, that's not it at all," he said. "The biggest problem is the accent of the teaching. They focus on dogma and discipline and trying to do everything right. The church loses its life. They do not teach on the grace of God. Some people think this teaching about grace is something new, but it's not. I've read biographies of men from different countries who ministered out of an understanding of God's love. These men faced the same problem with churches that left the basics of the Gospel. Paul addressed this issue in his letter to the Galatians: people thought they could satisfy God based on their works. If I live by the law, I am more concerned for myself, not the world."

He believed that evangelism and church planting were not that difficult. "Some churches make Christianity too complicated," he said. "Paul says in 1 Timothy 1:5 that the goal of our instruction is love from a pure heart, a good conscience, and a sincere faith. The basic Gospel message is simple. When people see God for who He is, they will respond."

His church had a significant track record, having started fourteen church plants in neighboring villages. "What methods do you use to start new groups?" I asked.

"We look to see where the Holy Spirit is working and try to follow His leading. Usually we try to start a church where there is someone seeking God. In one village, for example, there was just one Christian woman. She asked us to come and help. Her son accepted Christ in prison and got out, so then there were two believers. They invited people to her home. Now there is a house church there with ten baptized believers.

"Sometimes church planters use a series of tracts and take them door to door as a way to make contacts and find out who is open. Some groups started after Child Evangelism Fellowship began Bible clubs in that village and parents became open through their children. More important than the method is that the church planter must feel called to this work and have the desire to reach people for Christ. We can try many different methods, but if the heart isn't in it, it won't be successful."

He described how most of the new churches started as fellowship groups. "Earlier we thought groups should be study groups, but they died out because new people felt stupid when they started coming and didn't understand what the study was about. Now believers invite people to fellowship groups where they drink tea, sing, and feel free to talk about their problems. The leader says something from the Word of God since without that, needs aren't met either. People have a great hunger inside and need food for their soul. They need hope."

I felt proud and grateful that Sergei had studied with and now taught for the Training Center. He seemed wise for his twenty-eight years. Still, I expected his role was not easy and asked, "What difficulties come with your ministry?"

"This has been the hardest year of my life," he replied. "Sometimes, especially during the summer, we have had all capable leaders out evangelizing and leading groups in different villages in the surrounding area, so we were left without anyone to lead music or brothers to preach. We are also trying to build a new house of prayer. I've had so many responsibilities, I came to the place where I didn't have anything. No strength to go on. No words of wisdom to preach. I feared this death of myself, but when I came to the end of myself, I saw that Jesus is the resurrection and the life."

The girls and I joined Cory one brisk Sunday morning in February for Sergei's ordination. We arrived early at the village house-converted-to-church. Its bright blue door and window frames accented the whitewashed walls.

Sergei greeted us warmly. His young wife jostled a stroller to put their well-bundled baby back to sleep. Their two other small children looked on shyly. "We still have time," Sergei said. "Would you like to see the progress on our construction?"

He led us to an unfinished larger building around back. We stepped inside. "Now that we have the roof on," Sergei said, "people can keep working as long as it is not too cold." Noting the rough walls of large, porous blocks and the gravel floor, it looked to me like they still had a long way to go. Church members gave sacrificially for building materials and provided the labor—all volunteer.

"Of course we don't want to stop ministry for the sake of the building," Sergei continued, "so the brothers work on the building some days and some days they do ministry. I don't even know how it keeps getting built, but it does. I am surprised the work keeps going on."

Cory and other church leaders soon gathered in the "brothers' room" while I looked for a seat. The hall to the house church was filling quickly. The girls decided to play outside with other children, which was just as well with the tight seating. An overflow crowd stood outside in the cold and listened to the service from loudspeakers. They did need that new building.

Knowing that more important church leaders would be there, Cory had not planned to take part in the service—just watch and support. Nevertheless, they asked him to give one of the sermons and join the others in the "laying on of hands" and praying for Sergei.

Together, Sergei, his wife, and the leaders acknowledged the need for God's help, strength, and wisdom.

New churches begin through fellowship groups.

God provides hope for each generation.

Bible clubs for children open doors to parents.

12

Each Day Is a Gift of God

March – May 2001

J anelle and Alicia enjoyed their sewing class at the Center for Creativity for Children and felt accepted, even though they were much younger than the other girls. After sewing several stuffed animals by hand, they began making dolls and fabric flowers. On Janelle's ninth birthday, the students all brought goodies and chipped in to buy her a book of Russian fairy tales.

The students began the tea party by standing and singing the Sunday school songs Janelle and Alicia had taught them, complete with hand motions. "Fish in the water, birds everywhere. Loving the Savior..." It surprised me to see those teenage girls singing with such enthusiasm. Even the teacher sang. After cake, cookies, and tea, they played games.

Janelle came home with a big grin after her gymnastics class and said, "We practiced somersaults today and the teacher made *me* a teacher. I'm the third best in the class in somersaults, since most of the others forgot how to do them." She told how the teacher gave her a group of students to instruct. She looked pleased but said, "I was embarrassed."

This teacher rarely passed out compliments, so any affirmation went a long way. Earlier that week, I had watched students do somersaults and listened to her comments: "That's bad. That's bad. Bad..." Only exceptional students received any praise. The girls came home discouraged occasionally, but they learned a lot and did not want to quit.

The sewing teacher smiled easily and gave compliments more generously. One day she told me, "Your girls are quite talented." She turned her head to the side, pretended to spit with a "*ptu, ptu,*" and knocked on the table.

I had seen this spitting and knocking before but never understood it, so when Anya came for the girls' next Russian lesson, I asked her about it. "It probably goes back to the time people in Ukraine worshiped the sun and trees and things in nature," she replied. "They believed every house had a spirit who lived there, the spirit of an ancestor. People think if you speak well of someone, you give them the evil eye, and the spirit will make things go bad for that person unless you spit over your left shoulder or knock on wood."

This was our fifth year in Ukraine, but I still felt surprised by aspects of the culture—like the idea that people improve if criticized and will be cursed if praised. When Cory complimented his co-workers, they seemed embarrassed and uncomfortable.

Anya continued, "When I first started teaching, I always praised the students when they got the right answer. An older teacher heard me and scolded me for doing that." She still piled on the praise with her Sunday school class and with Janelle and Alicia. In return, they loved her and blossomed under her care.

Now into a routine with sewing, gymnastics, Russian, and homeschool lessons, the girls wanted to learn to play the piano. I asked around and learned that a piano teacher lived in our building, just a few doors down from us. She taught at the music school downtown but agreed to take Janelle and Alicia as private students in her home.

I went to the first lesson. The teacher sat near her piano and lectured about the different parts of the instrument, different composers, and different kinds of music. Alicia played with the cat while she talked. Finally, the teacher tested their sense of tone and rhythm.

"What did you think?" I asked the girls afterward.

"I liked it," Alicia replied. "She has a cat."

Janelle looked more doubtful. "I don't think I'll be able to answer her questions. She said she is going to test us next time, and I didn't understand half of what she said."

Before their next lesson, I suggested to the teacher, "Since they still don't understand so much Russian, it might be better if they can start learning to play. That way they won't lose interest."

I did not stay for the lesson, but Janelle came home smiling. "It was fun," she reported. "She said I'm very smart."

Alicia came home after her hour saying she liked it too: "I got to play with the cat." She prayed at lunch and again at night, "Thank you that we get to take music lessons."

I felt grateful for this answer to prayer, more evidence of God's ability to take care of little details. Homeschooling seemed like our best option, but I had hoped for outside activities. God provided, right in our part of town.

I learned with the girls as we studied ancient history. Picture books helped us see what life was like in Egypt when Moses and Joseph lived there. Janelle and Alicia drew scenes from Bible stories to paste on our timeline as we covered the Assyrian, Babylonian, and Persian empires.

While learning about the Greek period, we visited the historical museum downtown. Along with artifacts from other civilizations, we looked at Greek pottery fragments, masks for theater, and a mini statue of the goddess Demeter. The girls climbed on the two stone lions outside, recovered from a Greek shipwreck. Greeks had settled Feodosia in 500 B.C. and used Crimea as a source of grain and slaves.

Anya came for the girls' Russian lesson looking discouraged one day. She explained she had just come from a consultation with Dr. Bob, an American briefly helping the church clinic. Anya had never fully recovered since her heart attack four months earlier. She still lacked her former stamina and sparkle, but Dr. Bob offered no easy answers.

He explained that even in America her problem would be difficult to treat, requiring surgery and close observation. Because her heart did not function properly, it could kick out another blood clot at any time, which could hit the brain.

After her Russian lesson, I invited Anya to the kitchen. "We are all dying," I said. "None of us knows how long we have to live. Your condition is serious, but you have the chance to accept every day as a gift from God and look for ways to live that day for Him."

She nodded, but I wondered later if I had been too blunt. People in Ukraine were big on giving wishes for long life and happiness and avoided any talk of death.

After the next Russian lesson, we sat in my kitchen again and talked over tea. I said, "Maybe it was bad for me to say, 'You're dying. We're all dying...'"

She interrupted me. "Now you are acting like a Russian. A Russian would say, 'Everything will be all right.' It was good what you said, that I should look at each day as a gift from God. I have always been healthy. When I am in pain like this, I don't want to live, but every day is a gift from God. I just hope I will be well enough to work with camp this year." She seemed calmer than she had been for a while, more at peace.

Warmer weather brought fewer power outages. Spring rain washed away the coal smoke that hung over the city. The air smelled fresh on my early morning walk with Cory. Cherry blossoms brought color to bare tree branches. The weeping willow tree by our apartment building showed a tinge of green. I bought daffodils to brighten our table. My favorite milk lady returned after a winter absence, bringing milk to town on her bicycle.

With spring here, the Training Center leaders began holding monthly seminars in eastern and western Crimea, preparing Christians for an evangelistic focus that summer. Between the two locations, over 120 people attended from twenty churches. They learned practical tips on how to talk to people and ask nonthreatening questions, but most sessions focused on God's love for all and His gift of grace.

Cory told me, "Many people have always heard that acceptance by God is based on following many rules. Stefan counseled a woman not long ago who had gone to church for many years but had no assurance of salvation. She was afraid she had not done enough to please God. Stefan showed her from the Bible that our salvation is based on God's grace, not our works. She cried hearing that."

When pastors from all over Crimea gathered for their next meeting, Andre intended to promote evangelism in general and talk about preparations for summer outreaches. When Cory got home afterward, he said, "Feodorovich took up most of the time with his talk. He went on and on about how we need to make sure we are holy, and that we must promote holiness in our churches before we can do any evangelism. I think he's afraid that if too many new people start coming to church, it will dilute the status quo. If holiness is the main goal, you don't want a lot of unholy people around with their messy problems."

The pastor who spoke next put the emphasis back on evangelism. "Before a husband and wife can raise their children, they need to have children first," he said. "Similarly, the church needs new people before we can expect to influence them."

With just fifteen minutes left to the three-hour meeting, Andre finally got his turn. He took it into overtime. He stressed that Christ died for everyone, not just the Christians. Churches can get so focused on their programs, they forget the reason for their existence: to bring people into a relationship with Christ.

Fortunately, some were looking beyond themselves. When the men in the church planters' course came for training every third week, they reported on their outreach efforts. Now ten months into the course, all had seen results in their endeavor to start groups in areas without churches. Some saw great openness in their communities, even among a Muslim people group, but all faced challenges.

One man described the great opposition he experienced in one village where he led a group. The collective farm director, the most powerful person in town, viewed these Christians as a threat. She would not allow them to meet in any public building or public place, forbade any children's programs, and did what she could to hinder the work.

In another village, however, he had good relationships with town officials. He and his group of new believers organized a community celebration for "Women's Day" and sang Christian songs at the concert. That collective-farm director was so impressed, she set up appointments for him with officials in other towns so they could put on similar programs there.

Since June Johnson, our nurse teammate, planned to return to Ukraine late in April, we needed to find her an apartment. I hoped we could get something as nice for her as she had found for us. We finally located one, just in time, through a doctor acquaintance who knew of June's work. It needed kitchen cabinets and wallpaper but came mostly furnished.

Janelle and Alicia looked forward to her arrival and made a big "Welcome Home" sign for her new apartment. A couple weeks later, June took time out from apartment repairs and her medical work to call Janelle and Alicia into a secret conference.

I did not think much about it until Alicia said, "When June comes over tomorrow, you HAVE to stay in your room and then you CAN'T go out on the balcony." I obediently lay in bed reading while the smell of baking brownies filled the apartment.

On Mother's Day, the next day, they treated me to brownies and pudding, followed by a dramatic rendition of "The Tortoise and the Hare." It was the only time I had seen Janelle wear a turtleneck without complaining. Alicia lay down for a nap in her bunny ears. June played the hippo, wearing a pink comforter over pillow padding. She stood at the finish line cheering, "Go, Turtle! Go, Turtle!" Cory and I laughed and applauded their performance. No need for fancy outings when you live with such talent.

Spring made everything look better. Tulips followed daffodils. Lilacs budded. Then the sweet scent of locust-tree blossoms hung over the city. "You'll probably laugh," Cory said on our morning walk, "but I think I am starting to feel more at home and almost like it here."

I did laugh—a delighted giggle—since I had heard many verses of the "Life is Hard Here Blues." I had sung them too, but it's good to find joy in the place one lives, not merely long for pleasures found far away. I liked this time of year with flowers and greenery. The longer and warmer days already resulted in more produce at the market—lettuce, radishes, and new potatoes. I looked forward to the sun-ripened tomatoes of summer.

"What do you like?" I asked Cory.

"What?"

"You said you are feeling at home and like it here."

"No, I said I'm *starting* to feel at home and *almost* like it. Why are you laughing?"

"I'm just being sympathetic," I said, trying to stifle a giggle.

"It varies from day to day," he added, "sometimes from hour to hour. When we were in Budapest, I realized how oppressive it is here."

I remembered well our spring visit there. Cory noted how people could leave cars outside overnight. Janelle and Alicia loved the good playground equipment. It felt more European to me than Soviet.

Still, I pressed on and asked, "Okay, then, when you like it here, what do you like?"

Cory said, "I can finally deal with public officials without needing someone to do it all for me. For example, I got the gas meter and water meter installed. I'm used to the way they do things now, and so I don't get so upset when it takes three days instead of one hour.

"I like the guys I work with. I like seeing change in people. Some of the church planters have really grown. Great things are happening with Sergei and his church in Nizhnigorski. I guess I'm mostly glad just to be a part of what God is doing here. It's amazing to see that God is able to use me."

We had learned to persevere when nothing felt rewarding, but we could finally see fruit.

The stone lion came from an ancient Greek shipwreck, not far from Feodosia.

13

A Different Philosophy of Treatment

June 2001

Early in June the men being trained as church planters gathered for a final week of teaching for the one-year lecture phase. Cory told me, "This week we divided the guys among the leaders for the mentoring stage. We'll visit them during this next year to talk and pray and see how they lead their groups. And maybe make some suggestions. Since I have a car, they asked me to take the two who live on the far side of Crimea. You might get tired of me being gone so much."

I thought the girls and I would get along fine while he was gone. We kept busy, and June came over occasionally to visit.

With her birthday still six weeks away, Alicia had already figured out her guest list and what games they would play. "Mama, I want to make napkin rings for everyone," she said one day. "Can you help me make salt dough?"

I measured out salt and flour for her. Janelle soon joined her, creating shapes at the table. When I checked the cookie sheet later, I did not find many napkin rings. "Those are beads, and that's a jewelry box," Alicia said.

Janelle pointed to a square blob and added, "I made a bed for a mouse I'm going to sew."

When June came over on Saturday, the girls eagerly greeted her at the door. "We made you something," Alicia said, "but you have to look for it." They gave "hot" and "cold" as clues, giggling and hopping as she got closer. Eventually she found her prize: a necklace made from salt-dough beads, now painted fluorescent colors.

"Thank you!" she exclaimed. "It matches my clothes." At least the blue matched.

She wore her present when they walked to the park, but the girls told her, "You should put it inside your shirt. People are staring at it."

A few days later June called and asked, "Can you be my translator this afternoon?" She planned to meet with the clinic staff and had asked Tatiana to translate, but Tatiana had a sudden change of plans. June's Russian wasn't bad, but she wanted to communicate and understand fully. I didn't know how much help I would be, but I couldn't think of any other translator. Anya agreed to come a little early for the girls' Russian lesson, giving me the freedom to leave.

The meeting did not start at 2:00 as planned. The clinic staff first wanted to ask June how to treat some difficult wound cases. A cat scratch on the leg of a diabetic had become horribly swollen and infected.

Next, June saw an older woman with open sores on her leg, a complication of swelling from poor circulation. She typically sat for eight to ten hours a day on a stool selling sunflower seeds. June had seen her before with the same problem. The woman wanted some medication to heal her wounds.

June said, "You need to lie in bed with your feet propped up on pillows. You must stay home and do this for ten days. It might not take that long, but if you don't treat it now, it will get worse."

June often had repeat patients who wanted her to fix their problems but would not follow instructions. Does God feel similar frustration with people?

Finally, we sat down for our meeting. The clinic staff consisted of two doctors and two nurses, all Christian women. Besides seeing patients twice a week at the church clinic, they made house calls. They used their contacts to talk to people about God and pray with them.

Dr. Lidiya reported, "God has especially blessed the clinic ministry the last few months. The people who come now are seeking God. They ask for spiritual help, not just physical."

With her background as a registered nurse specializing in wound care, June had trained one of the nurses to take on her job while she was gone. June had no desire to work in competition with this nurse. "I would like to see patients on a consultant basis this time," she said. "If one of you has already seen the person, and you want my opinion, I will see the patient with you and use it as a teaching time."

The women nodded. One replied, "We want to learn everything you know." June also hoped to help church planters by doing medical outreaches in villages and perhaps provide training for city medical personnel.

About a week earlier, someone in the church had asked June to go see a woman in the hospital with a serious bedsore. June declined, saying, "It will do no good for me to go. They have such a different philosophy of treatment here. If I try to treat anyone who is still in the hospital, the doctor gets offended and takes it out on the patient."

The new wounds nurse went instead and reported, "The wound was so deep, so black, and so awful, I got frightened. I didn't know what to do."

She assured June that the head doctor had asked for her to come and even asked if she would provide training for the nurses at the hospital. June did go, but the woman had a stroke that morning and was dying.

June said she wanted to teach prevention since many problems, like bedsores, could be easily avoided using inexpensive materials and techniques. Besides relieving suffering, she hoped the teaching relationships would open opportunities for Christian witness.

My clinic visit confirmed that I did not want to take up professional translation work any time soon, but between the two of us, we understood and communicated what we needed to. I was glad to get a closer look at the clinic ministry. While busy with my little world at home, I did not see the needs out there.

When Tatiana called that evening, I discovered why she could not translate for June. "The director of the gallery suddenly quit," she said, "and I will take her place. God answered your prayers."

Tatiana came over the next day and filled in the details. The director was already six years past retirement age, and her superiors on the town council had tried to get her to quit for some time. She finally put in her resignation, giving three days' notice. The town council appointed Tatiana to replace her.

"My vacation was supposed to start this week," she said, "but I need to postpone it until I am more familiar with my new responsibilities."

"What do your co-workers think about it?" I asked.

"They don't know yet," she said. "When I go in on Friday, I will just go to the director's office, find the chair empty, and make myself at home."

The next week, I asked her, "How is your new job going?"

She replied, "Many people come to me with questions about everything." The former boss, especially during the final months of her reign, would walk around screaming, "I'm the director around here, and you will obey me!"

Tatiana took a different approach to leadership. She explained, "When people ask me what to do, I ask them, 'What do you think you should do?'"

June finished remodeling her apartment and inspired me to undertake some repairs in my own. When I first saw the wallpaper in my kitchen, I disliked it intensely but learned to ignore it. June suggested, "Why don't you get something you like better, something more restful?" I decided the landlady would not mind since the paper looked old and inexpensive.

With wallpaper as standard décor in every home, most women in Ukraine knew how to install it. One woman said she changed her wallpaper every spring because of mildew in her village home. Anya knew the art very well and showed me how to match patterns, wrap around corners, and cut holes for electrical outlets. It brought back memories of craft projects in grade school— this was just a bigger cut-and-paste job.

One home-repair project led to another. I painted the radiator pipes, but the cheap paintbrush kept shedding bristles, so we ended up with texture.

I told June, "I'd like to repair the water damage in the ceiling, too." She brought over a little bag of white rocks, left over from her apartment repairs.

Fortunately, I had seen these white rocks before. We once visited a couple who showed us how they made their own spackle and whitewash. They explained how they first put chunks of limestone in their coal stove. After the rocks had baked and cooled, they dropped the rocks in water, setting off a chemical reaction. The water bubbled and steamed as the rocks got hot and broke down into white mush.

I wondered if it would work for me. I added water to June's rocks. At first I saw just muddy water and rocks, but the water started boiling, and the rocks disintegrated. I used the thick mush to replace missing plaster in the ceiling. Lacking proper tools, I smeared it in place with a kitchen spatula.

I thinned the remainder down for whitewash. My motivation to whitewash the whole kitchen ceiling did not last long since it was hard to apply and dripped all over. Part of the ceiling looked brighter anyway. It had texture too, from my lumpy whitewash.

Valentina, our neighbor with a garden, called and asked if I wanted to buy some strawberries. I went to her apartment and got a dishpan full.

As Janelle helped me clean them, she asked, "Why did you buy strawberries that are so small and sour?"

"I wanted to help her."

"Can't you help someone who has sweeter strawberries?" They still made good jam and with a little sugar, tasted good with pancakes or cake.

Life wasn't all work. Janelle and Alicia went swimming as often as possible. As we walked to the beach, Alicia enthusiastically told me, "The water is a lot warmer now. When we went with June, it was really cold, but if you stay in the water long enough, your legs go numb, so it doesn't matter." I stuck my foot in the water and decided that if this was "much warmer," they must have polar bear blood.

When Cory returned home after the final evangelism-training seminar for churches, he told me, "Only fifty people came this time, but they seem excited about doing outreach this summer. They divided into thirteen groups to discuss their strategy."

He explained that most would work with church planters. Typically, they would go door to door, talk to people, and invite them to a meeting in the evening. They also planned activities for children.

"So will everyone go at the same time?" I asked.

"No, each group will decide what week works best for them. To me, it's exciting to see churches taking responsibility for evangelistic outreach."

During the next church service in Primorski, we heard from one woman who had attended the two-day seminar. Instead of traveling home for the night, she stayed with relatives and told them how she had become a Christian. To her surprise, they asked many questions about spiritual matters. "No one left, and we talked until midnight! I praise God for this training. It gave me confidence and the ability to answer their questions."

Everything seemed to be going well until Cory called me later that week. "I need to tell you about something serious," he said. "I just talked to Galina, our landlady. We are being evicted from our apartment and have one week to find something else."

"What do you mean?" I asked. "She said we could stay here as long as we wanted to."

"It doesn't matter what she said. Galina's mother died several months ago, and now she has problems with her stepfather. She hit him on the head with a pan during an argument. Now he says he will send her to jail for attempted murder unless she gives him her apartment."

"What?" My brain struggled to process this new information. "Why should she give him the apartment?" And I had just put up new wallpaper.

Cory gave scant information over the phone but filled in the blanks when he got home. She had moved from our apartment to her mother's house by the Black Sea. She fixed it up to take in summer tourists and ran a café. Then her mother died. Her stepfather now said if she wanted to keep the house, he would trade it for her apartment. She offered to let us stay in the house with her or else in another house in that town.

Neither option sounded good to me. I did not want to live in the village or share a house with her, but to find another apartment on such short notice seemed unrealistic. We had spent months trying to find an apartment for June. It would be even harder to find something now, with summer tourist season here and all available apartments rented out to Russian tourists.

"Can't she move out to another place?" I asked Cory. "Or at least give us more than one week? Her problems should not have to affect us."

Cory consulted with Stefan and Andre. They prayed together. The girls and I prayed. I poured my nervous energy into cleaning the kitchen and making cookies. I reminded myself that God took care of the birds, and we were even more important to Him. He would meet our needs and give grace.

With the electricity off, I could not listen to soothing music. I tried to make my own and sang, "Whatever my lot, Thou hast taught me to say, 'It is well, it is well with my soul.'"

Cory visited Galina again and told her, "We have a contract, and we cannot move out now. We cannot consider getting another place until after the summer tourist season is over, but we are praying for you."

She said she would likely move out and leave her daughter at the house. When he got home, I asked Cory, "So is it settled now?"
"I don't know."

Besides her medical ministry, June (left) helped with VBS day camps.

14

Progress and Opposition

July 2001

Cory left around 5:00 a.m. the next Sunday morning to drive to northwestern Crimea with Andre and visit Vanya, one of the church planters. He came home surprisingly cheerful at 10:30 that night, with enough energy to talk about his day. They first attended an older church, which felt a little stiff, but they enjoyed their afternoon with Vanya and his new village church.

Over lunch Vanya told how losing his arm to cancer three years earlier brought him back to God and helped reshape his priorities. He began to serve God with zeal, wanting to make a difference with his life.

Not long after he began his training as a church planter, he started the group Cory and Andre visited. Two people soon turned to Christ and were baptized. Now, one year later, twenty-five came regularly, and he planned to baptize fifteen of them soon. Cory and Andre noted the enthusiastic and loving atmosphere in the group. One woman in the back kept saying "Amen!" whenever the preacher said something profound.

"These guys are catching it," Cory told me. "They're putting into practice the things they learned. It's going to work. It's already working."

I don't get excited too quickly. "But isn't Vanya a little brighter and more motivated than others?"

"Some of the guys struggle more and lack confidence—but they are seeing results too. The fields are ready for harvest. People want to know about God, and they will respond when they hear the Gospel. As long as church planters spend the time necessary, they have success."

The road contained stones, however, as illustrated by their morning visit to the older church. The pastor seemed upset by a concept Andre had taught Vanya and the other church planters, calling it "heresy." He questioned Andre on his beliefs and teaching.

Andre had taught on "life in the Spirit" and said we cannot expect to produce significant fruit based on our own works, but the Holy Spirit empowers us for fruitful ministry. The pastor kept saying, "We must look to God, not the Holy Spirit."

I interrupted Cory's account by saying. "I don't understand what the big deal is. The Holy Spirit is also part of the Godhead."

"Of course," he replied, "but the Holy Spirit seems more uncontrollable. Guys like this are afraid of emotional extremes. There's no heresy, but they like to use that word to discredit someone they don't agree with."

Andre finally opened his Bible and read: "The fruit of the Spirit is love, joy, peace, patience, kindness, goodness, faithfulness, gentleness, and self-control." He looked at the pastor and added, "Search yourself and pray. See if you have that fruit."

Cory tried several times to meet with our landlady but never found her at home or at her café. When he finally saw her, she said she had been taking care of her boyfriend after a train hit him when he fell asleep by the tracks. She did not say why he chose that location for a nap, but we often saw drunk men lying in uncomfortable places. She agreed to let us continue living in her apartment and asked for a loan or a two-month extension on our lease, since she had spent all her money helping him. Cory gladly gave her money and got a receipt, relieved by her promise.

With that settled, Cory went to visit a church planter who lived three hours away. He found Vadim behind his house, stacking dried grass with a pitchfork. He had cut it with a scythe earlier, preparing winter feed for his livestock. Every bit of land was put to use with a large garden, cows, pigs, chickens, turkeys, ducks, geese, and two dogs to guard it all.

The road leading to his village contained many potholes. Vadim said that according to official records, it was recently resurfaced. Since no workers came and nothing was done, the funds likely went into someone's pocket.

Cory told me, "Vadim talked nonstop for six hours. It's like he's been on a deserted island. He got out some juice after I got there at 10:00 but started talking and forgot to pour it until 1:30. His wife came home about then and prepared lunch. She works as a doctor in the village."

"So what did he talk about?" I asked.

"Problems. Economic problems in his area. The lack of water. Problems from his past. Problems getting new churches planted."

Vadim became a Christian about eight years earlier, while living in Sevastopol. Four years into his Christian walk, his home church sent him to start a church in a village north of Simferopol. It thrived. The problem was, he had been divorced and then remarried some ten years before he accepted

Christ. Other church leaders in the region said he should not be in ministry and should divorce his second wife and reunite with his first. They took the young church from him and put someone else in charge of it, but it died after he left.

The pastor in Sevastopol still thought God could use Vadim and encouraged him to enroll with the Training Center. He resisted at first—he had never read a book in his life and had no interest in studying. He joined anyway and found supportive relationships and practical advice.

Starting over in a new village, Vadim invited people to his home for fellowship and Bible study. After a year around thirty people came to Sunday services, and he had sixteen baptized members.

He still received criticism. The pastor in a larger town, forty minutes away by car, condemned him for starting a group in "his" territory. Furthermore, he said Vadim had been divorced before, so he should not lead a church anyway.

Vadim told Cory, "I understand they will never ordain me, but God already has. God called all believers to go. I can't simply sit." He saw how people lived in hopelessness. They leaned on drugs and alcohol, which made their lives only worse. He wanted to tell them the Good News he had found.

While going door to door, he met one family where everyone drank heavily, even the twelve-year-old. He continued to visit them and help them. "Their house is very dirty," he told Cory. "I feel sorry for them. I gave them some clothes and other things."

He told of new people who now came to study the Bible. A younger woman had been in jail for two years. Her mother came too. He tried to talk to a brother who had been in jail, but the man cursed God, said he didn't believe in Him, and later committed suicide.

He worked in two neighboring villages as well. His wife helped with children's work, and he visited the children in their homes as a way to meet their parents. Children seemed to grasp spiritual truth more easily.

He said, "I can't imagine doing anything else," but spoke of opposition and prejudice. Some people still believed rumors spread during Soviet times—that evangelical Christians ate children and had orgies.

Cory prayed with him and prepared to go. Vadim escorted Cory to the car, where he tucked in gifts of homemade butter and cottage cheese along with preserves from their garden: jam, pickles, and tomato juice.

Driving one hour further, Cory came to Vanya's home. "It was the same there," Cory reported. "He talked nonstop. I didn't even comment or give advice. He just talked until late that night and then began again the next morning."

Andre continued to promote outreach. At the last council meeting for church leaders, however, Feodorovich thoroughly criticized him for allowing

Vadim and another divorced man to evangelize and form new groups. Andre told Cory afterward, "At times like this I don't feel like preaching anywhere or doing anything. I just get beat down."

His next meeting went better. He told pastors from all over Crimea about the 41 new groups that church planters had started with 500 people attending. He described the summer evangelism program: 120 people came for training from 20 churches. He also gave the pastors a letter for their congregations, inviting them to set aside the last Friday of each month as a day of fasting and prayer for evangelistic efforts. They could either come to a central location or meet in their own churches.

Cory attended the first gathering at the end of June. They planned to meet from 10:00 a.m. until 2:00 p.m., but they prayed two hours longer. Forty church planters and pastors came. We felt encouraged even if some church leaders still did not support these efforts.

I wondered if the reluctance to reach beyond church walls was a leftover attitude from the Soviet prohibition against evangelism. I heard more church history from Piotr's father, a retired pastor.

Since an American team had come to help his church with outreach, Piotr invited them and us for dinner. Janelle and Alicia ate with his five children in the kitchen, while eighteen adults crowded around a long table in the living room. Piotr's wife, Tanya, brought out rice, fish, fried eggplant, cucumbers, and tomatoes garnished with garlic and parsley.

While we ate, Piotr's father, Ivan Mikalovich, told about Christianity during the Communist era. The church in Feodosia was founded ten years before the Bolshevik revolution of 1917. During the campaign against religion that followed, the believers lost their house of prayer. Their pastor was sentenced to ten years at a prison camp for preaching the Gospel and for allowing children in church services. Five years later he was released in poor health, but died the day after he returned home.

Through the 1960s, the pastor acted as an informer for the KGB, cooperating out of fear. The congregation did not trust him and made Ivan Mikalovich pastor in 1972. "We used to hold baptismal services far from town," Mikalovich said, "so no one could see who was getting baptized."

Only four people in the congregation had Bibles: the pastor, a deacon, and two others. Bibles printed in Moscow were the only ones allowed, but they printed few Bibles, and officials restricted their distribution. If police raided a home, they seized any unauthorized literature. The choir director copied hymn books by hand since none could be purchased. She had asthma and when she could not sleep at night, she sat up copying both words and notes. Every Sunday she carried notebooks weighing over twenty pounds to the house of prayer for the service. She carried them home again, afraid that if she left them there, the KGB or someone else might take them.

Even though the authorities tried to discourage religious activity, Christianity was legal. Ivan studied the codebook and knew his rights and the rights of the church even better than some of the KGB agents sent to harass him. He stood up to them, citing the code number and quoting the law. Even during the repressive Soviet period, he helped start new churches in towns near Feodosia.

"We had a large and active youth group," he said. "Sometimes they filled up the back of a bus and sang Christian songs. I scolded them for that, because it could have caused problems for them and for me. We used weddings and funerals as opportunities to preach the Gospel to people outside the church. Maybe that is why we are seeing such a big harvest now, from seeds planted years ago."

His son, Piotr, helped form the church in the neighboring town of Primorski in 1990. Piotr talked about new efforts to start additional churches, led by three men who went through our training program. He said, "In one of those villages lives a man named Iliya. Three years ago, a Muslim Tatar gave Iliya a New Testament. The Tatar told him, 'I have read it, but I have my own religion. You read it.'"

Iliya had never seen a Bible before, never gone to church, and never heard about God. He read the New Testament through twice but did not understand it very well. During the third reading, it became clear to him. He had always tried to be a good person, but he suddenly understood he was a sinner. This made him feel depressed. As he continued reading, he understood God loved him and made the way for him to be forgiven.

Iliya got down on his knees and prayed with tears. When he finally stood up, he knew God had accepted him. He had always been afraid of death, but he now felt peace and feared it no longer. He continued reading and understood he should get baptized, but he did not know any Christians.

Then someone invited him to see the *Jesus* film in his village. Yuri was using the film to make contact with people and start a Bible study. After the movie, Iliya talked at length with Yuri and said he wanted to be baptized.

Yuri told Piotr, "He is ready. I didn't do anything. God had already worked in his life before we got there."

The next Sunday morning, I attended a baptismal service at the Black Sea. Church members gathered on the beach to sing and watch as eight people in white robes waded into the water: seven women and one man. The man was Iliya.

Yuri pointed out for me Iliya's wife and eleven-year-old daughter among the onlookers. He said, "Besides that family, three other women come for meetings. I showed the film three weeks ago and have met with them every Friday since then." So far, only Iliya had given his life to Christ.

July brought hot weather, the kind that turns butter to soup if it's left on the table. We melted too. The milk lady complained, "My garden is burning up. The cows don't have much to eat, either."

Crimea's beaches filled with Russian and Ukrainian tourists who came to lie in the sun and soak up Vitamin D. Old women urged me to get a tan to avoid winter sickness, but I feared the sun's fierce rays and waited until late afternoon or evening to go swimming. By then we met a steady stream of people headed home in shades of tan and pink. The girls had turned into little fish, and I used our outing as a refreshing way to get exercise.

"I think she had a good birthday," I told June as we walked home from our final event, a swim in the Black Sea. Alicia had eagerly anticipated her party for weeks. She made a long guest list and planned out many games and crafts. I rose at 5:00 a.m. to cook and bake a cake before the house got too hot and then helped the girls decorate for the party. Three girls came, plus June and Anya, all bringing presents. It looked like everyone had fun.

"How was your day?" I asked Alicia who lagged a few steps behind.

"It wasn't very good," she complained. "Not everyone came and Lilya couldn't go swimming. And we didn't do everything I wanted to."

"It was a wonderful party and you need to be grateful," June scolded. "Your mother worked hard..."

Silently I cheered, but I didn't say anything. I saw the same tendency in myself: I build up expectations for how life should be, and it rarely works out that way. Instead of thanking God for the good things, I focus on the disappointments.

People flock to Black Sea beaches each summer.

15

People Are Not the Enemy

An American team came to help June and others from the church clinic with medical outreach and evangelism in villages. June said, "I've gotten used to some things that used to shock me: the primitive state of the village clinic, poor light, cramped quarters, lack of privacy, and the noise. I am still surprised, though, by what awful conditions some people live in. Their physical condition is often similar to their spiritual condition, but God uses poor health to reach people."

One team member told of their visit to the home of an elderly couple living in extreme poverty. The woman was confined to bed after a stroke. She lay on filthy, smelly rags that were crawling with worms. The husband, also in poor health, could not help her much. The visitors removed the rags and gave her something clean to lie on. "I know we didn't fix her situation," the visitor said, "but she was grateful for the little that we did."

Pastor Piotr said he thought medical work was an effective way to show the love of Christ to people without hope. "People are amazed Americans come to Ukraine, not for resorts or nightclubs, but to touch the sick and heal their wounds. People are attracted to Christ when they see love in action."

A church planter told of his conversation with a woman in her fifties who came to the clinic. She believed in God and prayed for her children, but said she could not pray for herself. She had had so many abortions, she felt unworthy of God's love. Her son went to prison, became a Christian there, and was released early. She and her son came to the afternoon meeting, where they heard more of God's forgiveness.

Anya called me in August, her voice bubbling over with excitement. "We have everything worked out for camp in Batalnaya," she said. She named different people planning to help. Most were new believers since the church was just five years old. One helper had once tried to keep her children from going to Sunday school and finally visited the church to see what attracted them there. She continued attending and was baptized that summer.

"I often tell you my problems," Anya continued, "I wanted to share my joy with you too. I'm so happy to see how God is raising up people in the church who can work with children. I can die now knowing the work with children will continue."

I knew Anya had heart problems but told her, "Or else you can start a group in another place."

She laughed.

Anya invited Janelle and Alicia to attend the day camp and asked them to present a skit illustrating the Good Shepherd's concern for the lost lamb. Stefan already had a full car but agreed to pick them up. They could sit on laps. Anya invited me also, but the laps were already taken.

Janelle and Alicia came home with a good report: "It was fun, but there were a lot of flies." Flies go with village life, just like animals and outhouses.

When Vanya invited Cory to a baptismal service on the far side of Crimea, I wanted to go too. We would have to leave very early to get there, but I wanted to meet this church planter and see something of his ministry.

We stopped to pick up Andre and his wife about 4:00 a.m. Andre got just three hours of sleep that night, after a late meeting with church leaders in another part of Crimea. Nevertheless, he and Cory talked most of the way.

Delara, his wife, told me about her family in Russia. With her father sick from throat cancer, she recently took him money for treatment. As soon as she got there, her mother started badgering her again, "Why have you left the faith?"

Delara replied, "Left the faith? What faith? You raised me as an atheist!" As Volga Tatar, they were culturally Muslim but never practiced the religion. Her mother started going to the mosque only after Delara became a Christian. She did not read the Koran since she did not understand Arabic.

The pressure continued throughout Delara's visit. Even though her sisters' lives were a mess, and she alone helped her parents financially, they still saw her as the "white crow," or black sheep, of the family. She tried to point out how God had blessed her with a good husband and children, but nothing helped.

When we arrived at the beach, Vanya met us with a big smile. Lacking a right arm, he extended his left to shake hands. His wife, Natasha, a friendly woman with short fluffy hair and a touch of makeup, greeted me with a peck on the cheek. Many people had gathered already. Some wore white robes. Natasha explained that twenty-one people planned to be baptized. Twelve of them had come to Christ through Vanya's efforts.

"I usually help Vanya with the ministry," Natasha explained, "but I was sick a lot this summer and ended up in the hospital. While there, I shared the Gospel with other patients and with the doctors and nurses. I talked to some Muslim Tatar too; many of them were open and ready to listen."

Natasha told about their church plant in a village about twenty minutes away. During the last few months, they started groups in two more villages. In one, they held services at a home for the elderly.

Cory had accompanied Vanya to this care center several weeks earlier. He said the place looked like a regular house, though rundown, and it smelled like urine and disinfectant. Someone looked after the ten or twelve residents there. Usually, the elderly lived with their offspring, but these had no one else to care for them. One person accepted Christ during Cory's visit.

"We share the Good News with the blind and the crippled," said Natasha. "Several people at that home have repented. It is better that they come to Christ late in life than not at all." She pointed out a woman being carried on a chair toward the beach. "She is one of two people from the home who is getting baptized today."

A youth group gathered and began to sing. With the help of loudspeakers, anyone who happened to be up and in the area at 8:00 a.m. could hear the music and explanation of the Gospel. A few beach walkers paused to listen.

The church leaders decided Cory and another visiting pastor should perform the baptisms. Cory protested, "There are other ordained pastors here. I don't need to participate." They insisted. At the appointed time, he waded out into the sea.

Janelle and Alicia loved having June as their babysitter in our absence. When we arrived home late that afternoon, they welcomed us with, "Why are you home so early? We want June to stay longer!"

Our landlady called late in August and asked us to come for dinner at her café. I was a little dismayed to hear dinner would be at 8:00 p.m. since I usually slept poorly after a late dinner, but we wanted to work around her schedule and wanted to get to know her better.

After dinner, Galina's boyfriend and Cory stood up. Cory explained to me, "He wants to go look at the car."

Galina chatted about her summer. I asked, "How are things going with your stepfather?" I hoped all had settled down enough so we were no longer in danger of being evicted.

"He is an evil man," she said. "He is not satisfied unless things are going poorly for me. He is so mean, it killed my mother, and it's killing me too. He returns evil for good. He comes to my café at any time, and I give him anything he wants to eat or drink. He gets a good pension, but I pay everything for him. Still, he is always cursing me. I work here from 6:00 in the morning until midnight or 1:00 a.m. It is hard work, and it was horribly hot this summer, but it's easier to be here all day than to go home. If he gets really drunk, I have peace for a day or two, but then it starts again."

"What about the apartment?" I asked. "Is that still a question?"

"We fight about it all the time," she replied simply.

Cory finally returned, and we left for home. "Did you two talk about anything interesting?" I asked. They had been gone a long time.

"Bad news. Her stepfather still wants our apartment and says we have to be out by September first." That was just one week away. I couldn't believe it; but as Cory continued, I figured they must be serious. He explained that the apartment had been in the name of Galina and her mother, but when her mother died, half went to the stepfather. "The house where they live is his, but he says she can have the house if she gives him our apartment. He says he wants to move to town. She offered to rent another apartment for him, but he says he wants what belongs to him."

"But we have a contract!" I protested.

"He didn't agree to it," Cory said. "Half belongs to him. Do you want to share the house with him? You forget where we live. We don't have any rights. I don't want to be here if he comes with the police on September first."

"That's just a week away. We can't find anything and move in that amount of time."

I didn't sleep well that night. The high-fat dinner sat like a bomb in my stomach, and the news rattled in my head. I prayed. I tried to remember that whenever anything bad happens to me, something worse happened to Jesus. The Son of Man had no place to lay His head. I tried to be grateful for what He did for me and trust Him to meet our needs.

Cory talked to Stefan the next morning. Stefan checked the ads for apartments to rent or buy but found nothing. He talked to a lawyer, went to see our landlady, and reported back. I hoped it was all a misunderstanding, but it wasn't. He said she apologized for the inconvenience to us and promised to return the money we had paid ahead.

"Does Galina's stepfather really have rights to our apartment?" I asked.

Stefan explained that according to the laws of inheritance, he had the right to half of the apartment. However, he did not have the document that gave him those rights. Galina had put off getting it, but the law said she had to within six months of the previous owner's death, and that was coming up soon. It might take two weeks to get the document, and then the old man would need to give us notice.

"You still have some time to work with," Stefan said. "I don't know how long, probably at least three or four weeks."

"Would he consider selling the apartment to us?"

"No. He would not even reason with me. He has no need for a three-room apartment. Galina told him that if he wants to move to town, she could find him another apartment, but no, he kept saying, 'I want what is mine.'"

The stepfather vowed to make her die in poverty. He planned to leave everything to the government when he died. He promised to strip the house of all the furniture when he moved out. Galina said, "My only hope is that he kills himself through alcohol poisoning before he can kill me. He has bad health and drinks a lot."

I felt badly for her. I felt worse for us. What a jerk. Later that day, I read a quote by Joe Aldrich: "Remember, unsaved people are not the enemy. They are victims of the enemy."

Still, I hated the idea of moving. I watched mosquitoes bounce off the screens June and Anya had installed outside our windows before our arrival. We would need to install new screens, but that was a small matter. We had accumulated so much stuff. Besides regular furniture, we had big wooden wardrobes since Ukrainian homes do not have built-in closets. We would take our new water heater, the stove, curtains, hundreds of books. Even the kitchen sink.

Like Galina, I could hope he did himself in before he could force us out but knew we could not depend on that. Cory did not want this ax hanging overhead, never knowing when it would fall.

I printed off and hung up ads around our part of town, seeking an apartment to buy or rent, but few calls came in. Stefan checked the ads in the paper and walked through several neighborhoods, asking, "Do you know of any apartments for sale or rent?" He did not find any rentals but found some for sale. He looked at many, Cory looked at several, and I looked at the best two, but none of us liked what we saw. Stefan visited the landlady and her stepfather again, but the stepfather was not willing to rent or sell to us.

I felt overwhelmed by the need to keep juggling the other balls in my life, plus catch this watermelon I had just been tossed. I would need to start school soon with the girls and can tomato sauce and pickles while produce was still available. When we finally found a place, we would need to put up new wallpaper and do repairs before we could move in. I leaned on the verse from Psalms, "The Lord gives grace and strength." I would need both.

About a week after the news, Cory asked some neighbors sitting outside, "Do you know of any apartments for sale or rent?

One woman said, "My husband and I were just talking about selling ours, but we have not told anyone yet. Do you want to see it?"

This older couple shared their three-room apartment—a living room and two bedrooms—with their son, daughter-in-law, and granddaughter. They decided everyone would be happier with two smaller apartments. They lived just one entrance over from us, also on the third floor.

I joined Cory and Stefan for a second visit. The stairwell looked almost frightening, with huge patches of crumbling plaster and graffiti scratched in the little paint that remained—but that could be fixed. Inside, the apartment was better than the others I saw and had the same floor plan as ours. I hoped we could get it.

The wife did most of the talking. "If you are interested, we want you to have it," she said. "You are the first buyers, so it would be a sin against God to sell to someone else." In spite of her reference to God, she seemed more superstitious than religious.

She said, "We found a one-room apartment for my son, but we are still looking for a two-room apartment for us."

"God will make it work out," Stefan said.

"I hope so, if there is a God," the woman countered.

Stefan couldn't pass that up. "Of course there is."

Before we left, the woman drew Cory and me aside. She offered to have a priest come and sprinkle the rooms with holy water, as some believe this water will chase evil spirits from a house.

"It won't be necessary," Cory replied. "I am also a minister."

We felt encouraged by this apartment option. We had hoped to stay in the same region, close to the market. Janelle had said, "We need to live close to my piano teacher."

16

My Help Comes From the Lord

September – October 2001

"What are we going to do this week?" Alicia asked. All their friends were heading back to school, and I felt we should start school too, in spite of everything else going on in our lives.

I called Janelle over to join us. "You know we have a lot going on right now. We don't want to move, but we will have to move. Sometimes when Daddy and I have a lot to do, we get grouchy. We are going to need your help."

They nodded. "What can we do?" asked Janelle.

"Can you do school on your own? Without me pushing you?"

"Sure!" they chorused.

"I don't have time right now to read to you much and do school the way I want to, but we can't wait until after we move to start school." They eagerly looked at their new workbooks for math, handwriting, and English.

I still began the day with Bible reading, a devotional story, and memory work. Monday's Bible reading was from Psalm 121: "I lift up my eyes to the hills—where does my help come from? My help comes from the Lord." They began memorizing the chapter. It applied well to our situation. Hearing them rehearse the words strengthened me.

The evening of September 11, 2001, a friend called, telling us to turn on the television. In disbelief we watched constant replays of two airplanes hitting the Twin Towers in New York and the buildings' collapse. I wished the girls did not have to witness such tragedy, but we wanted to know what happened. Guests stopped in and wanted to see it too. More replays.

Janelle said later, "I'm going to pray a lot tonight. I can't stop thinking about the person waving that cloth out the window." We did pray.

We received many phone calls from friends who expressed their regret, shock, and sadness.

Janelle was relieved to learn later that not as many died as originally feared. Many escaped, even from upper stories, and they found some people alive. She felt God had answered her prayers.

Locals asked us, "Do you think there will be war?" Older ones, who had lived through war, added, "It is awful." We checked the Internet news regularly for any developments, twice a day, if we could get on.

I wrote in my journal: "Uncertainty gnaws holes in my sense of peace. Like David, I wonder why the wicked prosper...and then, like David, I find rest when I look to God and remember He is still on His throne."

Would war affect our ability to come and go or our supply of finances? Cory said, "One thing I've learned here is that we can't be controlled by fear."

The Bible promised wars and rumors of wars until the end. We wondered what the future held, but we could not hide in a cave and still use our lives to make a difference.

I like to know what to expect; life in Ukraine had taught us to expect uncertainty. We never knew when the power would go out during winter. The water went off without notice. Workers installed pipes for natural gas and promised a regular supply, but the gas stopped because of a squabble between gas companies.

We still did not know when we could move or start repairs. Our landlady wanted us out as soon as possible, but the neighbors who promised to sell to us still sought another place to live.

Cory said, "This uncertainty about our apartment brought up the same uneasy feelings I had when we first moved to Ukraine—the stress of not feeling in control any more."

Uncertainty affected me too. I wondered if I would have the strength and whatever else it took to cope. Cory regained peace by remembering God is ultimately in control. Likewise, I could look to God for strength, enough to meet each need.

Andre collected statistics from the summer evangelism program and found the results were even better than expected. He learned that 420 people from 17 churches participated. They shared the Gospel in 53 villages and 183 accepted the Lord. Though 500 expressed interest in joining a Bible study group, 315 continued coming. Knowing these numbers represented real people, we thanked God for this response.

Cory and the other leaders met with church planters for a seminar late in September. Over the summer, the men had led evangelism programs and worked with their small groups. They also tended their gardens and got food ready for winter.

Leaders used this seminar to focus on the theme of fellowship. Men whose whole Christian experience stemmed from traditional church services usually fell back on the only model they knew. Most non-Christians, however, would rather go to an informal gathering with discussion instead of a lecture.

To help stimulate ideas, leaders asked the group, "What are some things you do to promote fellowship?" Some met with people one-on-one to hear their problems and pray with them. Some gathered for tea and cookies, singing and conversation. They all agreed people must feel loved to feel free enough to share their problems.

One church planter said, "I finally realized that small groups really do work. During our training, teachers said we should hold discussion groups and help other people learn to lead instead of trying to keep all the control. Nevertheless, I started holding church services as soon as I had a few interested people. More recently, I started several small groups and gave other people responsibility. The result is more growth."

While Cory attended this two-day seminar, Janelle and Alicia included the church planters and Daddy in their bedtime prayers. Alicia prayed, "Thank you that we can stay home, and we don't have to go everywhere with Daddy."

I was also grateful. Cory said the bed he used was worse than usual, very swaybacked, so he did not sleep well. Plus, other people now lived in the collective-farm dormitory where they stayed. The others made a lot of noise drinking, gambling, and fighting at night.

Though tired when he got home, he played cribbage with the girls and went to look at wallpaper with me.

We finally got documents for the new apartment, but the former owners said they needed another week before they could move out. Friends told us they would help us with repairs. Cory and I bought supplies, so anyone who showed up could work.

We got the keys on October 9. For the next week, a crew of nine to twelve people joined us every day. Before putting up new wallpaper, we had to take off the old. Those old layers seemed to be holding up the wall. When stripped off, plaster came too.

We heard that much construction from the Soviet period was of poor quality. Workers stole materials, and the Communist policy of equal treatment for all did not reward incentive and hard work. Many walls, steps, and side-walks showed workers had not mixed in enough cement with the sand.

In our case, our helpers were even more particular about doing a good job than we were. They removed all the crumbling plaster before swiping on new cement and gypsum. They sanded the walls smooth and put up new wallpaper.

Janelle and Alicia enthusiastically helped strip wallpaper the first day and painted the next. By the third day, they were ready to stay home and do schoolwork.

Cory and I started early and worked late. I fed the work crew lunch, ran for supplies, answered questions, pitched in, and collapsed in bed each night feeling like I had started an intensive exercise program.

Our friends worked wonders with wallpaper, paint, and linoleum. It would have taken us months to accomplish the same on our own. We had asked a couple of people for help, but many more showed up. They all had busy lives and good reasons not to assist, but they came anyway and worked hard. Eighteen people helped with repairs or the move. We felt honored by their loving sacrifice.

Janelle said later, "It's good to have friends. We couldn't live here without friends. Without friends it's like...like being in a hole."

If neighbors had not heard the gossip, they certainly heard the sound of repairs or saw the parade of furniture and boxes going out one entryway and into the next. "You got a good apartment," one neighbor told me.

I said nothing about the floors with waves in them from poorly laid concrete and nothing about walls without square corners. Our kitchen sink, for example, was set in a corner but the near side was almost two inches from the wall. I said nothing of the graffiti in the stairwell, or used syringes, or the pile of human waste I cleaned up in the entryway. "Yes," I said, "it's a good building in a good region. Quiet. It's close to the market. Close to the sea."

"You are smart to buy a home here," the woman continued. "Those attacks in New York were terrible. With war starting in America, you are smart to live here." People usually asked why I would leave the good life in America to live in Ukraine, but this was the first time someone congratulated me for the decision. She continued, "I hear some who emigrated are coming back here to live. Will your relatives come here to rest during the summer?"

I told her it was too far and too expensive, but I wrote home, "If you know what's good for you, you will move to Ukraine!" No one took me up on it.

Getting evicted had been a huge shock. I dreaded the process of finding, fixing up, and moving into a new apartment, but God provided. As the dust settled, it gave me great pleasure to have our own place and to fix it the way I wanted. God did not answer our prayers the way we wanted—He answered them even better.

Our former landlady's stepfather did move in. He often called Cory for help. "I can't figure out how to plug in the telephone," he said. "Come help me install a water heater," he demanded. "I have no one else." Our former landlady said he liked living in town, and they were happy without him, even though he took most of the furniture.

Alicia's creative streak showed up at unexpected times. While eating dinner one day, she said, "I wish I had pointy things on my tongue so I could drink milk like a cat. And I wish I had a long tongue so I could comb my hair with it."

Janelle, one year wiser at the age of nine, said, "Then you would cough up fur balls." This led to a discussion of what it would be like to cough up a fur ball—not the best subject for the dinner table.

At another meal Alicia announced, "I want to be president of the United States when I grow up."

"Why?"

"Oh, it sounds like an interesting job. And I would be famous because I would be the first woman president. After I'm done being president I will come down and be a nurse or a doctor."

Cory told her, "If you are president, you will have a bodyguard for the rest of your life."

"Maybe I won't be president then." Who wants a constant babysitter?

When their sewing class held a fall party, Alicia decided to go as a tree and wove a headdress of weeping willow branches. Janelle took bunny ears and a tail. While we hurried to their party, Janelle noticed an old woman with a rounded back, walking stooped over with a cane.

"Look at that woman," she exclaimed, showing her compassionate side. "I wish Jesus was here. He could heal her." Just then, we overtook another tiny old woman, bent almost double. She shuffled along with a cane and stopped to rest after every step. "Oh, this woman is even worse off," Janelle said, "I feel so bad for her."

Suddenly, the crick in my neck—from sleeping on it wrong, or locals would say from a cold draft—did not seem important anymore. As we sped past the woman, I thanked God for health, strong legs, and a straight back.

June saw problems worse than this in her medical outreaches and home visits. Along with a church planter and translator, she went to see a sixty-nine-year-old woman who had suffered a stroke over a year earlier. With her failing eyesight and fear of falling, she stayed in bed. As a result, she now had a pressure ulcer on her bottom that went to the bone, as well as a frozen neck, shoulders, hips, knees, and ankles.

Her daughter-in-law had three children and was seven months pregnant. She felt badly the wound had happened, but had tried to help.

For over an hour and a half, June described proper treatment and care. The young woman listened attentively and then quietly asked, "Will I lose my baby?" Two months earlier, a doctor said her baby would die because she was caring for her mother-in-law. Since her lower back often hurt, she thought she was catching her mother-in-law's "disease."

June explained that the mother-in-law's condition was not contagious. Besides, the baby was still alive and growing. June described proper lifting techniques and reminded her that back pain was common at this stage of pregnancy. The woman looked like a heavy burden had just fallen from her shoulders.

After reviewing all the instructions, medications, creams, and cushions, June offered to pray. Permission granted, she prayed for the grandmother, the unborn baby, and the mother.

Afterward, she heard the woman whisper to the translator, "I have never seen a doctor like this."

June said, "I thought the church planter might be waiting out in the car, wondering what had become of us. Not at all. During the time we had been with the wife, he was with the husband. He said they had a wonderful conversation and wished he could have stayed even longer. This family is Muslim. Until today the door for sharing the Gospel in this home was closed."

Our life at home had calmed down, but more upheaval awaited elsewhere.

Dressed up for a sewing class tea party.

17

Faith Gives Them Hope

November 2001 - January 2002

Cory heard about some conflict between Vanya and the pastor of his home church so he left at 5:30 the next Sunday morning to visit. Before the morning service started, the pastor told Cory that Vanya was trying to push heretical teaching on them about the Holy Spirit, and that he beat his wife.

Cory tucked the information away and brought it out when he had some private time with Vanya and Natasha over lunch. He mentioned the allegation and asked, "Do you beat your wife?"

Vanya said they had some marriage problems over six years ago, before he gave his life to Christ. Cory told me, "I watched Natasha, to see what her response would be when the subject came up. I don't think it's a current problem."

"I don't think it is either," I said. "When we were there for the baptism, it seemed to me like she really respects him. She enjoys helping him with evangelism. When she talked about their life before Christ, she said 'it was terrible' but didn't go into detail."

"My gut feeling is that this pastor is jealous of Vanya's success. About him teaching heresy, I don't think there's any heresy either. Apparently Vanya taught that the Holy Spirit empowers us for effective service. The pastor says it's God who empowers us. I think it's the same thing he complained about when Andre and I were there last summer. I told Vanya to focus on his church plants, not his home church. When he does preach in his home church, he should talk about things he knows they have in common."

After they ate lunch, Vanya took him to the young church that met in the home for the elderly. Twenty-seven attended, including some who lived elsewhere in the village. Cory told me, "Some of the younger women get grief from their husbands since they became Christians, but their faith provides hope, something alcohol can't give." He thought the two-hour service went quickly as different people participated with lots of singing and poetry.

When Cory saw Andre next, he told him about the accusation of wife abuse. "They had problems over six years ago," Cory said, "but I don't think there is anything now."

Andre explained, "Feodorovich is spreading this rumor around and trying to use it to discredit the training program."

A few weeks later, Feodorovich summoned Andre and the rest of the higher council to go meet with Vanya. Andre expected the worst. "They're going to chop off his head," he said wryly. Vanya was already missing an arm.

As it turned out, they decided the accusations had no basis. Vanya was not teaching heresy, and the problems with his wife took place before he was a Christian. The pastor was rebuked instead.

Cory and I felt relieved, glad it was settled. At least we thought it was.

In December a team of three came from Wichita, Kansas to teach in a seminar for church planters. They covered topics such as pastoral concerns, the state of Christianity in the world, and apologetics. The team said their favorite part was hearing ministry updates during the daily times of prayer.

Every day, right after lunch, the men took turns reporting on their ministries. They asked for prayer for wisdom in balancing family and ministry. For growth of groups. For helpers. For direction. Some needed places to meet since town officials would not let them use public buildings. They spoke of barriers like alcoholism, prejudice, and family problems. Women and children responded more easily, but how could they attract men? Poverty and unemployment affected their outreach. Sometimes men started to attend meetings but moved away to find work.

On Sunday I joined the Kansas group as they visited the Nizhnigorski church. June offered to stay with the girls, saying, "You need to go more than I do." Janelle and Alicia still lacked tolerance for lengthy church services and long trips, but I welcomed the outing.

I sat on a bench in the packed house of prayer with my knees bumping the row in front of me. Church members had been working on a new building for three years already, but it still wasn't ready. Even though they had started many daughter churches, they still had over 200 members.

A young deacon named Pasha joined us for lunch at Sergei's apartment. He had given the first sermon that morning and led the singing. I asked him, "How did you become a Christian?"

"My father drank heavily," he recalled. "I never wanted to be like him, but by the time I was ten, I acted like him and even worse. I wanted to be famous, either as an athlete or a thief. I played soccer, but I was more successful as a thief. I started by taking toys from friends and moved on to other things."

His father accepted Christ and the family atmosphere improved. Pasha was fourteen when he started going to church; he wanted to see why his parents and sister had changed. "I already knew I was a sinner," he said, "and I was afraid of going to hell. God worked in my heart, and I repented."

He realized he would have to choose between soccer and church, because soccer games were held on Sunday, and he lived over ten miles from the house of prayer. "I chose Christianity. I still lived surrounded by the things I had taken from others. I thought about burning them, but I finally decided to face the people I had stolen from and give everything back."

He began working with children and youth. Now, at the age of twenty-four, he served as a youth leader.

On their last evening in Ukraine, we joined the Kansas team at Andre's house for dinner. Stefan and Nadia came too. One visitor looked around the living room and asked, "Does everyone here have wallpaper? I never noticed it before."

"Yes, everyone has wallpaper."

Another said, "It's a 'guy thing' to not notice such details."

Cory translated into Russian. Apparently this trait was cross-cultural.

Stefan said, "When a man came home from work one day, his wife met him at the door wearing a gas mask. 'Do you notice anything different?' she asked. He paused. 'Uhhh. Did you pluck your eyebrows?'"

When the laughter died down, Larry Wren, the team leader, commented, "It seems as if our visits here have become more relaxed. There's more joking, more laughter. When we first started coming, we were afraid of offending anyone." Cory and I enjoyed the humor they brought since our life in Ukraine often felt stark and serious.

After Cory interpreted, Andre said, "Some Christians think it is wrong to laugh. They get that from Ephesians 5:4, which is not clear in the Russian Bible." The verse forbids "silly talk."

After dinner, Larry told the wives, "You play an important part in this ministry too. Your husbands are gone a lot and you make sacrifices."

Andre's wife stood and said, "When we attended university together, Andre was studying to be a geologist. He told me he planned to get his doctorate and teach, and said that if I marry him, I must understand he will be busy with other things. God led us in a different way, but I knew before I married him he would be busy."

Andre told about a pastor in Sevastopol: "When he proposed to his wife he said, 'If you want to marry me, you must understand my first priority is to serve God. I will come when I want. I will leave when I want. I will bring home any guests at any time.' She agreed and they got married."

The Americans all agreed: "That would not go over in my house."

In their sewing class, Janelle and Alicia prepared entries for a New Year's contest. Alicia made a doll by wrapping fabric strips around a wire frame and covered it with cloth "skin" and a fluffy dress. Janelle worked on a bee couple, which sat on a log holding flowers.

The teacher told me, "The girls need to come to every class—that's four times a week—so they can get their projects done on time."

Before heading to class, they put on two or three t-shirts, two sets of long underwear on top and bottom, two sweatshirts or sweaters, pants, and boots. "It's cold in the classroom," Janelle explained. "The teacher always pinches my arm to feel how many layers I have on and says I need to wear more."

The teacher nodded her approval when I brought in two round girls. "They should not take off their coats," she said. "It's only six degrees." From Celsius, that translated to 43° Fahrenheit. Her little space heater did not help much.

Both girls insisted, "I'm hot!" They got lots of exercise romping through the snow on our way to class.

"You will get cold when you sit," she said. "It was only two degrees (34°F) when I came this morning, so I sent the first group of children home with their projects and turned on the heater. It's a little warmer this afternoon, but not much. We will have a shorter class today, just an hour and a half, instead of two hours."

Their sewing class met on Saturday morning too, but with Alicia's cough and a bitter wind blowing, we decided to stay home. June saved the day by braving the elements to come and help the girls bake Christmas cookies.

June told me, "I'm planning to get a perm next week, and I'll invite Oxana to come do it. Would you like her to give you one at the same time?"

"Sure!" I liked a little curl and traces of the last perm had just about grown out. I preferred to endure the process at home where I had more control and could rinse off the chemicals as long as I wanted. At the salon they dumped just two pitchers of water over my head.

I was out of American perm solution, so Oxana brought Russian chemicals and used the local method. She wrapped my hair onto hand-carved wooden rods with rubber stays made from strips of bicycle inner tubes. She ran out of inner-tube strips, so I found some rubber bands, and she finished the perm.

She said, "We have a saying, 'Beauty requires sacrifice.'"

The girls hid in their room to escape the smell. When it was all over, they said I looked like Ms. Frizzle, the science teacher in the *Magic School Bus* books. Not quite the style I wanted. The perm and haircut cost just two dollars, so maybe you get what you pay for. Some heavy conditioner and another haircut helped diminish the poodle look.

The girls' piano teacher told me, "They would do better if they had a piano at home and could practice." She knew someone with a piano for sale and offered to look at it with me. We bought it for $90.

"How do you advise that we move it?" I asked the teacher.

"You can rent a truck, but it is cheaper if you can provide your own labor. Pay the men with bottles of cognac—that's what we do."

We knew someone with a truck and found enough young men to help. Instead of liquor, I gave them bags of tangerines and homemade cookies.

When I first asked the girls if they would like a piano, Janelle gasped, "Oh, Mommy, I never dreamed we might get our own piano!" They both promised to practice daily. They did for a while, anyway.

I had still not met our new neighbors and decided to deliver cookies during the holidays. The previous year it had helped me connect with the old woman above us, Valentina. She still called occasionally to chat and sometimes asked for help. When she thought her son sold their old car for booze money, she asked Cory to drive her to their garage way out of town, so she could see if the car was still there. It was.

I took Valentina cookies first. "Thank you! Wait a minute." She disappeared for a while and returned with several small, wrapped candies. "Give these to your precious girls. I was so sad you had to move. I don't have any other friends like you, but I'm glad you still live near."

I recruited Alicia to help me deliver the other cookies. Of the seven other doors in our stairwell, we found someone behind four of them. A thin old woman with several missing teeth and worn clothes lived above us. Across from her, a young mother with a six-year-old boy answered the door, and I heard a male voice in the background.

Across from us lived two young men in their twenties. When one of them opened the door, cigarette smoke billowed out, and I could see a New Year's Eve party in progress. Those few cookies would not go far, but I gave him the packet anyway with a holiday greeting in Russian. "Sank you," he replied. Either someone told him he had American neighbors, or else he heard English through the wall.

On the fifth floor, an old woman opened the door. When Alicia tried to give her cookies, she protested, "No, no! Not over the threshold! I can't take something over the threshold!" I had forgotten that superstition. I pushed Alicia through the open door. "Wait, wait!" she called as she went to the kitchen and soon returned with an apple for Alicia.

Putting on slippers and a housecoat, she stepped out and shut the door. "It's bad to talk over the threshold," she said. I later learned that ancient Ukrainians believed household spirits lived at the threshold.

"The Christian thing to do is stay home on New Year's," she said. "You can go out any other day, but if you want a close family, you need to start the year at home."

I didn't want to argue. "I plan to stay home too," I replied.

"Are you those people who moved here from the next entryway?"

"Yes."

"Where do your children attend school?"

"I teach them myself," I said and listed the outside classes they attended.

"What, were you trained as a teacher?"

"No, but I have good books and a good program. They will take exams later." Mentioning exams usually satisfied those who could not imagine parent-led education.

"I don't see why you don't enroll them in our schools. We have the best educational system in the world—better than any other country."

I had heard others complain about the declining school system and poor teachers, but I nodded as she continued her praise. She expressed strong opinions on several other topics. Not wanting to argue, I just nodded and wondered how I could end the conversation.

"And this stairwell is so dirty," she continued. "I lived in Germany for a while, and everything there was clean."

I didn't want to agree too strongly but wished her the best for the New Year and went home to be with my family and start the year off right.

On New Year's Day, we joined former neighbors for a feast of cabbage rolls, mashed potatoes, salads, and eggplant relish. The mother, grandmother, and daughter had lived near us when we rented an apartment downtown. Knowing they had applied to emigrate to the U.S. and join Grandma's sister, Cory asked, "How did your interview go in Moscow?"

Grandma replied, "The man wanted to know how long I had been a Christian." She got sidetracked and started telling about her childhood. I had heard the story before, but then I had not known enough Russian to understand her very well.

She grew up with four sisters and Christian parents. Another baby was born during the famine of the 1930s but died of hunger. Her mother did not get enough to eat and lacked milk for the baby. The father also died in the famine.

Christians were persecuted then, so neighbors were afraid to help them. The believers held their meetings in secret, in the forest. To avoid detection, families left at different times and took different routes to the designated spot.

Sometimes, when they had nothing to eat, her mother boiled water and added a little salt. It was winter and they prayed for food. They often went to bed hungry, but one morning they found a pile of wheat stalks on their doorstep. They could see no footsteps in the snow and received it as a gift from heaven. Rejoicing, they threshed out the wheat and cooked it. During the war, she and her sisters stayed safe, although soldiers took advantage of many others during that awful time.

Her daughter, Lena, rolled her eyes and interrupted, "Mama, you talk too much. You need to eat."

After Grandma downed a few bites, Cory asked again about their interview in Moscow. Of the many people interviewed that day, only their family and one other received refugee status. Grandma hoped for an easier life in America and hoped Lena would do the shopping. With her bad eyesight, she could not tell if she was getting good produce.

I had read in the news just a few weeks earlier that Ukraine had just marked the seventy-third anniversary of a man-made, Soviet-era famine that killed ten million people—about one-third of the country's population. The article told how Stalin used the famine to force peasants into giving up their private holdings and joining collective farms. Each village was required to provide a quota of grain that usually exceeded crop yields. The government seized all food and residents were not allowed to leave. Those who resisted were shot or sent to Siberia.

Stefan had told us of his father's experience in Western Ukraine during the famine. Authorities came to confiscate all their food. Stefan's father and his many siblings sat somber-eyed on a mattress on the large brick oven that also served as a bed. The official waved his gun, then snapped, "I will save my bullets and leave you to starve." He did not know the mattress was stuffed with grain, which kept the family alive.

One woman had always heard that her father died from an electrical shock but learned many years later the real cause was starvation. Her mother was close to death when she said in a fearful and hushed voice, "Daughter, when your father died, they told me I must tell everyone he was electrocuted. He really died of starvation during the famine. He gave his portion of food to me and to you children so we could live. I have kept it a secret all these years. You must keep it a secret too, or they will come after you."

Our own difficulties paled in light of what these people had lived through. We lived relatively carefree.

Janelle and Alicia brought their friend Masha home with us after the January Christmas service. With it getting dark so early, I decided it would be easier for her to spend the night than to try to get her home before dark. The girls danced in circles and cheered when I broke the news. They called Lilya and invited her to the sleep-over too.

We started bedtime preparations at 8:00, so they could have time to wind down. Cory pulled mattresses into the living room. For the next hour and a half, we listened from our room to giggles and repeated bits of the Russian Christmas carol, "On Christ's birth, angels came flying..." We heard a "thunk" and more laughter. When I went in for bedtime prayers, I found them "flying" from the couch and falling on the mattresses.

Their friends also prayed. "Thank you for this wonderful day. Thank you that we can come to this house."

They all woke up earlier than they should have. Instead of using the mattresses, all four slept together on the fold-out couch under a mountain of blankets. After a waffle breakfast, they bundled up to play outside. They slid, squatting on their feet, down an icy slope near our apartment.

Cold church buildings eliminate the need for coat racks.

18
Commitment Requires Sacrifice

February – May 2002

Training Center leaders needed a name for the ministry as they prepared documents for registration. They decided to call it "Efas," Russian for Ephesus. According to Acts 19:9-10, after the Apostle Paul gave two years of training in Ephesus, "all who lived in Asia heard the word of the Lord" (NAS). We hoped for similar results.

Needing a stamp of approval from the ECB Union headquarters in Kiev, Andre bought a train ticket. Before catching the evening train, he attended a regional church council meeting and told them his plans. Feodorovich rebuked Andre and said the training center was harming churches by spreading liberal teaching.

Even though most welcomed the Training Center's vision, Feodorovich continued to oppose it. Cory told me, "He can't control the results. New churches are popping up where women wear makeup. He is still trying to stop two of our church planters because of sins that took place before they were Christians."

Andre almost canceled his trip to Kiev, but others on the council quietly encouraged him to proceed with registration. He caught the train just in time.

In Kiev, the ECB Union president welcomed Andre warmly. He said he liked what he had heard about the Training Center and the resulting church plants. He gladly stamped the papers.

That weekend Feodorovich's term ended as head of churches in Crimea. Pastors gathered and voted in a new head who led a healthy church and supported the Training Center's goals.

Even though Andre took the heat from Feodorovich, he tried to explain the old man's perspective. Feodorovich had endured prison camp in Siberia for eight years because of his faith. He became a Christian and stood for Christianity when that decision required sacrifice. He believed true commitment to God still required sacrifice. He feared that if churches bent too far in trying to make worldly people fit in, the church would lose its savor as salt and any "decisions for Christ" would be too shallow to withstand the test of time.

"There is truth in that," Andre said. "It seems as though those who become Christians easily, easily fall away. He has good intentions. He is trying to protect the Church, but he does not understand God's grace. For example, he thinks that those who had some big sin in their past cannot serve God. That was the way he was taught."

Janelle and Alicia continued to enjoy their sewing class, even with a chilly classroom. They wore many layers and took jump ropes, since the teacher encouraged students to exercise when they felt cold. In spite of two electric heaters she brought from home, I could still see my breath in their room.

Some schools had closed early for winter vacations in December because of no heat and still had not resumed classes for the same reason. Other public buildings also went unheated, even the hospital.

The next week, a warm front came through. After weeks of overcast skies and icy conditions, we took advantage of pleasant weather to walk near the waterfront with June.

"It feels like spring!" exclaimed Janelle.

"I got my wish," Alicia added. "I wanted the sun to shine all day."

Janelle wrote about their outing for school: "After a long winter of boots, we finally got to wear tennis shoes. We walked almost to Masha's house and back. It feels good to run and have the wind on my ankles. It feels almost as good as going to America after being in Feodosia a long time."

I asked about her journal entry later as she helped me mix up cookie dough. "Sometimes I really miss America," she said. "It's easier to live there, but when I'm in America for a while I want to come back to Ukraine."

"What do you think about us being missionaries?" I asked.

"I think we are supposed to be missionaries. God has blessed us, and He wouldn't bless us if we weren't supposed to be missionaries."

Cory brought back a positive report from his next visit with church planters. "Around thirty-five or forty people came to the meeting at Vadim's house. He has a big living room, but not everyone could fit." He and Andre ate home-grown chicken before driving on to Vanya's village.

Vanya's church plant continued to meet in an old folks' home. Around forty-five people gathered, which made crowded seating. The service took two and a half hours. "They love to sing," Cory said.

The congregation honored Vanya's birthday with flowers and a card. "They respect him," Cory added. "He has a good presence, but I think they appreciate him because he provides hope. It's a poor village and no one else has anything to offer."

In spite of his successful and vibrant church plants, Vanya continued to face criticism. I had thought discussion ended when the regional council decided God could use him after all. The pastor of his home church continued to complain, however, saying, "Vanya is out of control. He does what he wants and won't listen to anyone."

Members of the regional church council visited his church plant to see what it was like and how he led it. The new head for Crimean churches saw the joyful atmosphere and said, "I wish all our churches were like this."

That still wasn't the end of it. Feodorovich, the former head, remained on the council and declared, "It's another spirit." He said Vanya sinned, and God judged him by taking his arm, so he should not be involved in ministry. Feodorovich did not believe God could bless Vanya, so the apparent success must be a result of worldly methods or inadequate content.

Vanya's young church continued to grow as people came to Christ, even Muslims. His two church plants already had fifty members, with twenty more preparing for baptism when the weather got warmer. On the other hand, attendance for the church Feodorovich led continued to drop. He blamed it on people moving away, older members dying, and the lack of spiritual interest in his town.

Feodorovich continued to criticize Andre and the Training Center. Andre presented all his teaching material to the new head of Crimean churches, who read it and said, "This is what I believe too." Nevertheless, the battle continued.

"Churches here used to be so concerned about survival, they didn't spend much time thinking through their doctrine," Cory told me. "Now they need to think it through. When they lacked Bibles, they passed down traditions and judged people based on external appearance. Before, the 'enemy' was the outside world, but now they have more time to fight each other."

Spring's paintbrush brought relief from the drab tones of winter. Lush green grass, daffodils, and cherry blossoms brightened our neighborhood. Sunshine and blue sky replaced persistent cloud cover.

I remarked one day to a friend, "Even though it got cold this winter, we had heat in our apartment this year, and the electricity hardly ever went off." It was the first winter we went without soggy salt and moldy wallpaper from cool, damp conditions.

She replied, "That is because we have elections coming up. My mom says we should have elections every year."

I had also heard we had better heat because they now used natural gas instead of coal in the heating plants. I appreciated the cleaner air. Even so, our heat disappeared after elections.

The cold was blamed for a wide variety of medical problems, including tooth decay and infertility. Having endured a few winters in Ukraine, I understood why people feared the cold. I never could understand, however, the fear of drafts during the summer. To say, "I don't believe an open window causes sickness," was like claiming, "I don't believe in gravity."

When my back decided I needed a break from housework and put me to bed for a few days—giving too much pain to sit, walk, or stand—many people said I had "caught a cold" in my back. One woman described how her back caught a cold when she washed sheets in cold water in the tub and then leaned out the balcony window to hang them in the cold air. She suggested I wrap wool around my waist to keep my back warm.

Another woman said I should draw out the pain as follows: Light a match and put it in a small shot glass. Place the glass on the skin, creating a vacuum. June had seen patients dotted with red spots from the resulting burns and burst capillaries. She did not recommend that or another favorite treatment: injections near the spine.

Exercises eventually popped something back into place. Finally well enough to get around, I met Valentina, our former neighbor, outside. "How is your back?" she asked.

"It's much better," I replied.

"I think you are trying to fool me, so I won't get kerosene and rub it on you. Don't be afraid; it will help you. My husband had a bad back and thought I was crazy, but I kept after him. I told him, 'If you want to be in pain, that's your affair.' He finally gave in and said, 'Okay, bring the kerosene...and don't forget the match.' I rubbed it on him and he got better."

With a testimonial like that, how could I refuse? I declined anyway.

June estimated medical treatment in our part of Ukraine was about thirty years behind the U.S. She gave her patients one recommendation for treatment, only to hear later that local doctors contradicted her advice.

Because of her success in treating difficult wounds, some doctors and nurses began to invite her to share what she knew. Then Lidiya, the head doctor for the church clinic, asked June to teach at a large gathering of medical officials in Simferopol.

June told me, "Yes, I'm nervous. Knowing that I represent Christians, American medicine, and missionaries, I want to make a good impression. Lidiya told me I will go last though, so that relieves some of the pressure."

As it turned out, the main speakers came late, so conference organizers put June first. She spoke on wound care and took questions. Someone asked,

"How do you treat diabetic wounds?" Knowing the local treatment was different, June described the American method. Lidiya told her later, "They were laughing at you." Fortunately, June didn't know it at the time.

The main speakers finally arrived, experts from Kiev and Odessa. They spoke on modern methods of treatment and repeated the same guidelines June had just given. She told me, "It was great to hear Ukrainian doctors encouraging Ukrainian doctors to rise to a new standard of care."

When the women at the church clinic told her, "We want to learn everything you know," June took them seriously. She paid Tatiana to translate and Anya to type up current treatments for various diseases, as well as patient teaching information. She also translated dosage and usage for medicines she shipped over. These fat three-ring binders became a resource for their practice.

She and other clinic staff held medical outreaches in various villages to support the efforts of church planters. After one outreach, she told me, "It really got to me this time. That village is steeped in alcohol."

A church planter named Yuri had worked there for four years with the result of just one baptized believer. "I'd be so discouraged, if I were in his place," she continued, "but he keeps going back. Many children come for Sunday school, though. The kids love him."

She told of a twelve-year-old boy. "He looks like he's eight since he's so malnourished. He lives in horrible circumstances but attends Sunday school. Another little girl hung around us and started to cry when we went for lunch since she rarely gets any affection."

June described how Yuri tried to talk to people about spiritual matters while they waited to be seen. "But it seemed as if they weren't even listening. They were too busy telling each other about their aches and pains. Yuri was so patient. When the conversations died down, he just tried again."

Even though the adults seemed hardened, June saw hope for the younger generation. "I'm trying to think of a way to help them have a VBS camp this summer," she said.

After Cory returned home from a meeting with Andre and Stefan, he told me, "They are both pretty depressed and anxious about the future." Andre reported that the last regional council meeting went poorly. Feodorovich continued to oppose the Training Center, calling it a "source of evil." He finally got enough council members to agree to force Vanya out of ministry. Vanya lived and worked in his region, making him the most obvious target.

Cory said, "They say Vanya is too proud, and he won't submit. It's like the Russian proverb, 'The tallest blade of grass gets cut first.' Those who show initiative get pushed down."

Andre went to tell Vanya and reported, "Vanya doesn't like the decision, but he is at peace and believes God will eventually allow him to get back into ministry. His main concern is for all the new believers and seekers he has been working with."

A few days later, Cory decided to visit Vanya after calling on another church planter. Upon arrival, Cory apologized, "Sorry I didn't let you know ahead of time I was coming."

"It's better this way," Vanya said. "If I had known you were coming, I would have waited by the gate all day and would not have gotten anything done."

He said Feodorovich now led Sunday services at his church plant. The new believers and seekers complained that they did not get fed through the legalistic sermons he brought. Vanya did not feel he could or should abandon these people, so he continued to visit them.

Cory told me, "Vanya seems to be doing okay. He thinks some of the opposition is because he tells people the most important thing is to love God instead of teaching them to follow rules. He thinks the rest of it is based on lies. He believes it will eventually be worked out. His wife is really struggling with the whole thing, though. They won't let her work with children anymore, and she already put a lot of effort into preparing for a big Easter program."

"What has she done wrong?"

"She hasn't done anything wrong. She's related to Vanya. She is expecting a baby in the fall but went to the hospital not long ago since they were afraid she might miscarry. She had a miscarriage once before. Afterward, some Christians said God was punishing her for her sins."

I felt angry and grieved by the news. I could do nothing to change it but pray. "Oh, Lord, hold this couple close. Give them the ability to forgive like You and to love like You. Give them wisdom and peace. Please bring a resolution to this in a way that You will be glorified and Your Kingdom will not be hindered in this part of Crimea."

19
Rescued

Ministry looked brighter elsewhere. I looked forward to attending the ordination for Pavel, a church planter from our first training course. Once a member of the mafia, he now served as an effective evangelist and church planter. Pavel had already served as pastor for five years with his first church plant and started groups in other villages. His trial period before ordination was longer than usual, but he had a rougher background than most.

As a young man, Pavel wanted to become a paratrooper, but he could not control his temper. During his military training, he started a fight that ended only when many men jumped on him and tied up his hands and feet. Instead of flying, he ended up in a submarine.

The ill-fated expedition left port late in November 1975. While passing through the Mediterranean Sea, the submarine and crew of 120 men entered an area with many minefields left over from World War II. Maps showed these mines, as well as underwater caves, which submarines used like corridors through the minefield. They had taken this shortcut before. This time, however, their smooth journey abruptly stopped.

Pavel felt a violent jerk. The lights dimmed and went out. They lost all radio contact. The chief officer on board assured the men, "This is only a drill."

The crew eventually understood it was not simply an exercise. Their submarine had hit something. All nine men in the front of the craft died in the collision. With their power source now covered with water, the survivors were trapped in total darkness 180 meters under the sea.

They could not send out divers to check the damage—they would have died immediately from the water pressure at that depth. The captain ordered them to release all the gas and oil so it could rise to the surface. Someone might see it there and know of the accident. Because of the mines, however, ships avoided this area, and waves soon washed the spot away. They threw out an alarm buoy, but it caught on a rock and never reached the surface.

The days became weeks. The weeks became months. They had plenty of water, especially since they did not use it for washing or cooking; the water was much too cold for showers. They ate dried sausage, dried fish, and canned food. Since the refrigerators did not work, someone salted the meat stored there. They ate it and no one complained.

The men had enough air, water, and food, but they all wondered, *is this my grave?* They were buried alive in the depths of the sea. Who or what could they count on? None of them knew God. The men began dying in their sleep, mainly from the stress, from the lack of hope, and the constant fear of death.

The hardest part was the absence of light. Their eyes eventually adapted, so they could see even in total darkness—not like one can see in the light, but they could see. They still got many bumps and black eyes from various levers, handles, and hatch lids sticking out.

The submarine was equipped with special air filters, which turned carbon dioxide to oxygen. Each filter was good for twenty-four hours. After five months, however, they started to economize on air filters.

By that time, fifty men had died. Since Pavel was strong, it was his job to shoot the bodies from the torpedo launcher. After putting the body in the torpedo hold, he sealed it and opened the valve. That was the whole funeral ceremony.

Far away his mother received a letter from the Minister of the Navy saying that her son had died at sea. She held a funeral, too, and placed a memorial for Pavel in the village cemetery. Relatives came, cried, and covered the memorial with flowers.

Pavel may have been one of the strongest on board, but the stress, diet, and poor air quality affected him too. After handing out food to the men one day, he went to his bed to lie down. He decided to stand up. He stood, but at the same time, he could see his body still lying down. He thought, *How can this be? There are not two of me!* Pavel saw his hand clearly in the darkness. *Why was it so clean?*

Then he flew. Nothing could stop him, not the submarine, not the rock, nor the sea. He flew through all these things and stood before a great light. He felt better than he ever had before. Nothing hurt. The light attracted him, but some invisible barrier did not let him go further. A soft voice told him, "It is too early for you to come here." Pavel protested but the voice repeated more sternly, "It is too early for you to come here." He flew back to his sick and dirty body.

When he later told his friends what had happened, they thought he was going crazy. At that peak of atheism, it was forbidden to speak or write about the supernatural. Unbelief gripped even those trapped 180 meters under the sea. They did not know God, but God had not forgotten them.

One day they heard the noise of a ship and then heard explosions. With excellent acoustics under the water, Pavel said it was like putting a bucket on your head and hitting it with a hammer. They wondered if a war had started.

On the surface, a ship from the Soviet Union was clearing the minefield above them. This was the only time in history when the USSR and NATO agreed to work together to clear the mines in neutral waters. Most countries had already cleared mines from their own waters, but no one wanted to spend money to clean out the neutral waters. Now, over thirty years after the war ended, they worked to clear this minefield.

They could have cleared the mines and left without finding the submarine, but the long cable used for clearing the mines got caught on an underwater rock. Some men on the ship wanted to simply cut the cable and go home, but the captain ordered divers to go unhook it.

The crew in the submarine could hear the propeller of a ship above them. They heard the ship stop. The commander yelled, "They found us!" But they had not yet been found. They waited with anxious anticipation.

Long hours passed as the divers put on their equipment and prepared to go underwater. They found their cable about 100 meters down, caught on a rock. They were still 80 meters above the submarine. Then they saw the signal buoy, caught on the same rock. The divers knew what it was and knocked Morse code on the buoy.

The crew in the submarine heard it and rejoiced. The acoustic specialist on board immediately replied with Morse code, "We are alive."

The answer came back: "You are found. We will lift you up. Wait."

It seemed like an eternity before a special ship arrived from Sevastopol, equipped to lift the disabled submarine. Pavel could not remember the rescue. He woke up in a pressure chamber.

When they retrieved his submarine, they found the other party in the collision: a small American sub. The two men on board had died in the crash. They lifted that sub, too, took it to Russia, and learned what they could from it.

Pavel spent the rest of his military service in hospitals and rehab centers. At first he and his shipmates received very dark glasses, similar to what a welder wears, so little light got through. Over time, doctors changed lenses to let in more light.

His eyes, stomach, and heart still bothered him when he went home. He received disability benefits, but he did not like his new status. With a sledgehammer, he broke his memorial at the cemetery, shouting, "I am alive and I will live long!"

Doctors did not share his optimism. Although he was just twenty-two years old, cardiologists told him that no ninety-year-old would envy his condition.

They said he would not live to his twenty-fifth birthday. He fainted often. When he saw his fingernails turn blue, he looked for a place to sit.

He tried to get the most out of whatever life he had left. He got married in the fall of 1976, several months after returning home. He loved to joke, so people in the village often asked him to be the master of ceremonies at wedding parties, and since he was strong, he could keep order. Those who got too drunk, he picked up, threw over his shoulder, and hauled off to bed.

He joined the local mafia, but he told them up front he would never kill since he had seen too much death on the submarine. He didn't mind punching people though. When his gang heard of those who had stolen something, they went to them and demanded a percentage. The thieves could hardly go to the police, so it was a good set-up for extortion.

They found a police uniform that fit Pavel perfectly. He wore it to call on people who made alcohol illegally. He confiscated their stills and collected fines. Sometimes he simply gave warnings.

He drank heavily and recalled, "Doctors expected me to die any day because of my bad health, but I was afraid to die."

In 1991 Pavel began secretly watching a television program about healings by God. With everyone still asleep at 7:00 a.m. on Sunday morning, he could watch it without anyone knowing. At first Pavel saw it as a fairy tale, but the healings were verified by doctors and witnesses.

He watched the program for eleven months. By this time, his health was so bad he lost consciousness every day. One morning the preacher said, "If doctors are not able to do anything for you, and they refuse to give you treatment, then only God can help you. You can turn to him in prayer." For the first time in his life, Pavel prayed, repeating the words of the preacher. Kneeling before the television set, he felt he had nowhere else to turn.

Pavel did not feel anything special or notice anything different. When he went for his next medical check, however, his cardiogram showed a normal heartbeat. The doctor asked him, "Why did you bring someone else's cardiogram to me?" Pavel went out and asked them to repeat the cardiogram and took the new results to the doctor. The cardiologist cried, "Why are you trying to fool me? This is not your cardiogram. This is the cardiogram of a healthy person. Here is yours." The doctor opened the thick file with Pavel's medical history. "You are seriously ill."

Pavel answered with a smile, "That means God healed me."

As he got dressed, he heard the doctor tell the nurse, "Here is one more follower of a sect who has gone crazy."

Pavel laughed inside. "You can think whatever you want, but God healed me. It's a fact you cannot hide."

Still, God seemed far away, unknowable, and unapproachable. No one had ever told him about Christ. His wife, Vera, had grown up in a Christian home, but she suffered so much ridicule in school because of her parents' faith, she left the church. Her father had died before she met Pavel. Vera's mother was afraid of Pavel, but she prayed for him, for Vera, and for their children.

Pavel drank heavily. Even if alcohol did not solve life's problems, it pushed them away for a while. He smoked more than two packs of cigarettes a day. One day he realized he was trapped. Unless he found an exit, he would die of alcohol poisoning like some of his friends.

The healing of his heart gave evidence of God's existence and power. Maybe God could somehow help him with this, too. Pavel began visiting churches and started reading the Bible. He had heard evangelical churches described as a shameful sect, so he knew they were not for him. The opinion of others meant too much. At one Orthodox church, the priest suggested that he become a deacon. This fueled his pride even more.

When he came home drunk one day, he stumbled and broke ten liters of white paint—at that time paint was sold in jars instead of cans. Vera was furious. The expensive paint was now ruined. She grabbed a metal bucket and raised it, planning to smash it on Pavel's head. Her swing was blocked, as though someone had grabbed her hands from behind. She tried again. Again, something blocked her. Her anger melted into shame. *I could have killed him,* she realized. *Oh, God, what am I doing?*

The next morning Vera asked Pavel to take her to the Evangelical Christian Baptist House of Prayer where her mother attended. "I cannot live this way anymore," she said.

She went forward at the end of the service to give her life to Christ. Pavel saw immediately she was a different person. She stopped screaming at him and nagging him. She smiled. She spoke kindly to him despite his condition: "You are such a good husband to me, such a gift of God."

Pavel wondered what had happened to her. At first he liked the changes, but then envy took over. She must have another man on the side to act this happy! Even if she didn't, he believed evangelical Christianity was a strange cult and tried to make her give it up.

Before she turned to Christ, she often beat him when he was drunk. She hit him and pulled his hair. Now, he beat her, and he was much bigger and stronger. She sometimes ran away to save her life. She often slept in the woodshed since he locked her out of the house.

The war went on for half a year. Vera simply grew stronger in her faith. She was ready to die as long as she could remain with the Lord.

One morning their fourteen-year-old daughter told Pavel, "Papa, you beat Mama so much last night."

Pavel could not believe it. "Me? Mama?" If Vera had told him, he would have thought she was making it up, but this was his daughter. "Is that really true?" he asked.

"Yes, Papa, you were throwing her around by her hair, back and forth."

The shame cut him like lightning. How could he have fallen so low? A seaman lift his hand against a woman? The mother of his own children? He went to the bedroom, locked the door, and knelt down. "Lord, save me, I am dying. I am even losing my memory. I don't even know what I am doing." For the first time ever, he prayed to God from the heart.

That did not stop him from drinking though. Late one night Vera heard him slam the gate. Then he banged through the door. She could tell he was drunk, and he was angry. "Pavel, calm down," she pleaded. "Pavel, please, it's late. The neighbors are trying to sleep." Still, he roared. "Pavel, please calm down. Go to bed." He drew closer, like an irate maniac.

Vera recalled, "I was small and thin then. It looked as if he was ready to choke me or tear off my head. I called out, 'In Jesus' name, Satan, leave him alone!' He came even closer, with his hands ready to grab me by the neck. I called again, 'In Jesus' name, Satan, leave him alone!'"

Suddenly he came to his senses and cried, "What am I doing?" His hands fell limp.

After that day he stopped getting drunk. It did not matter how much alcohol he consumed; he remained absolutely sober. His drinking buddies began avoiding him. They said, "Pavel is coming. He will drink everything and still leave sober."

He later learned that Vera had prayed, "Lord, give him a sober mind so he will understand what he is doing."

Alcohol lost its appeal. *It only stinks*, he told himself. He quit drinking. God cleared his mind to understand the Gospel.

Not long after this, he decided to go fishing. He was a good fisherman and always caught many fish, but that day his bobber did not even move. He tried all kinds of bait, but nothing worked. This had never happened to him before. It was like all the fish had died.

He opened his bag to get something to eat before heading home. While looking for a knife, he found a Gospel of John. Vera must have put it there. He usually threw away all Christian literature she brought home, but this time, he had no one to show off for. He decided to see what it said. When he started to read, he forgot about everything else. He forgot to eat and forgot it was time to go home. He read it from beginning to the end.

Before, he knew he was a big sinner but did not see any way out. Now, he understood Jesus Christ was the answer. He read and prayed the sample prayer at the end of the booklet, asking God for forgiveness and help.

The next Sunday he went to church with Vera. It felt like everyone was watching him. Of course, not long before he had promised to bring a canister of gasoline to burn the place and see how those sect-followers jumped out the windows.

He went because Vera had told him some Americans would be at the service. American visitors were rare then and he thought, *I must see them. Because of Americans, I sat for half a year on the bottom of the sea.*

With a sense of hostility, he entered the property. Too many people came that day for them to hold the service indoors, so they met outside. When Pavel saw those Americans, each one well over six feet tall, his anger cooled. One man told how people laughed at him after he became a Christian, and Pavel's resentment disappeared. More than anything, he hated to have anyone mock him. These Americans were his brothers.

The pastor invited him to come back the next Sunday. He did but stood in the entryway and listened to the service through the open door. He returned again. When he finally felt ready to enter the room, he sat on the last bench. The Word of God worked in him, and he decided to repent publicly the following Sunday. At the end of the service, the pastor said, "Anyone who so desires and whoever the Holy Spirit touches can turn to God right now."

Pavel grabbed the chair in order to stand up, but his hands became glued to the seat. He could smell strong paint fumes and thought, *Why didn't they tell me they had painted it or put a sign on the chair? How will I look when I go forward, and the whole church sees me with paint? That would not be repentance, but a circus.*

The church service ended and everyone left the room but Pavel. He decided to wait until everyone left even the yard, so he could go home unnoticed. The young pastor came up, put a hand on his shoulder, and asked, "Pavel, why are you still sitting?"

"You painted the chair and I sat on it."

"We did not paint anything."

At that moment, the smell of paint disappeared and Pavel's hands became free. "I can't understand this. I could smell fresh paint, honestly."

The pastor smiled and said, "You probably wanted to turn to God. Let's pray right now."

"No, I don't feel like it now. Maybe next Sunday."

As he drove to the house of prayer the next Sunday, he decided not to sit at all and stood through the service, waiting for the altar call. In his thoughts he addressed his invisible enemy: *You will not get me this time!*

As soon as the pastor gave the invitation, Pavel realized with shock that his body from his waist down was paralyzed. His legs felt as though they were filled with lead and each leg weighed a ton. He could not even move his leg, much less take a step.

When the service ended, he continued standing in the middle of the aisle, getting in the way of people leaving. His feet still felt glued to the floor. People walked around him, smiled at him, and shook his hand. The pastor came up and asked, "What happened?"

"You see, I cannot move from this spot." At that moment his legs returned to normal.

At the next church service, as soon as it began, he went quickly to the front without waiting for the altar call. When he fell to his knees, the beautiful prayer he prepared at home evaporated from his memory. Later, he couldn't even remember what he said, but when he opened his eyes, the whole church was crying.

The believers cried, rejoiced, and congratulated him, hugging him. The persecutor who tormented their sister and promised to burn the house of prayer had repented. For half a year, they had prayed for him. God answered and the church rejoiced. Only Pavel did not feel anything special.

He thought, *Probably God did not forgive me, such a big sinner.* He remembered how Vera practically flew with joy after her repentance.

Every free moment that week, he searched the Bible for an answer but found none. As they prepared to leave for church the next Sunday, he put his hand in his coat pocket. He was surprised to find a pack cigarettes. He hadn't smoked all week! He didn't even think about it, never had a craving. It was impossible, something only God could do. He understood God had forgiven him and received him.

Baptism for new believers.

130

20
Like a Light Went On

June 2002

Pavel explained, "There are only two ways to leave the mafia: to go crazy or become a Baptist. I became a Baptist, which they think is the same thing as going crazy."

A year after Pavel turned to Christ, the pastor began to ask him to preach. Each service included three sermon slots and the young congregation had few men. Pavel always chose the same theme for his sermons: the love of God.

In 1995 he enrolled in a distance education course that prepared him for ministry. In 1998 he joined our training program. Four years had passed since then. The time had come for his ordination.

I found a seat behind Vera and kissed her cheek in greeting. "It's a wonderful day," I said. "I'm glad to be here."

"Yes," she agreed, "God has brought us a long way from the time we were living in darkness, and now, this." She shook her head. "I have to tell you, though, I'm scared. I cried all morning. So much responsibility."

I found her openness refreshing. "God will help you. It is better to know you need Him instead of thinking you can do it alone."

Several pastors from other churches preached. Afterward, Pavel and Vera knelt in front and prayed, committing themselves to God's service. Church leaders laid hands on them and prayed too.

Early the next Sunday morning, Cory dropped me off at Pavel's house before heading on to the train station to meet a team from Texas coming to work with Pavel.

I found Vera bustling about the yard, feeding chickens, and collecting water. "The water is on for only two hours in the morning and two in the evening," she said, dumping another bucket into a bathtub under a fruit tree.

131

She hurried to the summer kitchen, a shed behind their house, stirred a pot on the stove, and accepted my offer to help make lunch. While peeling potatoes for borscht, I learned she would be feeding the group all their meals all week.

"I'm not afraid of the work," she said. "I'm used to feeding evangelism teams from the Bible college, but I do hope they stay healthy. American stomachs don't always adapt well to different food."

She said they had hoped the Americans could stay in apartments with indoor toilets, but church members with apartments felt too embarrassed to invite Americans to their homes. Pavel decided to host the team of six. She felt a little nervous about it, though. "I heard about a group of Americans who stayed in a village. They made a big deal among themselves after one of them used the outhouse. The hostess did not understand what they said but understood very well what they meant."

I tried to assure her, "This group has been to Ukraine before. I'm sure they will be fine." At least I hoped so.

Later I sat with the team around a simple table set outside for lunch. "What did you think of our church service?" Vera asked them. They said they saw more joy, more enthusiasm, and more young people than they had seen during previous trips to Ukraine.

Pavel explained, "We have a young church, just two years old. Most of the members are new Christians and have a living faith. This village is just one of eight where we have started groups. It's hard to cover them all since there are just seven days in the week. I hold at least one meeting every day." Four young believers helped him, and he was training three more.

After lunch Pavel discussed the plan for the week with the team. With so many villages to cover, the team would split into three groups of two. Translators and Pavel's helpers would accompany each group. Every morning they would go door to door. "In all these villages, people are open to the Gospel," he said "and they are expecting your visit."

They would eat lunch at two o'clock, hold a team meeting, and then visit the residents of Pavel's village. He had formed groups in other villages but saw little response in his hometown until that spring when over 300 people came to a showing of the *Jesus* film for Easter. Sixty attended the first follow-up meeting. Fewer continued to attend regular meetings, but he hoped the team would promote extra interest.

"They all knew me when I was a hooligan," he said. "For a long time after I became a Christian, they did not believe I could really change. It's been ten years now, and they see God has made me a new man. Now they defend us as belonging to 'the true faith.'"

He told the team they would visit a home group in a different village every evening. "During the day, you can invite people to these groups," he said. "In the evening, you can minister to those who come, new Christians and those close to the faith."

When I saw the team again the following Sunday, I asked them about their week.

"It is going to be hard to leave this time," said Loyall Watkins, the team leader. "Much harder than our last visit to Ukraine when we stayed in a hotel. Pavel and Vera have been so good to us. For example, they worked hard to keep the 'solar heated' tank over the outside shower filled."

One of the women said, "Even the outhouse wasn't bad. It had fresh wallpaper and a can of deodorizer."

The team felt good about their outreach. Yes, it was hard. Some people yelled at them. Many complained about hardships and claimed life was easier under Communism. Some did not want to hear their message, but they found many ready to listen. Sometimes they visited people Pavel or his helpers knew. Sometimes they simply initiated conversations at the market or as they walked down the road.

One woman said she would just call out to someone, "Hello!" and her translator would interpret. If the person stopped, she continued, "I have come here from America to talk about my faith." She told about a woman who invited her home, cried as she heard about God's love, and then prayed to receive Jesus.

Another told of a woman in her mid-forties who said she had no reason to live and felt empty inside. He explained how God made us with an empty place that could be satisfied only when we are in relationship with God. Jesus made the way for this relationship. She wanted that and prayed.

 Several said they could see a spark of life in people's eyes when they recognized reason for hope, like a light went on.

One told about a negative experience that turned around. A middle-aged woman started yelling at her, "Why do you bother to come here? You don't understand how hard life is in Ukraine. God has abandoned us." She decided any conversation would not be very fruitful and started on down the road. Then an old woman working in the garden, the mother of the first, started to yell at her too.

She told me, "I wanted to 'shake the dust from my feet' and move on, but I felt prompted to say, 'Why are you mad at me?'" The barrier came down and the older woman listened with tears about God's love and prayed, accepting that love. She later brought team members fruit juice and pastries as they waited on the road near her house.

Of all the villages, they felt best about the response in Pavel's hometown. About 130 people came to the meeting held there on Thursday.

Pavel seemed pleased by the team's contribution. Vera added, "They became like family. I will miss them."

Our two-year term had passed quickly, and we planned to fly to the U.S. for a six-month furlough early in July. When church planters gathered at the end of June for prayer, Cory told them, "There's a rumor going around that we are leaving and not coming back. We already have return tickets. Stefan even saw them. Someone told me he heard we plan to move on to something higher. There isn't anything higher than Feodosia." They laughed.

In our absence, we hoped Stefan could make more progress than we had on the problem in our basement. When we moved into our new apartment, we planned to fix up the stairwell. With large patches of missing plaster and abundant graffiti, it looked worse than most. We also wanted to install a security door at the entrance to keep out drug addicts and other undesirables. After moving in, however, we understood moisture from our flooded basement had weakened the plaster.

We didn't know our apartment came with an indoor pool until Cory noticed a gushing sound—not simply a drip—and saw someone descend the basement stairs wearing hip waders. That pool made a lovely breeding ground for mosquitoes, which continued to hatch and hunt us down all winter. They snuck in every time our door opened.

Fumes from the basement smelled like a sewer. Janelle and Alicia usually grabbed their noses before dashing through the entrance and did not breathe again until they reached the second floor. Until we solved the water problem, a security door would simply trap more moisture, mosquitoes, and odors inside.

Neighbors had said, "The housing department has known about the problem for a long time, but they don't have money for repairs."

Stefan suggested to Cory, "We could offer to buy pipes, and the housing department might install them." He agreed to work on it while we were gone.

21

Will We Be a Normal Family?

July 2002 – January 2003

Our furlough schedule included speaking engagements at supporting churches and several mission conferences. Janelle and Alicia looked forward to seeing cousins, riding bikes, picking strawberries, going fishing with Daddy, and "a hundred more things." I would be able to drive and looked forward to grocery stores with shopping carts. I liked Oregon's beauty.

Alicia asked, "When we get to Eugene, are we going to be like a normal family?"

"What is a normal family like?" I probed.

"Well, they live in a neighborhood, at least that's what I've read in books. Umm. And kids do chores."

As a sociable child, I think she hoped for a neighborhood with other children more than extra chores. Fortunately, we lived in a furlough house at a Christian camp with other missionary families as neighbors. God provides.

Our months in the U.S. gave opportunity to touch base with supporting churches and renew ties with family and friends. We got medical and dental checkups. We shopped for clothes and homeschool materials. Janelle and Alicia joined a kids' choir for a Christmas musical.

In Ukraine I occasionally longed for an outing to break up the routine. In the U.S. I wished for more routine. The Apostle Paul said he learned to be content both with abundance and in need. Ecclesiastes says there is a time for everything—everything is good in its own season.

June wrote us from Ukraine: "I feel like calling you tonight but perhaps an e-mail is better. Stefan told me about something terrible that took place. Feodorovich excommunicated Vanya from the church this week. The reason? Because believers were getting together with him for fellowship. From Stefan's point of view, Vanya did nothing wrong. In fact, he went above and beyond what he was told and encouraged believers to go to church. His wife is due in two weeks. My heart hurts for this man and his wife."

With the distance, all we could do was pray, so we did. We prayed for Vanya, for his wife, for the new believers, and that God would somehow use the situation for His glory.

Andre also wrote a few weeks later: "I am sorry for not writing for so long. You know that life contains times of difficulty and uncertainty. It is hard to write during such times. I am not one to write about the weather, but I write about the will of God and His works. When I don't understand God's will or what He is doing, I wait for understanding from Him."

He said that some church planters no longer had time for ministry after they finished their training, since they stopped getting stipends and had to return to work. The local churches could not pick up their support. Churches seemed less interested in evangelism and church planting.

He had traveled around Crimea but could not find more than fifteen interested men suitable for training as church planters. His conversations with pastors revealed several reasons for the low number.

In many churches few men had come to Christ within the last three to five years. Longtime believers already had their own ministries and were not ready to focus on starting new churches.

With rising inflation, most men spent all their time and energy on earning a living. They were reluctant to devote themselves to ministry, especially such a difficult ministry as church planting.

Many pastors still believed their main duty was to care for the existing church, not to worry about other people or villages. They were not ready to let men in the congregation minister elsewhere either, believing they should also work in the established church and help the pastor reach his goals.

Andre continued: "Furthermore, some pastors still try to hinder the ministry we are trying to promote. Although this group is not strong, they have influence and make our job difficult. As we saw all this, we asked the Lord what we should do to change the situation and how to find those who can plant churches."

He prepared a questionnaire for churches to get feedback on their activity, vision, and how they thought the Training Center could help them. He would get forty minutes during the next regional pastors' conference to go over it.

In conclusion, he wrote: "I have not been in a hurry to begin the start-up courses because it is not clear what we should do. Maybe you have some advice. It's too bad that you are not here so we can discuss these things in detail."

Cory called Andre and told him, "Ministry will include times of growth and plateau. Don't be discouraged. If you are not ready to start another training session in January, there's no hurry. Perhaps it is better to spend more time visiting churches and give more general training in evangelism for a while."

As we prepared to return to Ukraine in January, Alicia said, "I can't wait to go home. The first thing I'll do when I get home is hug June; then I'll run upstairs, get in bed and hug my pillow. I will hug it every night and maybe every day."

"Why will you do that?" I asked with a grin.

"Because we will be in the same bed for a long time, and it's my bed."

Janelle said, "I can't wait to go through the toy box—and see June and Christopher, of course."

I looked forward to a slower pace. My own pillow and bed seemed inviting too.

Enjoying fresh snow near our apartment.

All are precious to God.

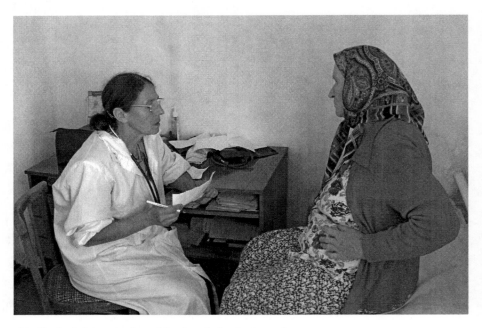

Medical ministry meets spiritual and physical needs.

22

Serving Even in Difficulty

February 2003

When we returned to Feodosia late in January, we immediately pulled out boxes with our warmest clothing. After a mild winter in Oregon, we now needed boots, hats, sweaters, scarves, and heavy coats.

Masha and Lilya came to see Alicia and Janelle, now nine and ten years old. They compared height and shoe size. Lilya, twelve, was tall and thin; but Janelle had almost caught up with eleven-year-old Masha.

June stopped by too. "I'm as tall as you are!" Janelle said.

June replied, "Oh good, now I can start wearing your clothes."

The next day, a girl from their sewing class came over. "You came back like you said!" she exclaimed. "We've been counting down the weeks. We missed you. We still sing the songs you taught us. We meet in a different building now so I will come on Monday to show you how to get there."

Later, Andre dropped in after his meeting in Simferopol. He wore a big smile, pleased that forty pastors came from all over Crimea to discuss evangelism and church planting. He reported, "There was a big turnout even though they knew we would talk about evangelism."

As a way to lay the foundation for a summer outreach effort and for an evangelism course that spring, the new overseer for ECB churches in Crimea called the meeting. He began it with a sermon on God's concern for the lost. Paul grieved for those around him. Do we have the same attitude?

Andre asked the pastors, "What factors in your church help with evangelistic outreach, and what hinders it?" They listed positive points such as prayer, children's work, people who could evangelize, and giving. Their list of negatives was much longer. We lack vision. We have not learned to evangelize. We have not learned to give. One said eighty percent of his congregation was of retirement age; the elderly lacked energy and resources.

Andre did not have time to address all the problems, but he told Cory, "The last few months I have felt discouraged and very tired every evening. But after this meeting, I felt as if I had drunk a liter of coffee! For once, no one argued with the need to reach out."

Cory attended the next Training Center leaders' meeting and told me afterward, "It warmed my heart to hear about church planters who continue to serve even through great difficulty and with few resources." He also heard of men with various personal problems no longer in ministry. He mentioned one going to school in Moscow, one with marriage problems, and one who wasn't walking with the Lord at all. Some got jobs after they stopped receiving stipends and now worked from dawn until dusk, six days a week, with little time or energy left for church-planting efforts.

I wanted to hear about the others, so my heart could be warmed too. Cory gave an update on several men and their ministries. Pavel still worked in several villages with help from the men he mentored. Leonid had gone to a sick church, which was doing better and planning an evangelistic outreach that summer. Nicholi worked in three villages without a regular income. When he ran out of money, God provided through gifts of produce.

Sergei, who served as pastor of the Nizhnigorski church, told how he called a meeting to promote a summer outreach. He expected around thirty people, but sixty-five came. Training Center leaders planned to hold seminars in Nizhnigorski and Simferopol during April, May, and early June.

As they discussed this course, Cory told them, "I don't have to teach. You know my pronunciation and grammar aren't the best. It's hard for some people to listen to a foreigner. I don't mind giving you my lectures and letting someone else teach them."

"You are not getting off that easy," said one leader.

Andre added, "Those of us who have been in the church for a while learn all the proper religious words. We use them and hear them without thinking. You say the same things we do, but you choose different words that are fresh and help us understand these truths in a new way."

God uses even our weaknesses.

After a week in Ukraine, Alicia complained, "I wish the electricity would go off." Nostalgia for the good ol' days, I guess. When the lights went out the next evening, I heard a cheer from the living room. Janelle and Alicia brought their craft project to the kitchen, where I washed dishes, and we had a rechargeable battery lamp. "I wish the electricity would come on again," Alicia said. "We can't listen to our story tape." We lacked power just forty minutes, nothing like the marathon sessions we once endured.

Our radiators got the temperature up to just 61 or 62 degrees. Keeping the oven on all day added a little more warmth, but I still "dressed like a cabbage," as Anya would say, with a hat and many layers. At the market, vendors looked like even bigger cabbages. I was glad I did not have to stand outside all day, stomping my feet for warmth. Others suffered more than I did, but I still disliked the cold weather and gray skies of winter.

One morning I woke up to a cold apartment feeling grouchy. I opened my Bible and came upon James 1:9-10: "The brother in humble circumstances ought to take pride in his high position. But the one who is rich should take pride in his low position, because he will pass away like a wild flower."

I thought about that verse all week. I pondered it when tramping through the mud. It came to mind as I entered our stairwell with crumbling plaster, mosquitoes, and foul smells. We lived on a low rung according to American standards, but compared with much of the world, we were rich. We ate well. God met all our needs. Could I take pride in a low position? Could I rejoice in a humble lifestyle for the sake of eternal issues?

I liked comforts and beauty, but like the flower, these pass away. If I can use my short stay on earth to make an eternal impact, I have reason to rejoice.

June gave us an update on her work in villages. For two years already, she and her co-workers at the Primorski Church Clinic had held medical outreaches to support church planters and their efforts.

The chief medical official for the region east of Primorski heard about them and invited them to work in seven villages in his region, even with evangelism. June explained, "Even though some town mayors oppose this outreach, his stamp of approval overrides their disapproval."

Poverty and alcoholism characterized these villages, which ranged in population from around 100 to 8,000. This strip of Crimea, between the Azov Sea and Black Sea, was used as a "prison without walls" during the time of the tsars. With poor soil and no good sources of fresh water, those sent to live there often died within three years.

It was still a difficult place to live. With few jobs available, many moved away. A church planter could work years and still have few believers to show for his efforts.

June told us of her conversation with one church planter who had ministered for two years in one of these villages, but few came to the meetings he held. She asked him, "Do you get discouraged by that?"

He replied, "Some who used to come moved away. I used to get discouraged, but then I remembered something. God asked me to evangelize. That is my job. I am not responsible for the number. That is God's work. I am to sow the seeds, so that is what I keep doing."

The medical ministry helped break down walls of suspicion and build goodwill—at least it usually did. They still weren't sure what to expect for their next outreach in one village. The last time, they found locked doors.

June described the village as "little more than a shamble town, minus the tumbleweed." Once a collective farm, it was located well off the main road and hidden in a small valley. It held about 1,000 people.

Four months earlier, the medical team held an outreach there and saw thirty people. The day went smoothly and they felt well-received. The next week, Yuri, a church planter, took medical supplies to some people. It gave him a chance to get to know them better. They invited him to return, so he arranged to show the *Jesus* film the following week.

June recalled, "When we arrived, there was a padlock on the door where we expected to show the film, and no one was around. Yuri went to the home that had invited him back. He could see people through the window, but no one answered the door. Mystified, we went to the house where Dr. Lidiya was seeing a patient."

Nina, the patient's wife, told them what happened. Two days after their medical outreach, the Orthodox priest came to the village. When he heard about the visitors, he shouted at the people, "They are a dangerous sect. Today they give you medicines. Tomorrow they will come and demand that you pay for them! If you don't pay, they will take your homes!"

Nina looked angry and said, "I saw everyone you treated. All of them are better!" Dr. Lidiya had wanted to visit the five most-serious cases. Nina went with her, but only three people opened their doors. Nina shouted through the closed gates, "You call yourselves Christians, yet you take their medicines and then lock your doors!"

Yuri and the medical team hoped another medical outreach might help. Perhaps enough time had passed that the villagers would not feel threatened.

Time, need, and answered prayer brought out the people. June reported, "We saw seventy people! There were many difficult cases, but we had all the right medicines and enough for everyone. Yuri did not stop talking the whole day, and people listened. One woman said she had prayed a long time for Christians to visit her. She and Yuri talked for four hours. Two families invited Yuri to return for more conversation."

After escorting Janelle and Alicia to their sewing class, I heard the sound of a piano coming from a building across the street. A sign by the door read: "Music School #2." I went in and inquired about lessons. The receptionist called a teacher, who told me she had an opening. We took it.

Alicia may have liked her former piano teacher's cat, but she never liked the teacher. Both girls were ready to try someone else and liked their new instructor, in spite of her stern manner and appearance. Another mother told me, "She loves her subject, and your children will learn a lot from her if they practice."

The teacher suggested two hours each week at the school and one hour at her home since she lived near us. At home she seemed kinder, more open. She pointed out a framed photo of her mother who passed away just three weeks earlier. "She had stomach ulcers. They gave her one operation. She was dying, but they did another operation anyway, just for the money. Such a thing never happened in Soviet times, before perestroika."

She said the funeral included a meal, of course. Nine days afterward, she held another meal in her home for family and friends in honor of her mother. To mark the forty-day anniversary, she planned to use a café. "It's a good tradition," I said, "but I know it's expensive."

"God provides," she replied. "I got paid this week for my work at the music school last year."

Cory and Andre drove across Crimea to see Vanya, the church planter with one arm. When they arrived around 10:00, he greeted them with tears and a hug. During the next seven hours, they talked and prayed together. Seven months had passed since he had been excommunicated.

Not long after they arrived, Dima came over. Even though church members were not to fellowship with Vanya, Dima continued their friendship. When the pastor told him to stop, he asked for a week to think about it. He finally said, "I cannot throw away my brother." He was also excommunicated.

Dima, Vanya, and Natasha began meeting every Sunday afternoon for their own worship service. Soon two non-Christians joined them and one accepted Christ.

Vanya and Dima wanted advice and asked, "What should we do now?"

Cory kept quiet and let Andre answer. "Are you attending church services?" he asked, referring to the home church.

"No, we have been excommunicated."

"Just because you've been excommunicated does not mean you cannot attend. Go, simply go, even if no one speaks to you. The important thing is to try to build relationship. No healing can take place without that. Were you in sin when they excommunicated you?"

"No."

"Are you in sin now?"

"No."

"Maybe God will convict them and change their hearts through your presence. Live as you should. If they tell you not to come, then you are free."

Vanya's wife, Natasha, struggled with the sense of rejection even more than Vanya. She was not under discipline, but none of the church members would talk to her. She had served in that church and thought she had friends there. After she gave birth to a son in October, no one visited her or even asked about her baby.

On the long drive home, they reviewed the situation. Cory still thought the pastor built a case against Vanya out of jealousy. Andre said, "Of course, if one person is not having success and another is, it's hard not to be jealous, but only God can judge what is in a person's heart. I cannot."

This pastor had been Vanya's sports teacher in school. Through him, Vanya became a Christian. "Of course, he has made mistakes, but so has Vanya. Vanya should have done a better job communicating, explaining his vision and what was on his heart. If he had taken the time to nurture relationships with the brothers, it might not have turned out this way."

Whatever the root cause, they hoped for a peaceful resolution. They discussed what the Training Center might do to ensure it did not happen again. It was counterproductive to invest time, energy, and funds into training men to be evangelists if they were going to be rejected.

Cory explained to me, "From the beginning, we have trained only those who had the blessing of their home church, but some men, like Vanya, are rejected later."

They expected to discuss qualifications of an evangelist at the next church leaders' meeting. At the last gathering, Andre handed out a questionnaire addressing different aspects of this issue. It included questions such as: What qualifies someone to be an evangelist or a pastor? How do you deal with Christians who have been divorced?

Andre believed every member of the Body of Christ should serve in some useful function.

23
God Makes Up for Our Weakness

March – May 2003

Many winters in Feodosia passed without enough snow to go sledding or build a decent snowman. This winter, however, snow stubbornly stayed on the ground until the end of February. We bundled up to go out, but bitter wind still nipped our noses. Small children wore so many layers their arms stuck out like miniature snowmen.

Finally, a breeze from the south brought warmer weather. Huge icicles crashed to the ground, accompanied by a steady drip from the roof.

Janelle and Alicia often invited Lilya or Masha over on the weekend—sometimes both girls came. With the arrival of warmer weather, we walked Masha home one Sunday afternoon the long way, by the beach. Masha and Alicia looked for shells and colored bits of smooth glass, while Janelle drew in the sand: "I love Jesus" and later, "Jesus loves me." It made me smile. Even if she could not sit through a two-hour Russian church service, she had the important things down and worshiped God in her own way.

When I heard the girls' piano teacher would soon commemorate the fortieth day since her mother passed away, I asked Anya to tell me more about the tradition. I wondered how I could properly support her.

Anya explained, "Friends and relatives gather on the ninth day to eat, drink vodka, and say, 'May the ground be for her—or for him—as down.' That's down, like feathers. On the fortieth day, they get together to do the same. People think the spirit remains in the home until the ninth day, maybe until the fortieth day, I can't remember for sure, but they gather to tell the spirit goodbye and to go in peace."

I decided to bake some banana bread and took it over that morning. She met me at the door with fuzzy hair and in a bathrobe. I could not remember how to say, "May the ground be as down" in Russian, so I just apologized for coming early.

She said she had been up since 6:00 a.m. cooking and invited me to come for a meal at noon. I felt I would be intruding on a family event and declined. I agreed to drink tea though. I sat in her kitchen and sampled her rice dish and poppy seed rolls.

"Since it is Lent," she said, "I made chicken soup for those who don't fast and borscht for those who do." She made "fasting rice" with soy bits instead of real meat. Likewise, she made rolls without eggs.

"I started teaching your girls soon after my mother died," she said. "They brought joy to me in a difficult time. They are such good girls."

I was glad she thought so. Maybe it was the homemade gifts they gave her on Women's Day. They chattered to her about their bird and friends. They also practiced and progressed.

She continued, "I told my cousin I teach American students on the piano, and they come to my home for lessons. She was shocked and said, 'Don't you know that Americans live so much better than we do? They must be appalled to see our poor conditions.' Tell me honestly, what do you think of my apartment?"

"Your apartment is nice," I said. I didn't think to tell her about our first home in Ukraine, which lacked indoor plumbing and a refrigerator. Even though she decorated differently, with a rug on the wall, our apartment was not better than hers.

We had still seen no progress toward getting the broken pipe in the basement fixed. Mosquitoes still hovered in the stairwell and snuck in every time our door opened. I tried to slip out the door quickly with my bag of trash and an empty jar when I went for milk in the morning.

Overflowing bins showed the garbage truck did not come often enough. The street sweeper for our region gathered trash spread around by birds, dogs, and the wind. She lit a fire in the bins to try to reduce the stack. The smell of burning plastic stung my nose. I longed for beauty.

I had a harder time readjusting to life in Ukraine this time—perhaps because we came during the winter and spring dawdled. When we returned the previous term, our lives had improved dramatically with a better apartment and an automatic washing machine, but my gratitude wore off. "Lord," I prayed, "give me Your perspective."

Jesus left a pure heaven for a polluted, sin-marred earth. His feet got muddy. Outside Jerusalem, the trash heap burned constantly in the valley of Gehenna. Jesus referred to hell as Gehenna. He came to save people from the garbage pile and give them life. Then He said, "As the Father has sent me, so I send you." May I find my joy in Him.

I passed two women delivering notices who paused by our entryway. Seeing its rundown appearance, one woman said, "I don't go into stairwells that look like that." It did look scary, with missing chunks of plaster and paint.

In the girls' book, *Red Sails to Capri*, the artist said, "I look for beauty no matter where I go." Could this apply to our stairwell too?

Then one day I saw it—the outline of a bear cub going down the stairs. I studied another patch of missing plaster and saw a whale, which grew weekly in size. On the other wall, I found a baby elephant. Our stairwell suddenly became friendlier, with walls decorated like a kindergarten instead of a slum.

While I got used to the appearance, Janelle and Alicia got used to the smell. When we returned to our apartment after a trip, they even said happily, "Ah, it smells like home."

The sewer-like scent from the basement grew stronger, however, so Anya suggested, "You should write a letter and get all the neighbors to sign it. Send it to the mayor's office, with copies to the sanitation department and housing department. A letter is better than going in person." It sounded easier too. She helped me write it and typed it for us.

It was one way to meet the neighbors. They all signed, but no one thought it would help. The old woman on the fifth floor said, "I have been down to the housing department so many times, they hide when they see me coming. I have been to the mayor's office so many times, they told me not to come any more."

We eventually got a letter back with a promise to replace the pipes "during the third quarter of the year." It looked like good news to me. Stefan advised us, "You should still wait to fix up the stairwell since a promise is not the same as a completed job."

Anya gave a little more encouragement, saying, "If they don't fix the problem by October, you can complain again."

Even if we could not fix up the stairwell, Cory got some manual labor by working on his new garage. He had rented before, one of some 600 garages at a garage cooperative. When he had to move out, he bought one. The new garage came with a lot of junk as a bonus, but it was well-built and included a basement where he could store humanitarian aid and potatoes in the winter.

Though just a fifteen-minute walk away, I still had not seen it. Cory always went for the car when we needed it and picked up the girls and me outside our apartment. I did not drive in Ukraine—the market was closer than the garage.

Besides, the garage cooperative was pretty much a men's club. On hot summer nights men sat around in their underwear drinking vodka, playing cards, and escaping their wives. Some people lived in the garages, especially during the summer when they could rent their apartments to tourists, so it was not entirely a men's hang-out.

With repairs complete, Cory invited me to go see the new garage. It was a fine day for a walk. Laundry hung from balcony windows like flags waving in the breeze. Daffodils had begun to open. We passed the gate to the cooperative and entered the maze with row after row of garages, each one looking much like the last, except for the numbers painted on the doors. Cory pointed out the newly whitewashed tree trunks by his garage and the bright blue door. He eventually unfastened a giant padlock and three more locks. It was another good reason not to drive: no automatic garage opener.

Inside it looked like a garage, just cleaner than most. Stefan had helped remove junk, patch holes in the wall, and whitewash it.

Cory lifted planks in the middle of the floor, uncovering steps to the basement. Downstairs he showed me the coffin, unused, left by the previous owner. The solid wood looked much better than the typical fabric-covered, pressboard boxes. The man had made it for himself but did not want to store it in his apartment. After Cory bought the garage, men of neighboring garages asked him, "Did he leave the coffin?"

On Easter morning, we drove to Primorski for church services and pulled in behind an old bus. Many children got off. They had come from villages where church planters and a Sunday school teacher formed groups—the same villages June and her medical team served. More children than adults responded to their efforts, but a wedge of light must start somewhere.

Believers greeted one another with *"Kristos Voskres!"* (Christ is Risen!) and replied, *"Voistina, Voskres!"* (Indeed, risen!) Some repeated the greeting and reply three times, smiling widely and shaking hands vigorously.

The village children, wearing well-worn clothes, took part in the service. I knew most came from homes with alcoholic parents, poverty, and neglect. Their hair and skin lacked the glow that comes with a healthy diet and good shampoo, but their faces radiated hope.

They sang off key, perhaps from the lack of music in their lives or because their Bible teacher was not musical either. They sang anyway. The church pianist moved to the piano and began picking out notes, softly at first. By the time they reached the end, she played a superb accompaniment.

I sat and thought: *God is like that!* Our best efforts sound flat. God sees our hearts, picks up the melody, and makes up for our weakness.

Janelle and Alicia invited Masha and Lilya over on "Easter Monday" to decorate Easter eggs and play. After a few rounds of hide and seek with eggs, they played a Russian game. Two girls tapped boiled eggs together; the winner's egg remained unbroken.

Janelle and Alicia played "I Spy" on our way to visit a village church the following Sunday. They watched for a horse and wagon, a woman on a bicycle, a green car, a pigeon, and a tree with whitewash around the trunk. On our way through the village, we noticed many people headed to the cemetery with wicker baskets.

Leonid apologized for the light turnout that morning. "Some of our church members think it is important to keep the tradition of going to the graveyard on the Sunday after Easter."

On this holiday many in Ukraine joined friends and family members for a picnic at the cemetery. After visiting with the living, they left a food offering for the dead. Scavengers with sacks often collected the food later. One woman told me, "They get more impatient every year. Sometimes, they sit nearby waiting for people to leave. It's not that I expect my mother to reach up and take the food, but it's in poor taste for them to be so bold."

Leonid's small congregation met in a former kindergarten. Janelle and Alicia sang a song Anya had taught them. Cory preached, along with two others. Although children of believers sat calmly near parents, several in the back struggled to sit through the whole service. Tamara, Leonid's wife, told me later that they were the children of alcoholics and drug addicts but came to Bible lessons each Saturday.

I first met Tamara and Leonid when he attended the Training Center's first course for church planters. They were newlyweds then. I loved Tamara's friendliness and candor. She told me how she had visited Nizhnigorski from Kiev as part of an outreach to children and met Leonid. She hesitated to leave the city for such a small town when he proposed, but she soon made friends and found many opportunities to minister to children.

When Leonid was asked to lead the congregation in a smaller village about twenty miles away, Tamara did not want to move. She felt settled, had friends, and Nizhnigorski was rural enough for her. Their landlord kicked them out of their apartment, however, and God gave them a house in that village.

I looked forward to having time with Tamara again. After the service she asked me, "Will you come for dinner?" When I agreed, she added, "Good, because you wouldn't get away that easily!"

Like most houses in the village, their compact yard contained a garden, geese, chickens, beehives, and fruit trees covered with blossoms. Leonid gave us a quick tour of the house while Tamara heated the borscht. Their four-year-old son shared a small room with Tamara's mother. The baby slept in a tiny sitting room. Their little bedroom doubled as an office.

We crowded around a small kitchen table. Dinner included turkey gelatin. The girls skipped it, as well as the green-pepper relish and the salad with lots of onions, in favor of boiled potatoes and bread. They soon excused themselves to finish assembling a puzzle.

Leonid told about a new church member, a Tatar. I remembered seeing him on the back bench and noted his darker features. His wife opposed his

Christianity. Even though she was not a practicing Muslim, she feared losing her family and culture. He had stopped drinking, smoking, and running around, but she still tried to get him to turn away from his new faith.

Over tea and cookies, Leonid outlined his vision for the church. He wanted the congregation to become more active in outreach to surrounding villages. They held Easter services in several places, and fifty kids in a children's home heard about the Lord. He asked for advice on how to continue training the congregation for evangelism.

As we drove home, Cory told me, "It's exciting to see how Leonid has caught the vision and is trying to pass it on to others."

Before Easter Cory had heard that Vanya was in the hospital with pneumonia. After three weeks, he was still in the hospital, so Cory and Andre got money and medicine and drove the four hours to see him. They eventually found him at home, preparing to go to Kiev for more tests.

Vanya told them, "One lung does not expand properly, and doctors drained off a cup of liquid. Tests show it is not pneumonia." They now suspected cancer. He had lost an arm to cancer five years earlier. Had the cancer returned? Some in the church said Vanya's sickness was God's judgment, proof he was in the wrong.

Cory told me, "He looks okay, but he coughs, especially at night."

Not all pastors believed sickness was evidence of sin. Piotr taught one Sunday on sickness and pain using the story of Jesus healing the blind man. The disciples assumed the man's blindness resulted from sin, but Jesus did not agree. Piotr said sickness and pain can come from our sin or the sin of others, but some sickness simply comes from living in a fallen world. The Apostle Paul had an ailment to keep him humble. Piotr urged his listeners to look at pain as an opportunity to depend more on God and less on themselves.

24

Some Came from Muslim Homes

June – July 2003

A team from Texas came again for another outreach with Pavel, planning to stay a little over a week. Since Cory had worked out the details for their visit, we traveled up to see them.

Vera ladled up bowls of borscht, which Pavel passed around the table. He joked, "Russians eat cabbage and water for first course, cabbage without water for second course, and water without cabbage for the third course."

When the team emptied their bowls, Vera served cabbage rolls with mashed potatoes and salad. Finally, she brought out cookies and poured cups of strawberry compote.

Even with jet lag and a long trip, the team looked enthusiastic. Linda Pippin, who had come the summer before, told me, "It was so good to see a man in church that I witnessed to last year."

She explained how God used what she thought was an interruption for a divine encounter: "A man from the church went with my interpreter and me around the village. He stopped and talked to a woman who just wanted to argue. I got impatient and wanted to move on, but my interpreter told me to wait for God to lead. Soon an older man came down the sidewalk. We talked to him, and God softened his heart. I asked him 'Are you tired of living the way you are living? Would you like to start over again?' I told him Jesus had sent us to that street to talk to him because God loved him and had a better way for him. He began to cry and said he was wishing for something else in life. We prayed with him, and he asked Jesus to come into his heart and change his life. It's great to see he is still coming to church."

That afternoon we returned to the house of prayer for an open-air meeting. Pavel started by turning up loudspeakers for the taped music, while others set up benches outside. Some people passing by stopped to listen to the singing, testimonies, and message.

Cory visited the team several times that week, taking drinking water and e-mail messages. Some of them held a camp for youth and children. Others went door to door in several villages using a cube with pictures portraying the basic Gospel message and invited people to an evening meeting.

"Sometimes I was certain we would be tossed out the door," said Timon, a new Christian who accompanied an American and a translator. "But I asked those people to give us three minutes to share the story of Christ, and then we would go quietly. I was amazed to see how God worked in people who were not interested at first but became open to hearing about Jesus and His love. Some listened not just three minutes but over an hour. Often those same people repented and after they prayed, they said how God had lightened the load on their hearts."

Two weeks later, we drove north again to attend a baptism for Timon and twenty-nine others in a canal running through the steppe. Sergei, pastor of the Nizhnigorski House of Prayer, baptized ten. Pavel came with twelve new believers, and another church planter brought eight people from two villages.

Pavel pointed out Timon among the group dressed in white robes—the young man with blond hair—and said, "He is my Timothy. He used to work as a department head on a collective farm, but now he helps me." Several years later, I learned that Timon had belonged to a rival gang at the same time Pavel was in the mafia.

Adults sang hymns while children threw rocks in the water and tested the temperature. Sergei and Pavel gave a few words on the meaning of baptism.

"It's like when a couple decides to get married," Sergei said. "The decision is an important first step, but the ceremony before witnesses is also important." They prayed, and then, one after another, the new believers waded out into the canal.

Pavel and his wife, Vera, invited us over for lunch afterward. Vera said, "The house isn't picked up, but we would love to have you come. I cried when the team from Texas left. I need some guests."

I knew she had been feeding over twenty people for ten days and laughed. "You didn't cry from exhaustion?"

She laughed too. "No, God knit our hearts together. They were a blessing. My son's mother-in-law came to Christ through that team. Some sisters from our church helped me in the kitchen, so I didn't get very tired."

While Vera fried potatoes in the shed she used as a summer kitchen, I cut up cucumbers on a crude table outside in the shade. Two men also waited for lunch. Oleg, the smaller, darker fellow had been baptized that day, and I asked him how he came to Christ.

"I was friends a long time with Vasili," he began. Vasili helped Pavel with evangelism and now helped Vera in the kitchen. "We used to smoke and drink together and do other bad things. Then Vasili came to Christ and his life changed. He shared the Gospel with me, but I wasn't ready. Then I fell over on my bike when I was drunk and skinned up my arm. I didn't break it, but it hurt and took two weeks to heal. I think God allowed this to happen, because it helped me to turn my attention to Him. I used to come home after drinking, and my wife would yell at me, and I would yell back, and then I would leave and go drink some more. My life has changed, and my wife came to Christ too, not long ago."

When Dave and Annette Dryden arrived early in June as interns from a Bible college, they decided to go by "Daveed" and "Anya" so people could remember their names more easily. On their first Sunday in Primorski, Piotr introduced them to the congregation. When he said, "Daveed and Anya will be here for six months," I heard a murmur of approval. The church had seen many visitors who usually stayed for little more than a week. Six months would allow more meaningful contact and contribution. Dave and Annette planned to help that summer with day camps in villages east of Primorski.

Piotr had asked if Dave and Annette could live with his family, saying it would give his children an opportunity to practice English. I wondered if the family had enough room, with five children and three bedrooms, but the living room became a bedroom, and his children became guides and translators. Janelle and Alicia liked that arrangement, expecting to see Masha more often.

Piotr and his wife, Tanya, invited us to a meal for Dave's birthday. Dinner was not yet ready when we arrived at 6:00, so I joined Tanya in the kitchen.

"I thought I would make pizza," she said. "Americans like pizza." While she mixed the dough, she gave me potatoes to grate and onions to chop and then mix with boiled egg, bologna, mushrooms, and mayonnaise for a topping.

"How much mayonnaise?" I asked.

"Just put in the amount you would," she replied. I had never made pizza with mayonnaise or potatoes before, but the result tasted fine.

After studying Russian for a couple weeks, Dave and Annette traveled with June and other helpers from the Primorski church to a village for camp.

Dave, in charge of games, told us, "My t-shirts are getting all stretched out from kids hanging on me. The kids like to chase me. They don't know what to do with me when they catch me, but they think it's fun. And Annette...she has even the troublemakers doing the hokey pokey in her English club."

Camp attendance ran around fifty-five to sixty children each day. Some appeared much younger than their real age, obviously malnourished. Most lived with poverty, alcoholism, and neglect. A few came from Muslim homes. All lapped up the attention.

On one of their free days, I took Dave, Annette, and a visiting team on a tour of Feodosia's oldest part of town. I always liked going to the fortress walls, built by the Genoese in the fourteenth century. I wondered if Christopher Columbus had ever visited this port city before seeking a shortcut to the East—after all, he came from Genoa. Columbus was twenty-four years old when the Ottoman Turks gained control of Crimea in 1475. They expelled the Italian merchants from their fortified coastal cities and hindered access to the Black Sea, thus giving Columbus reason to seek a different trade route to the East.

We walked around a few old churches from the fourteenth century and then headed down the hill to the old slave market, now a park. Next to it stood a fifteenth century mosque, built by Ottoman Turks.

Previously I had seen workers repairing the old mosque. This time, however, the gate stood open, and I thought I saw tourists inside. That was all the invitation I needed. Seeing them remove their shoes at the door, we did too and followed them into the big room—bare except for carpets. I hoped to learn something from the guide but caught just the end of his talk, something about that being the women's section over there because when we come to worship, we must focus our thoughts on Allah and not on the pretty woman next to us.

The Tatar guide showed us a 700-year-old silver coin. "This amount of money could have bought a camel," he said. "If you drop the coin in a cup of water and let it sit overnight, the water will be good for upset stomach."

The other group left, but we lingered. Janelle asked, "Do you give the call to prayer here?"

The Tatar said, "I give the call to prayer myself. I don't use a microphone for the first call, at 5:30 a.m., because not everyone in this neighborhood is Muslim. Many are sleeping and don't want to be disturbed—but I use a microphone for the other calls." Our guide was a mullah, an Islamic religious leader.

When asked how many people used the mosque to pray, he said, "Sometimes just thirty, but on special feast days, a thousand people might come. They roast a cow. Of course not everyone can fit into the mosque compound, so they spread out into the street and the park nearby."

Janelle asked, "Do you use the tower for the call to prayer?"

"Yes. I climb up there five times a day. Does anyone want to see it? The stairs are very narrow, and it is dark in there, but I could take a person or two."

He took more than that. Alicia and Janelle came down reporting 87 steps, but the mullah said there were 99 in all, when you count steps before the tower.

He told us how he and 200,000 other Crimean Tatar were packed into cattle cars and deported from Crimea right after World War II. About half died during the journey or from hunger and disease during resettlement. He returned to Crimea in 1990 but found someone else living in his home. Gray hair, visible around his skull cap, confirmed his age.

I already knew that conflict between Russians and Tatar did not start with World War II. The Tatar traced their origin to the Mongolian empire, which invaded Russia in 1223. The Tatar ruled Crimea for 250 years and then cooperated with the Ottoman Turks for another 300 years, until Russia expanded into Crimea.

The British went to aid the Turks during that struggle for Crimea, and the nurse, Florence Nightingale, went to help British troops. The famous poem, "The Charge of the Light Brigade," commemorated one battle in this conflict. Russia won in 1777, and Katherine the Great, ruler at the time, invited farmers to come and settle the land. The Tatar continued to live in Crimea until Stalin deported them to Central Asia, accusing them of helping the Nazis during World War II.

Tensions flared as the Tatar began returning to Crimea in the early 1990s and found Russians living in their homes. Some Tatar received property, but many simply squatted on unused land, putting up crude huts until they could build something more durable. Few Tatar actively practiced Islam, but Arab nations sent money for mosques and Islamic education.

For the most part, the Tatar mixed with the rest of the population and did not wear special clothing. When Christian evangelists went door to door, they often found the Tatar more hospitable and willing to talk about spiritual matters than Russians and Ukrainians.

About one-third of the children at camp in Batalnaya came from Tatar homes. During the week, the kids prepared skits and made invitations for a closing program for their parents. Cory and I attended the program on Friday afternoon along with twenty-three parents who didn't usually attend church.

Afterward, the leaders met to review the week. One teacher said, "When I asked the children what they liked best about camp, I expected them to say, 'ice cream' or 'going to the beach,' but they gave very different answers. One said, 'I like learning Bible verses.' Another said, 'Before, I didn't know there was a God, but now I know He is there, and He loves me.'"

We made friends with a cat downstairs and I fed her occasionally. When I came home with the milk one morning, she followed me upstairs and slipped through our door. A second later, she dashed across the floor and grabbed poor Christopher, our parakeet, who was out for a morning stroll. With three females screaming, she dropped him and ran away.

Christopher seemed shaken, but was alive. Relieved, Janelle said, "If he had died, I would cry for two weeks." We all hoped he would be okay.

Christopher was like a member of the family, having lived with us almost seven years. He had been through a lot. When we first got him, three-year-old Alicia used to stuff him in her purse. He often followed the girls around the house or went looking for them when he got lonely.

He could open the latch of his cage and let himself out. When I sat on the couch reading to the girls, he would hop on my foot and climb up my leg. Once he reached my shoulder, he would "groom" my neck, peck at my earring, and chatter.

We all loved him, but he was officially Janelle's bird. She could catch him when no one else could. She knew his moods by the way he ruffled his feathers, whether scared, content, or playful. He sometimes slept on her lap or shoulder.

The next day, Christopher was worse. I held him as he died. When the girls came home from camp, we cried together.

We got a small package from America that afternoon, which someone had sent four months earlier. It arrived late but right on time, in God's time. The enclosed card read: "Brighter days are just ahead waiting there for you, for I know you hold within your heart the faith to see you through."

Do pets go to heaven? I don't know, but I dreamed that night Christopher was still alive. We buried him in a secluded spot near the fourteenth-century fortress wall. When Cory dug the little grave, he found a small piece of pottery with green glaze. Janelle saved it to keep with one of Christopher's green feathers.

Almost two weeks later, Janelle felt ready to get another bird. She reviewed our book on budgies and poked holes in an oatmeal box for carrying home her pet. A green and yellow parakeet became the newest member of our household. She named him Timothy, or Timofae in Russian.

25
Needing Prayer

August – September 2003

Dave and Annette moved into June's apartment in August, after she went to the U.S. for a seven-month furlough. With camps now over, Dave began leading the Primorski youth group and spent time with Cory. Annette helped with music ministry and figured out how to buy and prepare local foods. She also held a "Bible club" for Janelle, Alicia, and their friends Masha and Lilya.

Alicia had many ideas for games and activities for their new club. "And we need rules," she said. "And we have to decide, if someone breaks a rule, what's the punishment? I know—she gets tickled for two minutes."

The club provided a fun outlet, but it did not fill up much time. With September approaching, the girls asked, "When will we start school?"

"Not yet," I replied. "I need time to get ready."

I organized bookshelves to make room for new arrivals. The girls eagerly pulled new books from boxes and exclaimed, "It feels like Christmas!"

Again they asked, "When can we start school?"

"Next week, on Monday."

"That's not soon enough."

"Okay, we can start on Saturday, if you do your Saturday chores on Friday."

With their jobs almost done, they staged a protest march on Friday afternoon. Alicia wrote signs with felt markers: "We want school!!!!" and "Start School Now!!!!" Cory took pictures, to encourage them along when their zeal grew cold.

Janelle asked, "Can we at least do math?"

I was firm: "You need to finish cleaning your room first."

Janelle prodded Alicia along, saying, "Hurry and clean, Alicia, so we can do our math."

Maybe the girls were ready to start school, but I wanted more time to get organized and to can tomato sauce. I could buy tomato paste, but why plunk down extra money when I could break my back making my own concoction?

I found a trailer-load of good sauce tomatoes at the market and bought as much as I could carry. I soon returned with Cory, who told the vendor, "She brought her mule." He packed more home while I bought fresh basil and hot peppers. I'd make hot sauce for Cory after messing with the tomatoes.

The next morning I pasteurized milk and cooked pudding in the same pan I had used to make hot sauce. I had washed that pan well, but the milk and vanilla pudding still left a burning sensation in my throat.

Janelle and Alicia ate half a bowl before Janelle noted, "This pudding doesn't taste right."

I explained. They ate it, but Alicia said, "I don't see how Daddy can stand hot sauce."

I served the spicy milk to Cory alone. The girls suggested I could turn the pudding into a chocolate-banana smoothie. Extra chocolate covered the taste but the ice did not take away the tingle.

Before summer's end, we still needed a picnic outside town. I baked a cake and invited Anya, as a belated birthday outing.

On our drive up the hill she told us about her guests that summer: "Every morning, very early, the boy started screaming. Whenever he was upset, he screamed and cursed his mother and sometimes hit her. I asked the woman where her son learned to do that. She said her father treats her that way, and the boy imitates his grandpa. Americans have the right idea—they move away from home when they get married."

The woman had stayed with Anya before, during earlier summer visits to Feodosia. This time she knocked on Anya's door with her mother and four-year-old boy in tow. She begged to stay there since no one else would take in a child. She said they could sleep on the floor. Anya decided she could use an extra 300 hryvnia ($60) for their eleven-day stay, but her daughter said it was not worth it.

Anya's daughter and son-in-law had come from Moscow for a month's vacation by the Black Sea, and Anya's divorced son also lived with her now. Her tiny apartment was barely big enough for two people. I could not imagine where seven people slept or how they shared the tiny kitchen and tiny refrigerator, but such was life in the resort town of Feodosia.

All of Anya's guests had just left. If I had known how tired she was, I would have planned her picnic for another day. "No, this is good," she said. "Picking blackberries and hearing the sound of wind in the trees is refreshing."

I loved getting out of town too, especially since our quiet part of town was no longer quiet. All summer, we heard the sound of jackhammers, drills, and cement mixers as workmen transformed the abandoned kindergarten next door into a tax office. They knocked out inner walls and window-frames for a complete renovation.

Neighbors told me, "They have money to spend on themselves while we live like this, with broken sewer pipes." We still had a mosquito hatchery in our basement.

All over town, we saw new construction. Unfinished apartment buildings, abandoned when the Soviet Union fell apart in 1991, finally filled out. Several stores sprouted between our apartment and the market.

Many new gas stations also pointed to a better economy. When we arrived in Ukraine in 1995, there were no gas stations. Instead, drivers bought fuel from trucks beside the road.

With summer as the busiest time of year in Crimea, the Training Center did not try to hold seminars then. Churches were too busy with camps and visitors. People tended gardens and tried to make enough money during the tourist season to last the rest of the year. Nevertheless, the Training Center leaders met weekly to plan and prepare for sessions in the fall.

They also continued to hold prayer meetings for church planters on the last Friday of each month. The men reported on camps and other outreaches. They talked about their joys and frustrations and shared prayer requests. Cory passed on some highlights after he got home.

Leonid said the Tatar Christian in his church was growing. The Tatar's wife, who had opposed his conversion, was softening and asking questions. Six children accepted Christ at a camp.

Sergei told how a woman in his church was hitchhiking one day and got a ride with the head of a collective farm. As they drove, the woman talked about her faith. The man asked her to bring someone to share this good news with all the department heads on the collective farm.

Sergei described how he and two others spoke to a full room of attentive listeners. Some women who worked in the office cried when they heard the message of hope and forgiveness. Sergei said, "We just started praying for this village, and God is already answering. The collective farm boss invited us to come again and speak to the other workers on the farm. He also said we could use a building to hold Bible lessons for children."

Andre also needed prayer. Cory visited him at home and found him reading with his foot propped up. Andre said, "When I lower my leg, my foot turns blue."

Something had hit his leg two weeks earlier, and an egg-sized lump developed from internal bleeding. A doctor cut it open to relieve the pressure but damaged a vein or artery. It got infected, and Andre began taking antibiotics.

Andre and his family had been hit by one problem after another. His oldest son recently lost fifty-five pounds while away at college. Doctors put him on insulin since his blood sugar was high. Andre's wife had a sinus infection. His oldest daughter was losing her hair, and doctors did not know why. Another daughter was almost hit by lightning. Andre had dreamed something bad was going to happen.

Andre's responsibilities at a church one hour away were more challenging than ever. He began leading that congregation when the former pastor emigrated to the U.S. He had hoped to quickly pass on responsibilities to a local brother, but he ran into problems so complex he did not know how to untangle them.

His wound and troubles for the family happened after he began addressing problems in the church. Satan tempted him to stop preaching the truth through the reoccurring thought, *If you will stop preaching this, you will get well.*

Andre told Cory, "At first, this was scary, but I realized it was more important to live in truth with one leg than to live a lie with two." His leg began to improve.

Cory told me the story when he got home and added, "On the positive side, this injury forced him to slow down. I haven't seen him looking this relaxed in a long time." Andre was not the only one with health concerns, however.

After we heard that Pavel had a heart attack, we went to visit him. His six-month stint in a crippled submarine almost twenty-eight years earlier had damaged his heart, but stress in ministry triggered his most recent problem. He made a tough call in a difficult situation, and people criticized him for it. He also felt the burden of trying to minister in eight villages.

Vera told me, with tears flooding her eyes, "I thought we would lose him. Pray for us."

During the church service, Pavel told the congregation, "Some people say I should slow down and rest. They say I work too much, but when I read the Bible and look around at so many people who don't know Christ, I hear God telling me to keep working. So I must obey God rather than men."

When I asked him afterward about his health, he said, "Praise God, I'm better today. But I met with the brothers last night and asked them what they would do if I went to be with the Lord. They agreed to help more with the ministry and lead small groups."

Pavel looked better when we attended the official opening of a new church in his home village three weeks later. We arrived early, having attended the morning service in a nearby town. Vera was setting out lunch: spaghetti noodles topped with fried carrot and bits of hot dog, with tomato salad on the side. She waved the flies away and urged us and several others to come and eat. She often fed a crowd at her outdoor table.

She told me, "We have someone living with us again. He is a non-Christian and drinks, but he needed a place to stay. Pavel reminded me, 'Faith comes by hearing the Word of God. How can they believe unless they hear?'" They hoped something would sink in.

Approaching time for the 2:00 service, we walked down a path through the garden, past the guard dog, outhouse, and chickens. "We meet in the kindergarten," Vera said as we walked down the street.

At least it used to be a kindergarten—it looked like an abandoned building. Peering through a big hole in the wall where a window should have been, I saw no floor. The wood had been taken for other use.

Pavel's group met on the other side, in a room with windows and a floor. Cory helped line up benches for the service, and villagers began to come.

Pavel told those who gathered, "I have lived in this village for thirty-four years. I once thought I was a Christian because I had thirteen crosses. When I finally read the Bible, the words it used to describe a sinner fit me perfectly. I wondered, 'How does this book know all about me?'" He told how he turned to Christ in October 1992 and began sharing his faith with others.

"I was very excited about it, but people looked at me like something had fallen on my head, so I kept quiet. People knew what kind of person I was. I had been in the mafia, and they didn't trust me. Over time they saw the Gospel of Jesus Christ is strong enough to change even a person like me."

Toward the end of the service, I joined Vera and several other women as they hurried to her house to prepare tea and sandwiches. One of the helpers was a new member of Pavel's church in a neighboring village.

"I regret I didn't come to Christ sooner," she told me. "I wasted so many years. I still have problems, but God helps me each day. Before, I did not even want to live."

"How did you start coming to church?" I asked.

"When an American team was here, my son invited me to go with him to the meetings. I was nervous about going, but the people were friendly, and the music and preaching touched my heart. My son rarely goes now, but I attend every meeting in the week. I want to know the Word of God more.

"I still regret the sinful life I led. I have been married five times. I had so many abortions, I can't even count them. I'm embarrassed to say it, and I still ask God for forgiveness. I would go to the clinic and then go to work afterward, like it was nothing."

"God forgives," I assured her.

She expected her co-workers to respond negatively when they learned she had joined the evangelical church, but she was pleasantly surprised. She read to them from the Russian version of the *Our Daily Bread*, a devotional booklet, and they seemed to like it. She reminded me of the Samaritan woman—after a brief encounter with Jesus, she became an effective evangelist in her village.

I always enjoyed visiting Batalnaya with its friendly congregation, more informal service, and Stefan's personable leadership style. People felt free to interrupt the sermon if they had a question. Many who once attended Anya's Sunday school class as children remained in the church as teenagers.

Katya, who accepted Christ as a teen, now led the youth group. She told me she had wanted to leave the village but believed God called her to stay and minister to youth there. "They get so much bad influence from television. I want to give them something good. They like to meet, and they ask many questions!"

When we attended the church's Harvest Day service, the youth recited poems and gave skits. I told Katya afterward, "The youth did a great job."

"We need some boys," she said, "But these girls are such good girls. Others in the village are drinking, smoking, and getting pregnant. One of my girls looked in the disco but decided, 'That's not for me.' These girls decided they want to have Christian homes."

I knew Katya hoped for one too, but her fiancé had not committed to any particular date. He worked in Moscow doing construction. At the age of twenty-three, she still lived with non-Christian parents in an unpleasant environment. June had described the house to me as "dark and dirty, except for Katya's room." The parents drank heavily, sold liquor, and opposed her Christianity. I once heard Katya pray, "Thank you, Lord, for teaching me patience through my parents."

Stefan came to our apartment the next week and said, "Please pray for Katya's mother in Batalnaya." Weeks earlier she had been bitten by a dog when she went for the cows. The wound became infected, swollen, and hot.

The village doctor did not know how to help her and advised, "Take her to the *babka*," or local witch doctor. Katya took her to the Primorski church clinic, but they could not help either. Some people said there was no cure, and the infected wound would result in her death.

Katya visited the *babka* and asked, "What treatment do you use, herbs or something else?" The woman said she used a type of prayer and herbs.

When she accused Katya of following Satan by going to the evangelical church, Katya understood the opposite was true. Furthermore, she knew if she took her mother to the *babka*, it would compromise her witness in the village. People would say, "You say you believe one thing, but you go to the *babka*." She decided to ask Stefan if church leaders could come and pray for her mother.

Cory joined Stefan and Andre when they drove out to Batalnaya to meet with her. Before they prayed, Andre held up a book and told her, "If this was my book, then I have the right to do with it as I want. God has the right to do with you as He wants. You are willing to receive healing from God. Are you also willing not to be healed, even if this sickness leads to death?"

She agreed, and they prayed for her.

When Stefan came to see Cory a few days later, I asked, "How is Katya's mother?"

Stefan broke into a big grin. "God worked two miracles," he said. "One is physical healing. Her leg is much better—there's no redness, pain, or swelling. She came to church Sunday and told us God had healed her. She said that when the brothers prayed for her, she felt like how a king or queen must feel when they have been crowned. She also said she understood that even though life contains difficulty, she now knows God is with her, and she needs to live for Him no matter what.

"The other miracle is a big change in her spiritually. Katya told me that when her mom gets up in the morning, she won't do anything until they have prayed together. She even reads the Bible to visitors who come over. Everyone in the village knew about her leg and was waiting to see if she would go to the *babka*. She is telling everyone God healed her, and people in the village are talking about it."

Even though Katya's mother and father did not have an official bar or store in their home, everyone knew they could buy alcohol there. On Sunday, the mother said that she understood she should stop selling liquor and cigarettes. Instead, they were going to try to sell staples like macaroni, rice, and oil.

A village church celebrates Harvest Day.

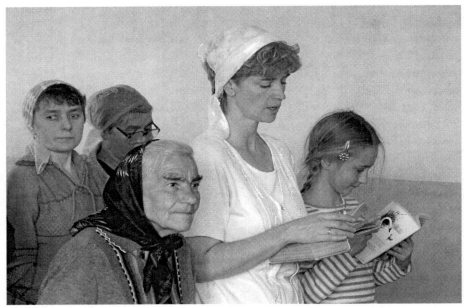

Caught reading in church.

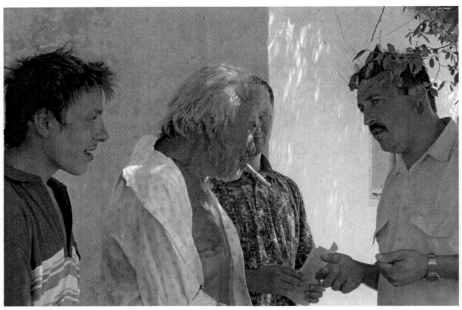

Evangelists share hope.

26

Reaching Out Was God's Idea First

Although we helped host many short-term teams throughout the year, I felt most intrigued by a group of Mennonites from Canada. The parents or grandparents of most of them had come from Ukraine. Some had been born in work camps of Central Asia, where their parents were sent after World War II. These Christians now came to Ukraine wanting to bless the land of their roots.

"My mother lived in Crimea until after World War II," said one woman. "At that time, they started to persecute anyone of German descent."

She explained how Mennonites settled in Ukraine during the late 1700s, fleeing religious persecution in Germany. Katherine the Great wanted people to work the land, so they came, planted crops, and built villages with schools, churches, and hospitals.

They prospered for over one hundred years, until the Bolshevik Revolution of 1917, which targeted landowners. Some Mennonites fled; many were killed. Those who stayed and survived that ordeal were later punished as "Germans" during the 1940s.

"My husband and I tried to find the village where my mother had lived," she continued. "We knew where it was supposed to be, but all we could find were some trees in a field, along with a few bricks and humps of soil that covered the ruins. After the war, Russian officials destroyed all German villages, wanting nothing left as a monument to their existence. Fortunately, we met an old woman who remembered the village. She showed us where different buildings had been, like the hospital and school."

Walter Loewen, another Canadian, hoped to see a church started in the village where his mother was born. His grandparents' house still stood. The person who received the order to blow up German buildings in that town refused, as the Mennonite home and barn were more solidly built and more beautiful than Soviet structures. He went to prison for his disobedience, but the large house now held the post office and other government offices.

During Walter's previous visit, we linked him with Mikhail, a member of the Nizhnigorski church who went through our training program. Mikhail and his wife, Yulia, agreed to move to the village and try to form a new congregation there.

They sought to build relationships in the village through acts of kindness. They gave out Christian literature at the market and invited people to their home for a Bible study. They also worked in two neighboring villages. Many listened but did not want to follow Christ. Yulia reported, "They can be miserable, but they are afraid of the Christian life. They say, 'If I become a believer, I will have to stop drinking and smoking, and I will have to live honestly.'"

Mikhail once told us, "Many people die here from alcohol, very many. In the last few months only one person died of natural causes, an old woman. The rest died from alcohol."

Resistance increased when the Orthodox priest told villagers they would lose their salvation if they took literature from this "sect" or read a Bible that did not have the Orthodox cross on the front. Few people ever went to the Orthodox Church or read the Bible, but they claimed to be Orthodox Christians because they were born in Ukraine or Russia.

Still, some responded to Mikhail and Yulia's kindness and faithful witness. Eight were baptized that summer. A small but growing church began meeting in a room of the post office building, the former Mennonite house.

Yulia wholeheartedly helped her husband. Looking through her photo album, I asked her if she missed her old home. "Not a bit," she declared. "I can live anywhere if I am doing God's work. I am glad we moved here. I think it is better to live in the village where we work. People can get to know us and see how we live."

Walter came to his grandparents' village to help Mikhail and Yulia with evangelism. During the middle of his two-week stay, Cory and I drove up to see how things were going. Several weeks earlier, Yulia had told me, "I'm a little nervous about Walter living with us since we have an outhouse." As I helped her in the kitchen before dinner, she now reported, "He is like family."

Yulia and her helpers from the church had prepared a feast in honor of Walter's birthday. I thought the first course made an adequate meal: three salads, bread, and stuffed green peppers. Yulia later brought out *cutleti*, a kind of meat loaf patty, then mashed potatoes and fried chicken, followed by three kinds of cake and assorted candies.

"My time here has gone very well," Walter said. "I am so pleased. This is my best trip to Ukraine so far." He described how they went door to door each morning with a translator. After lunch, they rested a while and then went out again in the afternoon. When people heard about his grandparents, some asked if he had come to reclaim the land. Walter chuckled as he told us. He sought to assure them that he came only to share God's love.

Two weeks later, an article appeared in the local newspaper about the Canadian who spent two weeks in the village where his Mennonite grandparents had a large farm. It questioned his motives. Did he come to try to get the land back? Not likely. Did he come for a pleasant vacation in our land? Hardly. Did he come from curiosity about his heritage? Probably not. Did he come to promote his faith? No, "the Mennonites are a very small, insignificant sect." The real reason, the author decided, was that his grandparents buried some of their wealth before they were chased off the land, and Walter came here to find it and dig it up.

Cory laughed out loud when he heard the author's theory. "People believe what they want to believe," he said. Many did not trust Jesus and the purity of His motives, so why should they trust us?

A year and a half had passed since Mikhail and others in the second group completed their training as church planters. Training Center leaders had put off taking on a third group but finally had enough suitable candidates—at least they hoped they did. Twenty men expressed interest.

Before accepting them to the two-year program, however, the leaders decided to see how they responded to a shorter course. They invited the men to attend a series of seminars, held every other weekend for three months. Those who completed the assignments, showing they had the gifts and motivation for evangelism and church planting, would be accepted for further training and receive a stipend.

When Cory came home after the first session, held at a large church in Simferopol, he said, "I didn't sleep very well. I had a sway-backed cot. And with fifteen men, the room we stayed in smelled like a men's locker room. And I didn't have any coffee when I got up. Next time I need to go better prepared— at least take some drinking water."

No one else complained, and the men who came seemed pleased with the content. Cory gave me a summary: "Andre talked about vision. Reaching out to the lost was God's idea first, motivated by love. Sergei explained the Gospel, that we are saved by grace. I taught on godly character, that leaders need to live with integrity—not just know the Bible but practice it too."

He told me about one of the students, Timon. "Remember when we went to the baptism at the canal last summer? He's the one who used to work as a manager on a collective farm, and now he helps Pavel. His wife got baptized at the same time. He said he and his wife used to fight all the time, and they were about to get divorced, but their marriage has really turned around."

Timon told how he came to Christ after his mother died in a car accident. He previously thought of himself as a good person, but he realized that if he died as unexpectedly as his mother had, he would go to hell and never see her again. At the funeral, he felt God speaking to him: *You are not living as you should.* He determined to change and began reading the Bible.

Before long he quit his job as a section manager on the farm since it required him to lie and to cheat people. Besides, he had time for nothing other than work. His mother had been active in evangelism—he wanted to take her place and continue the work she had done.

As a new Christian, he first watched Pavel lead groups. Then Pavel began giving him that responsibility. "I felt nervous at first," Timon recalled, "but I saw the power of God in my weakness. Like the Bible says, 'Rivers of living water will flow from you.'"

Though work with a third group had begun, Cory kept contact with church planters who had already graduated. One of them, Vadim, planned to hold a church dedication soon, and Cory invited me along. Cory had told me much about this simple man who loved people and wanted them to find hope in Christ.

Janelle and Alicia happily agreed to spend Saturday night with Stefan's family, giving us the freedom to leave early for the three-hour drive. "You'll like Vadim's wife, Sveta," Cory told me as we neared their village. And I did.

A thin woman came out to meet us after we drove up. She gave me a strong hug and kissed my cheek. A smile brightened her face and revealed several gold teeth. "I'm so glad you could come," Sveta said. "Come in and have breakfast with us." We had already eaten, but we sat and drank some tea.

Although they had indoor plumbing, they lacked constant running water. Sveta dipped water from a full bathtub and poured it over my hands.

Showing us their large living room, Vadim told how they had prayed for a home big enough to hold Bible studies. They found an acceptable house for $3,000 and scraped together half that amount. They returned to the village and met a man ready to take $1,500 for a house bigger and better than the one they intended to buy. God answered their prayer.

With no jobs available, the village was dying. Some houses simply stood vacant until taken apart for building materials. Nevertheless, Vadim and Sveta intended to bring hope to the people who remained.

The group outgrew their living room. They purchased another house and hoped to knock out an inner wall when they had more funds for construction. We walked down the road to this new house of prayer.

Sveta's sense of hospitality clearly extended to the congregation. She greeted everyone and made sure they had a place to sit and a song book. Besides the usual group, many visitors came for the dedication.

We sat on backless benches for the service, which lasted a little over two hours. Between each of the six sermons, we stood to sing a hymn. It renewed circulation and kept bones from fossilizing.

Cory read from Isaiah 56 and noted how the temple was called a house of prayer for the nations. "The church fills that role today," he said. "It must not turn into a social club nor lose sight of the need to reach people without Christ." Watching Vadim nod vigorously, I knew he shared that goal.

After the service men brought in rough wooden tables, which women covered with sheets of plastic, plates, and food. In proper Ukrainian style, they served a four-course meal, starting with borscht. Guests ate first and dipped into various salads on the table: pickled cabbage, pickled tomatoes, beet salad, and carrot salad with garlic. Next came mashed potatoes and chicken. Finally, servers brought tea, sweet bread, and hard candies.

While Cory talked to men outside afterward, I asked Sveta how she became a Christian. "I grew up in a Communist home," she began. Her family lived in a closed military city in the Ural Mountains. She never heard about God, except from teachers who mocked "foolish" people who believe in God. Like most other children, she joined the Pioneer club and then the Communist club for older students, *Consomol*.

"I did not become a Communist as an adult though," she said. "The Communist leaders did not live by the same morals they taught, and I did not like the hypocrisy." She suffered in a bad marriage and divorced after giving birth to two children. She later met and married Vadim who was also divorced and had two children.

Vadim's mother had been a Christian, but none of her children followed in her footsteps until after she died. One by one, Vadim's three sisters turned to Christ. Vadim and Sveta laughed at them for their belief. "I thought I was a good person and did not need God," she said. "I did not drink or smoke. I helped people. I was a medic and even went on calls at night."

She and Vadim had been married ten years when their only child together, a girl, died at the age of eight from congenital heart problems. "I came to Christ through my daughter," she said. After the girl died, Sveta dreamed her daughter was in a beautiful garden, which she recognized as heaven. She wanted to go to heaven to be with her daughter, so she began attending church and reading the Bible. She understood she was a sinner. Her good deeds were not good enough, but Jesus provided the way. She soon accepted His love and forgiveness.

It took Vadim a little longer to come around. He had always had a drinking problem, but it became much worse after the death of his daughter. Every day he drank heavily.

Vadim joined us and filled in the rest of his story. One day he got in a car accident, which he survived with severe injuries. He found a Bible in a drawer of his room at the treatment center. He pulled it out and said, "You don't give up, do You, God?"

He knew God had spared his life and decided to get right with Him. His sisters invited him to church for a special occasion. "I felt like the pastor was talking directly to me," he said of that service. "I wondered who told him all about me. I looked around, but no one was paying any attention to me. At the end of the service, I went forward to pray. I felt light afterward—like I could fly. From that day, I lost all desire for cigarettes and alcohol."

Vadim listed ways the Training Center helped him and prepared him for ministry: "I learned how to work with people, how to share my faith, and how to preach. The fellowship was wonderful. I grew spiritually."

Even more, he appreciated the Training Center's purpose. "Before, if anyone talked about doing evangelism or starting a new church in a village, we were told to shut up and stop being foolish. I can't tell you how many times I was criticized for talking about the need to reach people for Christ. The Training Center has this vision."

Ukrainian hospitality.

27

In Dependence, With Gratitude

Andre continued to work with church leaders trying to encourage outreach. He sent out a questionnaire and talked to pastors to find out what activity was taking place. When pastors gathered for their next meeting, he shared the results. The survey showed some congregations had started several new groups, but many did nothing. Even with 60 churches and 100 new church plants, there remained 1000 towns and villages in Crimea without a church.

Andre said that if the church was not doing evangelism, it was not fulfilling God's will and the Great Commission. If the church did not have people involved in outreach, it should seek to empower them. According to Ephesians 4:11-12, church leaders are to equip people for ministry. God intends for the church to reach the world. This includes financial support for outreach efforts.

Having church activity or non-activity printed out in black and white made some pastors uncomfortable. Feodorovich, who had long opposed our church-planting effort, stood and said, "I see nowhere in the Bible where we are told to start new churches. What we need is more holiness in the churches we have." He talked about proper attire for women and the need to get rid of televisions.

The new head for Crimean churches got the discussion back on track. He referred to Bible passages where the Apostle Paul started new churches and appointed elders and deacons for new churches.

Though not all pastors embraced the vision, we saw progress.

As Dave and Annette, our interns, prepared to return to the U.S., many urged them to come back after they finished Bible college. In six months, Dave had learned Russian well enough to preach in it his last Sunday. They looked forward to seeing family, but talked about the things they would miss.

"I will miss speaking Russian," Dave said. I took this as the sign of a true linguist. "I like going to the Training Center leadership team meetings with Cory. The guys joke around with one another so there's a joyful spirit, but they're working toward a serious goal. I also liked visiting the villages with church planters and seeing the kids who came to camp."

Annette said, "It seems as though the believers here take their faith and prayer life more seriously than many Americans. I learned from them. I will miss those relationships." She noted how they prayed before and after meals and before leaving a home. When a girl from the youth group came to help her buy meat, she suggested that they pray before going to the market so they might find good meat.

I also saw how believers prayed about the details and thanked God for small blessings like water, electricity, rain, good crops, and strength to get their work done. I heard them talk about a woman who said of her time in the U.S., "I became weaker in my faith there because I did not need to pray as much. Everything was provided."

We often heard stories of how believers saw God's faithfulness as they leaned on Him. Pavel and Vera ate produce from their large garden, but also depended on income from their honeybees. During an especially long and harsh winter, most of their bees died. Spring started late and with few colonies left, Pavel did not expect much honey that year. Instead of taking his hives to the countryside, he kept them in his yard.

He did not have time to sit with the hives, anyway, to make sure no one stole them—not if he was to continue working with church plants in eight villages. He said, "The bees kept multiplying, and I kept adding extra boxes. When blossoms faded by the first of July, I didn't know if they were working or just flying. Later, I realized they had discovered a field of sunflowers about five kilometers away."

After a busy time of ministry, he finally checked the hives and found them packed full of honey. It turned out to be one of his best years.

Giving another example of God's faithfulness, he told about a late spring frost one year. Though the potato patches of his neighbors got frosted and turned black, his potato patch remained green with just a few black plants around the edge. "It was as if God placed His hand over my garden," Pavel recalled. "When my neighbors saw that my potatoes survived, they wanted seed potatoes from me. I told them they were ordinary potatoes, and God protected them, but they didn't believe me."

Though we knew their life and ministry in the village included many difficulties, Vadim and Sveta often spoke of God's faithfulness, too. They told how God even helped their livestock so they could minister on Sunday. Most people stayed with their animals when they let them out to graze, but with various church services all day, Vadim and Sveta did not have time for that. They let out a fairly new cow to graze one Sunday on public land. It would have been a great loss if she wandered away or if someone stole her. God watched her, and she came home by herself, even though she had not lived with them long.

Vadim said that when sows give birth, the piglets usually came one every twenty minutes. The process could take all day, and someone had to stay near and remove the babies so the sow would not lie on them and kill them. One Sunday morning, a sow began to deliver, but all the piglets popped out quickly, before the church service began.

I saw God's provision in unexpected ways as well. Our businessman neighbor on the fourth floor got tired of finding used syringes in the stairwell and installed a security door on the outside, for the sake of his children. It may have kept out unwanted people, but it increased the problem of mosquitoes, moisture, and a bad smell in our apartment.

Stefan suggested, "Perhaps we could seal off the door to the basement with bricks and plaster."

He proposed this to the housing authorities, but they said our entryway provided their only access to the basement. The director admitted, "I would not want to live like that either," and agreed to Stefan's other idea of installing a metal door with a rubber seal. He also explained that they had tried to pump out the water to fix the pipes, but water flooded in as fast as they could pump it out. The apartment had been built on swampland.

Stefan found a door maker, who replaced the rotten basement door with a new metal door on the day before Christmas. Cory added a rubber seal and filled cracks around the door frame with expanding foam. It was my best Christmas present that year.

A large church in Wichita, Kansas sent us shoebox Christmas gifts as a way to help the church planters in their work with children. Cory pulled out two boxes for families in our stairwell.

When I gave a box to the businessman's six-year-old boy, his eyes glowed. The mother came down the next day with candy for Janelle and Alicia. "The gifts in the box were wonderful," she said. "Thank you. But I have a question." She pulled out some Silly Putty. "We cannot figure out what this is. My husband even tasted it, thinking it might be gum or candy." Janelle and Alicia rushed to get their grimy gray mass and eagerly showed mother and son some wonderful uses for Silly Putty.

I gave another shoebox to the woman who lived above us for her grandson. The woman told me later, "The gifts were incredible. So many things. Volva jumped up and down with happiness, and the shirt fit him perfectly." I later saw Volva making a snowman with his new gloves. He waved them and shouted, "Thank you for these!"

I made cookies again and delivered them to our neighbors. Those who were home received them gladly—except for the old woman on the fifth floor. "I do not take anything after dark," she called from behind her door. The previous year she did not want to take anything over the threshold. It must be nerve-wracking to follow all these superstitions, especially when ignorant foreigners don't live by the same rules.

I decided to take cookies to her the next day, when it was light, and imagined we would have a friendly chat. I knocked on the door.

"Who is it?" she called from within.

"Your neighbor!"

"What do you want?"

"I brought you some cookies."

"I already have everything I need. I don't need them."

I called the holiday greeting through the door and left. God tries to give gifts even better than mine, and He gets refused too.

We attended Christmas services at Stefan's church in Batalnaya on January 7. The youth put on a special Christmas program, which helped draw in relatives and some first-time guests.

Katya gave me a big hug after the service. She said life was again difficult at home. Though her mother began attending church after God healed her leg, she stopped coming. "She has a hard time believing God will take care of her and is wavering between heaven and earth. But I was that way in the beginning. Pray for her." Selling macaroni was not as profitable as selling liquor.

In other news, Katya and her fiancé still had not set a date. They did not have enough money for a house and did not want to marry until they could live separate from parents. He planned to leave for Moscow again in the spring to work on construction. "I am twenty-four years old and am ready to move away from home, but I remember that you were even older when you got married, and that helps me be patient."

"I felt impatient sometimes too," I said. "But I prayed God would work to make me the kind of wife I should be, so I would be ready when the right man came."

Getting married didn't end the need for more improvement. Cory left for meetings in Kiev, leaving me at home feeling sorry for myself. Before we got married, I traveled a lot and loved new experiences. At the age of thirty-one, God gave me a husband who preferred predictability over adventure. Our new roles required both of us to change, but Cory still found travel stressful, and I got tired of routine.

I tried to look on the bright side but had a hard time finding it. Another day at home. When I went out, I found gray skies above and mud underfoot. Then a phrase stood out from Jeremiah 31:2: "The people...found grace in the wilderness..." (NAS). I could use some grace for my wilderness.

I thought about it some more. The Israelites complained about another day of manna, but God continued to meet their needs in remarkable ways. Lord, forgive my ingratitude! He had also met my needs.

I enjoyed many things about my role as wife and mother. I appreciated the sense of partnership in a ministry bigger than I could have had on my own. Cory was good about sharing events of his day. I enjoyed being a part of Janelle and Alicia's growth.

The girls had already memorized several chapters in Psalms and other long passages and wanted a bigger challenge. They decided to tackle the book of Philippians. They were into chapter two when I read the next verse: "Do everything without complaining or arguing..."

"That's not really in there," said one with disbelief. It hit too close to home.

It really is. And children are not the only ones with that problem.

February brought an unusually heavy snowfall: around two feet, more or less, depending on the drifts. Janelle and Alicia enthusiastically burrowed into a drift near our apartment and made a snow cave. They crawled in snow and rolled in it. Concerned adults passing by asked, "Aren't you cold?" A child or two watched with envy, knowing their parents would never let them wallow in snow, fearing sickness.

Two weeks later the girls took delight in sunshine and a spring-like breeze. "Can we wear jackets to class and go without hats?"

When it was cold, I disliked the slick paths. When warmer, I grumbled about the mud. Ah, to see with the eyes of a child. God makes everything beautiful in its own time.

The Training Center leaders met with twenty-three men interested in church planting. The men took an exam on lectures from the three-month preparation course, and leaders interviewed each one. They wanted to see who was committed, capable, and had the support of his home church.

Cory told me later, "I am really impressed with most of these guys. They are sharp and feel a sense of call. For example, we talked to an older man today who said he has been looking for this type of teaching ever since he became a Christian ten years ago. He said he doesn't need a stipend, because he gets a pension; he just wants to attend the lectures and serve. Most of the guys are already involved in ministry and have shown initiative, but we have questions about a few of them. One said he feels uncomfortable sharing his faith, has no real sense of call, and doesn't get along with the pastor; but at least he was honest."

The next week the leaders met to discuss their impressions and decide which names they would submit to the Crimean church council for their approval. They added this step since Vanya was rejected after taking the training. Cory said, "I think the council will agree with everyone we recommend, but this step may prevent problems later."

Work begins on the abandoned building for the Efas Center.

28

Connect the Dots

March – June 2004

Early in March twenty men began the two-year course as church planters. Stefan arranged for this group to stay and study at a new church building in Beregevoya, a village not far from Feodosia. He found bunk beds, tables, and kitchen supplies for them to use.

The first session included lectures on vision for evangelism and church planting. Most towns and villages of Crimea and Ukraine still did not have any place people could gather to hear the Word of God.

During the discussion time, one person repeated a question of some older church leaders: "Where in the Bible does it say we are to start new churches?"

Andre told him, "With your pen, make dots in the four corners of your paper." As he talked, he illustrated on the blackboard. "Now, draw lines to connect the dots. What do you have?"

"A square."

"But I didn't tell you to make a square. When Jesus told the disciples to go, to teach, baptize, and make disciples, he gave them four dots. When you connect the dots together, you have a church. If we look at the Apostle Paul, what did he do when he fulfilled the Great Commission? He started churches."

The men gathered every third week for four days of teaching and fellowship. After sitting in lectures all morning, the men went out in pairs for evangelism after lunch. Some afternoons they worked on a service project, part of a massive undertaking Cory began reluctantly.

Three years earlier, a visiting American pointed out a partially-constructed hotel right next to the new church in Beregevoya. When the Soviet Union fell apart, many such building projects—hotels and apartment complexes—were abandoned due to lack of funds. "Maybe you should look into buying that and finishing it," the American suggested.

Cory initially dismissed the idea, but his local co-workers did not. During the summer months, many tourists came to the Black Sea, but good accommodations were scarce. The building could be used as a hotel during the summer and as a Christian training and retreat center during the other months of the year. It would provide jobs for Christians, and profits could support ministry.

The building was available. The purchase price was much less than the cost of materials already in place. Another American businessman provided a loan for the purchase. Cory decided that if it didn't work out, we could always sell the building and get the money back, since property values were going up.

Stefan said, "We have been doing training without it, but it would be nice to have our own place. We have had a gypsy lifestyle, getting bounced around, and some buildings we used have been far from ideal."

When Cory took me to see the building, it looked even further from ideal. He drove behind the Beregevoya church to a three-story skeleton of limestone blocks and concrete, with gaping holes where doors and windows should go. We climbed up stacked blocks to the open doorway and went in. Apparently, it had become a homeless shelter with a fire ring on the floor. Broken bottles, used needles, and trash lay everywhere. Graffiti covered the walls. It smelled and looked like an unofficial outhouse.

"We can knock out this wall for a larger reception room," Cory said. "We thought we'd put the office over here. We can close in this door and put a different door over there. It has a lot of potential. Here, let me show you the rooms; they are really big."

I followed him, carefully watching my step. All I could think was, *What a lot of work.* I certainly did not have the strength to clean the place. Cory led me up rickety steps to the top floor. It did have a nice view of the Black Sea. Still, finishing it off would take a lot more money than we had, not to mention immense wisdom and patience for bureaucratic hurdles.

We talked to our mission organization and some supporting churches. We had enough funds for initial steps forward, still thinking, "If we can't complete it, we can always sell it and get our money back." Stefan agreed to oversee the project. He made many visits to various offices to get building permits and other documents in order.

With the current group of trainees staying right next to our limestone skeleton, Stefan put them to work some afternoons during their training. "Twenty men can accomplish a lot," he said. They started by cleaning it. They did not have to walk far for their service project, but did not have any way to shower afterward, either.

Stefan worked on getting electricity to the site. He bought materials for a fence to keep out drug users and people needing a restroom or garbage dump. He met with a contractor about putting on a fourth floor and roof. He had the patience and people skills needed for the job, but often consulted with Cory for a second opinion.

June returned to Ukraine in mid-March. After leaving her luggage at her apartment, she came over for coffee and a chat. Janelle and Alicia jumped up and down, calling, "June! June!" when the doorbell rang. They showed her their birds and gave her a large serving of news from the last seven months.

"Thank you for taking care of my apartment while I was gone," she said. "It's nice to be able to settle in right away. This time I don't have to worry about finding a place to live or putting up wallpaper."

June had used her furlough to spend time with family, friends, and supporting churches. She renewed her nursing certification and packed boxes for Ukraine. Those boxes, filled with humanitarian aid, medical supplies, and materials for summer camps, now sat in Cory's garage.

After June and Cory had a chance to sort it out, Cory loaded his car with used clothes and took them to church planters for distribution.

Cory kept in contact with many of the men involved in evangelism through a prayer meeting held on the last Friday of each month. They talked about groups they led for children and adults, as well as individuals needing prayer. They praised God for small steps forward and shared their difficulties.

Pavel now worked in ten villages with help from the men he discipled. In the newest village, twelve people came to meetings, including a man recently out of prison. "The church is growing," he said, "but we need brothers to be involved in ministry. So pray for the Lord to send out workers into His harvest field."

Some spoke of their contacts with Tatar Muslims. A few of these had turned to Christ. Others seemed interested but feared rejection. Many Tatar children came to Bible clubs.

One praised God for the gift of a bicycle, which helped him get around. Another said he needed repairs on his moped since he worked in ten villages.

One said, "We had thirty people coming last year, but six moved away to find work and four died. We have some new people, though. Four are preparing for baptism."

Another reported, "I was working too many hours to have much time for ministry, but my boss now lets me work less time. I am grateful my wife supports my desire to serve God, even though it means a lower income."

They also prayed for Vanya, who was now fighting lung cancer. Cory and Andre had recently visited him and found him very thin after chemotherapy treatments. Doctors regularly drained fluid from his lung. Cory said, "He seems to be at peace but regrets his situation. His wife is more upset, facing the prospect of being a widow with two children."

With warmer weather and a door for the basement, the time had come to tackle the long-awaited repairs to our stairwell. We invited a local church planter to do it since he needed a job and had experience. He brought his brother-in-law along. The first day they knocked down loose plaster and concrete. I wished I had taken a picture of the bear climbing the stairs and the whale on the wall before they disappeared, but I looked forward to a cleaner result.

I invited them in for lunch every day and took them water. For the next three weeks, they filled holes with cement and plaster, whitewashed the ceiling, and painted the walls.

When they finished our stairwell, they helped Stefan with the unfinished hotel. He put them to work installing a fence around the property to protect building supplies and keep people from dumping their trash in the building. As a short-term deterrent, they stacked bricks in the windows and installed a door.

The basement was still full of garbage, but Stefan did not need skilled labor to clean it out. He approached a group of men waiting for the wine factory to open and said, "I will pay you 10 hryvnia a day ($2) to shovel garbage. But you have to work all day, and I won't pay you until the job is done." The rate was more than minimum wage. Several men accepted his job offer, and within two days they cleaned out the basement.

With the building now blocked off, neighbors complained: "Where are we going to dump our garbage?" Stefan told them to talk to the mayor. When he found new garbage in the building, he took it around to the neighbors and told them, "This is now private property. If I find you on the grounds, I am going to dump garbage in your yard." They all denied any guilt, but the garbage dumping stopped.

29

At Peace with God

July – October 2004

Janelle and Alicia counted down the days until their seventeen-year-old cousin, Tyler, came to Ukraine to help with summer camps. Though he later stayed with a Russian family, we kept him his first two weeks. Janelle and Alicia loved it. They gave him Russian lessons, played board games, assembled puzzles, and went to the beach.

At the end of his first week of camp, Tyler told me, "It's kinda sad that it's the last day." He explained how he got to know the different children—if not by name, by their personalities. They all tried to talk to him, practicing what English they knew. They seemed so open, so trusting. They smiled, not like most adults he saw. The little ones, especially the girls, wanted to sit on his lap or hold his hand. The boys tried to tackle him. He gave small children piggyback rides during free time.

"I don't know if I made a lasting impact with any of them," he said, "but I hope so."

"Most of them come from families with drunken parents," I explained. "The love you show them says a lot. They wouldn't want to hang around you and sit on your lap if they didn't feel loved. They will remember it."

June invited Janelle to help during Batalnaya's day camp for younger children. She left home with doubts, but came back with a big smile. She helped our friend Anya with the youngest group and held up pictures during the Bible story.

Anya assigned a five-year-old girl to her, who had never been to church before. Janelle reported, "On the first day, she was really shy. She hid her face and didn't want to talk, but the next day she smiled and talked a lot." Alicia decided she wanted to be a helper the next year too.

After another week of camp, June told about little Dima who came with his seven-year-old sister. Though he was too young for camp—just four—she looked after him, so they came as a package deal. Dima spoke on the level of a one-year-old. June eventually learned why. His father drank and tore up the house one day in a fit of rage, breaking windows. The kids saw it all, and Dima stopped speaking. June remarked, "We hold camp for children like this. Jesus said, 'Let the little ones come to Me.'"

The phone rang late one night mid-August. Vanya, the church planter with cancer, was not expected to live another day and wanted to see Cory and Andre. Could they go up? They planned to go, but early the next morning, the phone rang again. Vanya had died during the night.

I had hoped for a happier ending—but maybe it still wasn't too late. Cory and I prayed that those who had heard his testimony would be drawn to the hope Vanya had and that others would rise up to take his place. We prayed God would strengthen his wife and help her forgive those who had rejected her husband. We prayed for God to work in the hearts of church leaders, to bring renewal and revival.

The next day I rode with Cory, Andre, and Stefan to the funeral. We got there early, so we could have time with Natasha, his wife. She met us at the gate, wearing a black scarf, wiping her eyes with a handkerchief. She invited us in the house to see the body, which lay in a coffin set up on two kitchen chairs, the face waxy white.

"That's not Vanya," Cory whispered to me. "Vanya is gone."

Natasha described how Vanya had cried out with pain, day and night, for a week before he died. Doctors gave her morphine, and she would jump up from her bed to give him injections in the night. On the last day, the pain subsided. He wanted to eat. He wanted to hug his boys. Then he died.

"We washed him and dressed him," she continued. "A ready-made coffin was cheaper, so we got one of those. We put these branches by him to keep the body fresh, but it's been hot, and after two nights, there's already some smell. Is it okay that I put a Bible in the coffin? He loved the Bible...loved to read it." Andre nodded, blinking back tears.

The youngest boy, not quite two, put his finger to his mouth and said, "Shh. Papa's sleeping." The ten-year-old boy knew his father had died.

Others began to come. Men took the casket outside. Cory pointed out one of them and said, "He was one of the first to accept Christ in the other village; he is now leading the group there." That was one prayer being answered.

Over one hundred people came to the funeral, held in the yard. "Vanya was loved," I told Natasha.

A church leader who opposed Vanya officiated. After a song or two, he gave a "we're all going to die, so you better be ready" sermon. Another pastor spoke more warmly and told how he had prayed for his aunt, who lived in that village, and his aunt came to Christ through Vanya. Cory told of good qualities he remembered about Vanya: his smile, his jokes, his love for people. Those listening began to weep. People standing out in the road came closer to hear better. Cory called Vanya "my hero" and said, "He could do things I can't do... What we remember most about Vanya, though, was that he loved Christ and had hope."

After a prayer, they prepared for the funeral procession. Several women carried plastic flower wreaths in front. Next in line, four men took the casket lid, on which sat a round loaf of bread with salt filling a hollowed-out spot on top. Others moved the casket onto an old farm truck. It was clean, but rusty. The sides had been lowered to make a flatbed. Carpets covered the back.

The truck rumbled to life and slowly drove down the lane, past gardens, past geese grazing and cows resting in the shade, past neighbors who stood at their gates to watch the procession. Natasha, along with her mother, oldest son, and brothers, followed the truck. Church women followed them with their songbooks, singing minor-key hymns all the way. Cory said, "It seems surreal." I had to agree. We walked about a mile to a cemetery outside town.

The truck pulled to the edge of the road, and men lifted the coffin off. Someone had cut a wide path with a scythe through the weeds that led to an open grave. After another song, Andre preached.

"Vanya was a man who was at peace with God," he said. "That's not because he never did anything wrong. The Bible says, 'All have sinned.' Vanya, however, accepted the forgiveness that is available because of what Jesus Christ did by dying for us on the cross 2,000 years ago. That same forgiveness is available to all who believe in Him."

The local pastor invited people to "say goodbye." Some came near, spoke to the body, and kissed the forehead. When all who wished had come forward, men nailed the lid on the coffin and lowered it into the pit with ropes. Family members, including the ten-year-old son, threw handfuls of dirt onto the coffin. Others did too, and then men took turns shoveling dirt into the hole until a mound marked the spot. I appreciated the hands-on involvement of Ukrainian funerals.

Natasha called out, "Don't leave without coming to the table."

When we returned to the house, women began loading a long table outside with borscht, carrot salad, potato salad, smoked fish, fried eggplant, bread, juice, and more. It was a feast. As we sat to eat, they brought out mashed potatoes, ground beef patties, fried fish, and stewed chicken. I ate a little and then found Natasha inside. She looked tired.

"Did you get any sleep last night?" I asked. I knew of the tradition of sitting up all night with the body, but since it had been two nights, maybe she got some sleep.

"Oh, no!" she replied. "I had to cook all night to get ready for today."

That was more "hands-on" involvement than I would want.

The small son had said, "Papa's asleep." At least his body was—the rest of him was pain-free in the presence of his Lord.

Vanya's burial.

The church in Texas which previously sent teams to help Pavel with evangelism agreed to send medical workers for their next outreach, late in August. June ordered medical supplies from the U.S. and found translators. Pavel arranged for them to hold clinics and do evangelism in six villages.

Although Cory spent time with the team when they arrived, I waited until the end of their week to visit.

I asked June, "How was it?" Part of the team had gone door to door, part stayed at the clinic site to talk to people waiting, and the doctors and nurses saw patients.

"It was awesome," she said. "It's a real privilege to work with these people and be part of what God is doing in these villages."

Every night around the table, team members shared stories about the day. Encounters ranged from goofy questions to dramatic conversions where someone turned to Christ with tears.

One team member, Linda, told me, "I was sharing the Gospel with someone when a woman from the village came up and said, 'What these people say is true. My husband and I talked to them two years ago and gave our lives to Christ. My husband used to drink and beat me. He is a changed man. I am different too.'"

Linda saw that meeting as a gift of God. "This is my third time to come and work with Pavel," she said. "I continue sharing my faith without knowing if the seeds take root." She remembered the couple and later asked them if they were already considering Christianity before they prayed with her that day. No, the day she talked to them was the day they decided. They still attended church, and the husband now worked with a church planter doing evangelism.

Pavel later told us that over 650 people came to see the doctors and left their names and addresses. He figured it would take him all year to go around and visit them all.

T he Training Center leaders continued to meet every third week with the newest group of church planters. Every evening the men took turns sharing news of their ministries and prayed for one another. Cory told me about Victor, who wanted to go to Siberia to work. "He doesn't look as if he has much going for him, but he is smart and active in ministry." Victor originally came from Siberia and wanted to help the struggling believers there.

He and another man sent a video to the church. In it, they included a personal message with some lectures from the Training Center on topics like vision, the purpose of the church, and teamwork.

Victor reported, "I was afraid to send it. I thought one person might look at it and say, 'That might work for you, but it won't work here.'" Instead, the whole church gathered to watch it. The church had been on the verge of a split.

He told Cory, "I remember how you said that when churches don't have a goal to work toward and don't have vision, the members start fighting each other." Based on the video, the church decided to work together to plant a church in another village that had none.

Janelle began helping with VBS camps.

One way to get produce to market.

30

God Is Still on His Throne

November 2004 – January 2005

With another round of elections coming up at the end of November, Pavel complained that when he tried to talk to people about God, they wanted to discuss the presidential candidates instead. "All they can think about is who will give them higher wages and more comfortable conditions. They put their hope in man. After the vote, when their lives are still the same, maybe they will look for spiritual answers to their problems."

In many countries, election years come and go without significant change. In Ukraine, however, each new leader had altered the constitution. As Election Day drew near, the level of anxiety and tension in the country increased. What rights would remain? How would a new leader affect the economy? Would Christians retain freedom of religion?

Pavel did not seem to care what leader got elected. He said, "God is in control, and He will give what is right. If that means upheaval, then God will use it to draw people to Himself. The growth of house churches has improved the ability of Christianity to continue to spread if the church goes through another time of persecution."

I studied the news with a little more anxiety. Even if the Bible does say, "Blessed are those who are persecuted because of righteousness," this is not the type of blessing I want when praying "bless me" or "bless my country."

The first round of voting, three weeks earlier, narrowed the choice from twelve candidates to two. Election observers declared that vote was flawed, and democracy in Ukraine "took a step backward." Students and workers said they were threatened with expulsion and job loss if they did not file absentee ballots favoring the incumbent party. That candidate pushed for closer ties to Russia and promised to ban all "sects" but the Orthodox Church. The challenger wanted closer ties to the West and promised continued freedom of religion.

On the day after the second vote, authorities announced the Russian-backed candidate as the winner. However, some regions favoring him had more filed ballots than registered voters. Furthermore, exit polls showed the Western-leaning candidate was leading.

By that night, an estimated 100,000 people gathered in the streets of Kiev to protest. They called it "The Orange Revolution." By the weekend, ranks had swollen to an estimated 200,000 people calling for the election to be annulled. Many camped on the street overnight in freezing temperatures. They maintained a peaceful presence, but authorities condemned them as terrorists who threatened the stability of Ukraine.

The Parliament soon declared the election results to be invalid. Emotions ran high as the Supreme Court looked into irregularities. We heard rumors that Russian soldiers had come to Ukraine with weapons and donned Ukrainian uniforms. Hospitals in Kiev expected bloodshed and sent home non-critical patients.

The outgoing president said the economy was like a house of cards that would fall because of the ongoing protests. This led to a run on the banks as people remembered the economic collapse and hardship during perestroika. Food prices rose as people started to hoard.

Many in the older generation wanted stability more than anything else. They had lived through chaos and desired a strong leader with a strong hand, whether he be right or wrong. Those camping in the streets of Kiev wanted something more.

I checked news on the Internet often for developments. I read commentaries analyzing the news from different angles. What would happen? I finally decided I needed to spend more time looking at the situation from God's perspective.

The Book of Psalms reflects hard realities in life. It speaks of the ungodly who walk in pride and seem to flourish even though they crush the innocent. The psalmist felt disturbed, but when he looked up, he realized God was still on His throne. God would bring down the oppressor and defend the innocent. God was and is an anchor for the soul, a rock in a storm.

The Supreme Court ruled the election results of November 21 invalid and called for another round on December 26. I asked our milk lady what she thought of the decision. To her, the future looked bleak. "Of course, we are all very worried," she said.

I asked Stefan, "What are people afraid of?"

He explained, "There is a power vacuum now. People in government positions are not working. This is a top-down structure, and if they don't know who is on top, they are afraid to make a decision that will be the wrong one when someone else is on top. The president has lost his power base. The banks are unstable. People fear economic collapse and the uncertainty of the future."

Articles on the Internet reported that people in Ukraine were celebrating the birth of a new nation; though another vote remained, people now felt their voice mattered. Perhaps they rejoiced in Kiev, but in our region and other Russian-speaking areas, we heard of much anxiety and anger. Rumors fueled fear and frustration.

The girls' sewing teacher said, "I heard we won't get paid after December, and I'm sure it is because of Yushchenko." She recalled the period after Ukraine's independence when people worked without pay, sometimes receiving produce or a case of wine instead. "We will go without heat, gas, electricity, and water. That's because Yushchenko will have to pay back America for ten years all the money America gave to help him get elected. We get our oil from Russia, and they won't give us any if Yushchenko is president."

Others said that those living in the eastern, Russian-speaking areas would become second-class citizens under a Western-leaning president. They called for the eastern section to become autonomous.

Even children joined the nationwide attention to politics. During recess at one kindergarten in Feodosia, some children chanted, "Yu-chshen-ko," while classmates stood in another group and shouted, "Ya-nu-ko-vych."

Jesus came to earth during a time of political uncertainty. He did not come to set up an earthly kingdom but a heavenly one. He taught us to pray, "May Your kingdom come, Your will be done, on earth as it is in heaven." This was my prayer for Ukraine.

Janelle and Alicia counted down the days until Christmas. They started cutting out snowflakes at Thanksgiving time, and it soon looked like we lived in an igloo, with snow in every room. We lacked other reminders that Christmas was near, but the calendar was good enough for them. Their enthusiasm brought life to the season. They decorated our small, artificial tree and played Christmas music constantly. Hearing, "All is calm; all is bright," I wanted to believe it.

My fears for Ukraine's future settled as I heard, "God is not dead, nor does he sleep. The wrong shall fail, the right prevail, with peace on Earth, goodwill toward men."

Now eleven and almost thirteen, Alicia and Janelle were quickly turning into young ladies, but Christmas showed they were still children at heart.

"When are you going to put gifts under the tree?" Alicia asked.

Janelle added, "Make sure you tell Santa to fill the stockings, too."

I wrapped presents with a sense of anticipation and joy. The girls looked forward to opening gifts, but I also looked forward to giving them. As I wrapped, I remembered Jesus' words: "If you know how to give good gifts to your children, how much more does your Heavenly Father..."

The girls kept asking, "When are you going to put presents under the tree?"

"When it's time," I'd reply.

When I was young and single and wondered what the future held, I found a verse that became a favorite: "How great is Your goodness, which You have stored up for those who fear You..." (Psalm 31:19). I imagined God waiting for the right time to give the good gifts He had prepared. When older and married, I still didn't know what the future held, but God was still good.

The people of Ukraine are experts when it comes to giving well-wishes for birthdays, Christmas, and the New Year. Other holidays can also bring on the blessings. Calls typically came when I was in the middle of making dinner or sitting down to eat it. "I want to wish you happiness and health and everything good," said the voice on the other end. "May God provide all your needs and give you strength day to day. May your children be healthy, obedient, and grow spiritually..." And so on.

I used to think of this as an odd quirk but learned to appreciate this characteristic—as long as the blessing did not last so long that I burned the gravy. The Bible says much about speaking blessing to other people. By contrast, if American visitors tried to express affection using cutting jokes and sarcasm, it usually sounded offensive, even with a careful translator.

June brought us barbecued ribs for New Year's Eve. The girls baked cut-out cookies while I answered the phone to receive all the blessings and tried to come up with an articulate blessing of my own.

We played games, watched movies, ate popcorn, caught the countdown in Kiev on TV, and viewed fireworks going off all around us from our balcony.

Celebrations on television showed a packed Independence Square in Kiev, where people greeted the New Year, 2005, and cheered Yushchenko as their new president. Polls showed he received the most votes in the December 26 election, but his rival claimed to be the rightful winner and took his case to the Supreme Court.

Tension exists between political parties in the U.S., but there was more involved in this election. Many ethnic Russians felt loyal to their motherland and felt somewhat superior to ethnic Ukrainians, having been dominant during the Soviet Union. Ethnic Ukrainians wanted to shake off the old yoke. The girls' sewing teacher said, "I want to get cable TV so I won't have to listen to Ukrainian. I will watch programs from Russia only."

In the high emotion and uncertainty of the previous weeks, we thanked God that the transition took place without violence. It could have gone differently.

When Yushchenko was sworn in three weeks later, political analysts said he now had the challenge of healing a divided nation. For most people, however, political allegiance was less important than economic stability. If the paycheck and pension continued to come in, it did not matter much who sat in office.

We celebrated Ukrainian Christmas, January 7, by attending the "grand opening" of a new house of prayer. For several months, Mikhail and Yulia had worked to convert a house into a church building for their new congregation. They had outgrown the room in the former Mennonite house where they once met. Construction took longer than it might have, but Mikhail said, "I don't want to work more on the building than I do on building up the body of Christ through sharing the Gospel."

As Cory drove to the village on a narrow country road, he had to slow down several times to wait for geese to cross the street. Passing modest cottages, overgrown yards, muddy lanes, and villagers riding bicycles, I saw them with new eyes and asked, "Does it seem strange to be driving through Eastern Europe?"

"Thinking of it that way makes me feel nervous," Cory said. "It's hard to believe we have lived here almost ten years already."

It looked like a party in progress when we reached the site, with cars parked along the road, people milling about, and music playing from loudspeakers set up outside. Church members from other towns joined the celebration, along with visitors from the village. So many people came, some had to stand outside.

The service included special music and four sermons. Andre once said, "Whenever I preach, I try to have something for nonbelievers and something for believers." This time was no exception. As he spoke about Christmas, he said, "In school they used to tell us the story of Jesus was just a fairy tale. But they did not condemn people or put them in prison for believing in Little Red Riding Hood. People are not willing to die for their belief in Cinderella.... Jesus was a real person in history. The date of this year is used throughout the world and is measured from the time of His coming."

Before the next preacher could start, a woman went forward to publicly repent. I could not see her but heard her tearful prayer from my spot on a bench in an overflow room. An older man joined her and also prayed.

Mikhail's wife, Yulia, and some other women began cooking early that morning in order to feed guests from far away. Since we fit that category, she directed us to a back room after the service, to their living quarters where a meal awaited.

The new year began on a more somber note for Dr. Lidiya, a key leader for the church clinic where June worked. Dr. Lidiya had been sick for several weeks already. A chest x-ray revealed a walnut-sized tumor in her lung. Doctors suspected cancer. She checked in at the cancer hospital, and doctors scheduled her surgery for the following week.

June told us the news with a heavy heart. She had heard so many stories about complications from surgery, she felt worried for Lidiya. She also wondered how this would affect the future of the medical ministry. Dr. Lidiya's energy, her love for God and people, and her contacts with medical officials had all played a big role with the church clinic and village outreaches. Did she have cancer elsewhere too? Even if the tumor was benign and there were no complications, it would take a long time to recover from an operation.

In spite of this, Lidiya displayed a calm courage. She looked at it as an opportunity to share her faith at the cancer hospital. June sent out prayer requests.

Lidiya said later, "As I waited for my operation, I could not lie on my back, since it was too painful. I was reading in my Bible about God sending angels, when God sent Andre, Stefan, and Piotr to pray for me. After they prayed, I escorted them to the door and went back to my bed. When I lay down, I realized the pain was gone."

The next morning, the day of her operation, she developed a high fever. Doctors sent her home and told her to come back in two weeks. When she returned, they took another x-ray. It showed nothing wrong. They took several x-rays from different angles. They all showed that her lungs were perfectly normal. They would not need to operate after all. The doctors could not understand what happened.

Lidiya explained, "God healed me."

After a period of rest, she returned to her work at the clinic and told June, "My time of trial made me a better person. I see things with different eyes. My priorities are different now."

31

It Gives Meaning to Life

February - April 2005

Cory often spoke of different villages and church planters, but the names did not mean much until I could see them. Statistics came to life when I could visit people and hear their stories.

While Cory talked in the living room with Nicholi, a church planter who went through our second course, I stood in the kitchen with his wife. As she put the finishing touches on our meal, I cut bread and learned that they became Christians just five years earlier. Their infant son had been born with severe birth defects, which no doctor could help. "We visited different churches, seeking healing for him," she said. "This church did not promise healing, as some others did, but for some reason, we decided to stay anyway." Their son needed constant care until he died about a year and a half earlier. Several months later, God gave them another baby, a healthy boy.

Over bowls of borscht, Nicholi said he used to work as a refrigerator repairman. When the pastor first suggested he focus on church planting full-time and join our training program, he was afraid to leave his job. His wife did not oppose the idea though, so he joined.

He said lessons on doctrine helped him understand the Gospel better so he could share it more clearly. He also valued the practical advice. Since the teachers were all pastors, they taught and counseled from their experience.

Nevertheless, the work of evangelism was harder than he imagined. "I expected to see more results," he said. "It is one thing to hear lectures on how to share the Gospel and start groups, but it was not as easy as I anticipated. People did not come to Christ as quickly as I wanted."

He recalled how fellowship with the other church planters every third week provided a big boost for him. "It was like a breath of fresh air to see the other brothers and hear they were going through the same things I was. I liked the hour we spent every evening after dinner, sharing and praying for one another. When I think about those who lacked the support of their wives, I see God has really blessed me. My wife is so good."

Even without a regular income, he continued to work in two villages. "God does not take away problems but brings solutions," he said. He told how God provided for his family through unexpected gifts of money or produce.

That afternoon we visited a group he had started three years earlier. About thirty people gathered in a room at the kindergarten for the meeting. "It's great you have so many youth coming," I told Nicholi afterward.

He explained that most of them belonged to a family with eight children. The parents drank heavily and did not take care of their home or family. One boy started coming to youth group and became a Christian. Other siblings followed. Nicholi said, "They are socially backward, but they show more spiritual understanding than many Christians."

The next Sunday we visited a village by the Azov Sea. Nearing the village, I saw the huge silhouette of an abandoned nuclear power plant off the main road. The village was built to provide housing for workers, but after the Chernobyl power station in northern Ukraine blew up, and people in Crimea protested, construction ceased on this plant. The economy now depended on summer tourism.

Alexi met us by the market and showed us where the congregation met in a room they rented from the orphanage. The five-year-old church now had twenty-nine baptized members. I felt embarrassed when I realized I had forgotten my head scarf, but relaxed when I saw the other women did not wear one either. As a fairly new Christian, Alexi had not grown up with church traditions, nor did he push them.

With the break-up of the Soviet Union in the early 1990s, mafia gangs filled the power vacuum and crime was rampant. Alexi had belonged to the mafia in Kerch in those days. While he was out of town one day, the Special Forces came in and killed everyone in the gang except him.

His life had been spared, but for what? Alexi knew a Christian and decided to talk to him. He began attending church, gave his life to Christ, and attended our second course, which began in 2000.

He once told Cory, "The Training Center helped me develop as a leader. I got to see how others lived and preached. It was a privilege to fellowship with these brothers."

He appreciated topics like characteristics of a Christian leader and practical tips for ministry, but a better understanding of Christ's sacrifice gave incentive for service. "His love, grace, and mercy moves me to do something. I can't just sit in the back pew. I have to serve Him. I want to serve Him."

He said the Training Center had helped him set goals and analyze steps for reaching them. "The discipline was hard, but I needed it, and it helped me move ahead. I think that is why a church started here—I just plodded along and had a disciplined life."

Cory encouraged the young congregation to remain faithful and use what God had given them to serve Him and reach non-Christians in their region.

After the service, we went to a church member's house for dinner. While Cory and Alexi talked in the living room, I sat with Galya in the kitchen. She ran a second-hand shop and sold used clothes from England. With a twenty-year-old son, I guessed her age to be around forty. "How did you come to Christ?" I asked.

"I had been married three times before and was living with a man who was twenty years older. I knew I was a sinner. He became sick and died, but before he died, I saw him reading some book. He seemed interested in it, so I looked at it too. It was a New Testament. I found it interesting, unusual. The Sermon on the Mount, for instance, I had never read anything like it before."

After Jehovah's Witnesses came to her door, she went to their gathering. She visited another church but decided it was not for her either. Then a church leader from Kerch held an outdoor evangelistic event right outside her apartment. She listened and talked to the leader afterward. She prayed, receiving God's forgiveness. She and several others joined the group Alexi started.

"When I came to Christ," she said, "the burden of my sin fell away. I felt like a new person, and life became easier. Even though we did not have heat in the winter and the apartment was just six degrees (42°F), I had such joy I didn't even feel the cold. Before, I used to complain a lot about the cold."

With several others from her village, she attended the evangelism seminar we held in Nizhnigorski. "It was so interesting and informative. I want others to have the same freedom I found."

Meanwhile, Janelle and Alicia went to the Primorski church with June. They preferred spending time with her instead of visiting village churches. Besides, June needed help packing books for her move to a new apartment.

Knowing she would have to find another place to live, June began her search months earlier. With long-term rentals hard to find, she decided to buy. Her need for a new home turned into a test of faith as weeks passed with no good options.

Explaining her situation in a newsletter, she wrote, "I thought this was a simple search for four walls, a roof, and a floor, but God has used these last two months as a time of refinement. I want the kind of security I can touch and see, but God wants my security to be in Him. I've stopped praying for an apartment. God knows I need one. Now I'm asking for His help to trust and obey."

Ten days later she found an apartment she liked, located not far from us. The former owners eventually moved out, and repairs began. June counted twenty-seven people who helped her fix up the apartment and move into it. She invited each one to sign their names inside her pantry door as a memorial to God's faithfulness.

Stefan's repairs to our training center building took much longer. It now had a fourth floor and a roof. A large American church donated funds for windows and doors, so Stefan ordered those. An excavator dug a pit for a sewage tank.

Training Center leaders continued to hold sessions for the third group of church planters but decided to substitute one week of training with one week of labor on the building. From Monday to Friday the men knocked down some interior brick walls that did not fit our plan and built new ones. They lacked showers, but not spirit.

They began the day with worship, ate breakfast at 8:00, went outside at 8:30 for prayer, and then worked all day. Stefan said the neighbors stood around watching and listening. They finally asked him about his work crew. "They don't yell at each other. They don't swear. They don't take smoke breaks. They work hard all day. Where did you get them?"

Stefan told them, "They are Christians—true believers—the same men who come for training. But this week they have work therapy."

That spring, the Training Center leaders held another series of seminars on evangelism for churches. To get a feel for his audience, Cory asked, "How many of you are from Christian families?" Usually, long-time believers were the strong majority. This time, however, most came from non-Christian families. "That's great," he told me when he got home. "It shows there is new blood in the churches and these new Christians want to share their faith with others."

During his lecture on God's grace, Cory asked, "What does it mean that Christ died for us?"

Several responded. "We have forgiveness of sins," said one. "We have hope," said another.

Cory continued, "People need this message of hope. The Tatar are open and need Christ too." He told of Muslims in other parts of the world who now followed Christ.

Afterward, a young man introduced himself. He had become a Christian through the influence of Vanya, the one-armed church planter who died of cancer seven months earlier. "You are right," he told Cory, "the Tatar are open." He had married a Tatar woman, who also came to Christ through Vanya. He was now learning the Tatar language and tried to share his faith with these Muslim people.

It was good to hear that Vanya's vision had not died with him. His widow, Natasha, had also returned to teaching Sunday school.

Of the twenty men going through the current course for church planters, one of them was of Tatar background. After one session, Cory offered to drive him home to get to know him better and meet his family.

Salim was born in the Ural Mountains of a Russian father and a Tatar mother and grew up in Kazakhstan. Like other Tatar, his mother was forced to leave Crimea after World War II. Salim was raised without religion, like most people of the Soviet Union. His father drank a lot and often beat his mother. He recalled the anger, the fear, and the blood. He said, "When my father started bringing vodka home and getting my older brother drunk, my mother sent him away. They never divorced, but he moved in with another woman and started a new family."

In the army, Salim served as a musician, playing the tuba and drums. He later played with a jazz band and then worked as a sound engineer. When it became possible for the Tatar to move back to their homeland, the Crimea, his mother longed to go. For her sake, they left behind a settled life and moved in 1990 to nothing—no job and no home. She saw Crimea again, but died two years after her arrival. Salim said, "She was only fifty-five years old, but she had worked like a donkey for many years on a tobacco plantation, and she had many health problems because of it."

In 1993, Salim married Alma, a Tatar woman ten years younger. As a musician, he played in bars and at weddings and funerals—places where alcohol flowed freely. Salim drank heavily. When he became director of the town's cultural center, he drank with visiting musicians and often did not even go home at night. When he did go home, he was abusive, much like his father. Alma considered leaving him and taking their two children. Despite her Muslim background, she began praying for him in the name of Jesus; nothing else had helped.

Salim always thought there was a God, even if he did not live like it. He met some Jehovah's Witnesses and studied a one-year course with them. The Jehovah's Witnesses did not have their own Russian translation of the Bible then, and when they told him Jesus did not really die on the cross, he knew that could not be right and left them.

He developed a hernia and needed surgery. His employer was two years behind in paying his salary, typical then in the year 2000. His boss lacked any money to help fund the operation but suggested, "You should pray." With nowhere else to turn, he prayed—not to Allah but Jesus.

Soon afterward, two men invited him to their church. The first sermon touched him so much he began crying and gave his life to Christ. Church members took an offering for his operation. Salim recalled, "My own people didn't help me. My friends didn't help either, but Christians who didn't even know me, did."

Salim continued attending church services after his operation. His craving for alcohol disappeared completely. His wife liked her changed husband and soon became a Christian too.

Salim wrote to his sister, living in Kazakhstan, and told her how God had worked in his life and of his decision to follow Christ. She wrote back: "You are dead to me. You are no longer part of the family." Even though she was also half Russian and half Tatar, she identified with her mother's people and practiced Islam with her husband.

Salim traveled to Kazakhstan to see her and explain what it meant to follow Christ. When she heard him out, she decided he had not abandoned all that was good after all. In her mind, to be "Christian" was to be "Russian," which meant to drink, smoke, and have low morals.

Salim and his family lived in a village about three miles from a paved road. As Cory drove him home, the car slithered on the clay-based mud like it was snow—except snow leaves a clean car.

"The children have to walk to school in this mud," Salim said.

Soon after they arrived at the house, Alma set out a full meal. Cory was not hungry but ate so as not to offend. When Alma finished pouring tea and finally sat down with them, he asked her, "What did your family think about your becoming a Christian?"

Her father served as the local mullah, or Islamic religious leader. On one hand, he could remember when his mother used to pray to Isa Maseah, or Jesus Messiah, but for his daughter to become a Christian was a great shame for the family.

Her mother struggled even more. Salim used to drink and beat Alma, but that was more acceptable than conversion to Christianity, which she viewed as a rejection of culture and family. They rebuked Alma for "leaving the faith" and pressured her to recant.

Alma, however, had finally found peace in her own home and heart. She valued that more than the opinion of her parents or neighbors. She refused to give up her faith and told them, "Even if you kill me, I will simply go to be with Jesus."

At first, the family cut off any contact, but her siblings saw how Salim had changed for the better. Without his drunken rages, they were no longer afraid to visit her. Her parents eventually began coming again but continued to remind Alma how she had embarrassed them by becoming a Christian.

Salim told Cory that he worked regularly in three villages as an evangelist and helped in two others. He tried to reach everybody but especially the Tatar. Even though his own life changed dramatically after he became a Christian—from a rowdy alcoholic to a family man—other Tatar often told him, "You have betrayed our faith."

He replied, "No, you have betrayed our faith" and explained that until the fifteenth century, the Tatar were Christians. Salim knew the Koran better than most Muslims. He pointed out passages referring to Isa, or Jesus, and read further explanation from the Bible.

He told Cory, "Even though many Tatar agree with me and say they believe what the Bible says, they fear rejection by their relatives. They won't think for themselves. Even if they believe the Bible is true, they say, 'If the rest of my family is going to hell, then I will go too.'"

To further complicate matters, a group of radical Muslims, Wahabis from Saudi Arabia, tried to promote conservative Islam among the Crimean Tatar and stir them up against Christians.

Cory did not have many answers but knew God did. He and Salim prayed together, looking to God as the source of wisdom and strength.

Soon after Cory reached the main road, he saw a woman hitchhiking. She looked old, and it was already after dark, so he took pity on her and stopped. She was going to see her sister, dying in the Feodosia hospital. When learning he did not expect money for the ride, she said, "There really are good people left on earth."

As they drove, she told him about her life. She was Tatar and once had a big house in Kazakhstan but struggled to live in Crimea. "Why did you move?" Cory asked.

She said they moved because of fanatical Muslims trying to enforce a veiled dress code for women and killing those who did not comply. They ran away as refugees, so they could not sell their house. No one would buy it since everyone knew they were leaving anyway.

Cory asked, "What has Islam done for you?" She had no answer. Cory spoke of the hope that Christianity has given him.

She agreed, "Everyone needs hope." She said she had a New Testament and read it.

Grateful for fruit.

Church planters valued fellowship when they gathered for seminars.

32

"I Have Everything I Need"

May – June 2005

Janelle and Alicia worked hard in their sewing class preparing for an art exhibition and contest. Janelle made a doll and scene from "Little Red Riding Hood," while Alicia sewed Cinderella. Unfortunately, they could not keep the dolls or scenes, which became part of a permanent exhibition in the classroom.

I once asked the teacher if I could buy some of their handiwork, thinking it would help her budget. She seemed shocked that I would even ask. "Of course not! If everyone took their work, my walls would be bare. These are national treasures, like Aivozovski's art."

Aivozovski's paintings in Feodosia's art gallery were worth millions. I could not see the comparison, but did not argue.

When Janelle and Alicia began attending the class five years earlier, they were the youngest. Except for one other girl, they were now the oldest and helped the younger children.

At the music school, their piano teacher tried to put them on stage as much as she could. The school often gave concerts for visiting groups of elementary children and handicapped kids. It also held academic concerts and contests.

While listening to Janelle and Alicia practice, I complimented them, "You girls are playing better than I ever expected."

Alicia replied, "Of course! We have a Russian teacher. Whether we want to or not, we learn."

I had to smile. I remembered a time they went to their lesson unprepared. The teacher scolded them and then scolded me, "You must make them practice. If they will not practice, you need to beat them!" When I explained we had company during the weekend, she softened. "Why didn't you tell me?"

Alicia added, "Our teachers are all bark and no bite."

I felt grateful for the good musical education they received at such a low cost. We paid about $5 a month for three lessons a week.

"It's good we can learn to play piano here since lessons are so cheap," Janelle said. "And many classical composers come from this part of the world."

When other children in their sewing class asked Janelle and Alicia about American rock stars, they had no clue. They could have, however, discussed the differences between Beethoven and Tchaikovsky.

Months earlier, first one and then the other daughter said, "I'd like to learn how to play the violin." I let it pass a couple of times but kept hearing it. I finally conceded, "If you are serious, I'll look into it."

I talked to the piano teacher, who talked to a violin teacher, who agreed to work with them if we could get an instrument. "I suggest you go to the store by the music college in Simferopol," she advised. "Just don't buy one made by the Moscow Furniture Factory."

Cory drove us the two hours to Simferopol and dropped us off while he ran his own errands. The violin master at the store patiently explained the differences in instruments. We knew better than to buy the cheapest model, made in Moscow, and finally chose one made in Germany. It was a bit battered and rather old, but not too expensive. He said it was a good one. I had to take his word for it since I had no idea.

The girls decided to name it "Johann" after Bach and Mozart. When we got home, Alicia pulled the violin from the case and called out, "Janelle, we have a problem!"

Oh, brother, I thought. *We spent all that money, and now something is wrong with it.*

"We can't name it Johann," Alicia said, "because *skripka* (Russian for violin) is feminine."

Cory liked to be early—his definition of "on time." While waiting for the service to start at yet another village church, I decided to talk to an old woman who sat alone in the sanctuary. She greeted me warmly. I figured she might be good for a story or two to pass the time.

Though now eighty-nine years old, she remembered details about World War II as though it happened last month. She recalled a time of fear and hunger. Even though her father was a Christian, he had a position of authority on a collective farm. Christians were supposed to keep their faith to themselves, but he said one day, "Anyone who knows how to pray, you may go to the church and pray today for an end to this war." She recalled how they walked to the village, got down on their knees, and prayed with weeping. The next day, they heard no planes or bombs. The war was over.

She got married, had a child, and then, at the age of forty, was expecting again. The doctors said she was too old and must have an abortion. She told them, "I have never even killed a kitten, so how can I kill my own child?" Her baby girl became a gentle, kind woman who now had a daughter in Bible college.

Her son and daughter both lived in Germany. They wrote that life was easier there, and they wanted her to move to Germany and live with them. She refused. "I have everything here I need," she said. "I have a garden and some chickens. I am very rich. I don't need anything more."

Her words challenged me more than any sermon I heard that day. Her mismatched clothes obviously came from a humanitarian aid box. On her feet she wore dirty sandals with baggy boy's athletic socks with a red stripe and a hole in the heel. Her smell told me she did not have hot water or a washing machine, yet she said, "I have everything I need. I am very rich."

Halfway through the service, the pastor dismissed the children for Sunday school. Janelle and Alicia went with them.

As we drove home later, the girls talked about how well off we were. "They wore scruffy shoes that had holes in them."

"Their clothes weren't very nice, either. The nicest dress there was like our worst dress."

We all learned a little more gratitude that day.

I always enjoyed visiting Pavel and Vera and happily went along when Cory took up medical supplies for a medical/evangelistic team coming later that summer. Pavel told us, "Last year the team left me with the names and addresses of everyone who came to see the doctor. That list has kept me busy all year." When visiting these people, Pavel asked them, "Is there anything you'd like me to pray about?"

A few weeks later, he returned to see how God answered his prayers. God answered many of those prayers, a sign of His mercy, but that did not mean the recipients were ready to follow Christ. Pavel then simply asked, "Would you like me to pray for anything else?"

We planned to attend a Bible study with Pavel in another village, but Janelle and Alicia decided they would rather stay at his house and play with his daughter and a kitten.

"I'll drive," Pavel said. "I know a shortcut." Instead of taking the longer highway route, he drove on dirt roads through the fields in his boxy car with poor shock absorbers. We passed huge fields of sunflowers and recently harvested wheat. Then, out of place in the flat steppe, I saw a hill.

Pavel confirmed it was a burial mound for a Scythian nobleman, dating sometime between 500 and 100 BC, but the gold and other treasures had long since been stolen.

Arriving at the village, Pavel said, "I grew up here." He explained how he started this church plant by going to see people he knew. He later showed the

Jesus film and held other kinds of evangelistic outreach. "This is where I found Vasili." Vasili was now receiving training as a church planter and led the group in this village.

"How did you find Vasili?" I asked.

His mother was a member of the Nizhnigorski church, and his father was a drunk. Vasili went forward to accept Christ in 1993 but later stopped going to church. Pavel visited him and could smell marijuana in the room. Vasili excused his lack of attendance by saying, "I just haven't been able to get free."

Pavel suggested, "We could pray that you can get free." Pavel prayed for him.

Vasili also prayed and cried as he asked God for forgiveness. Pavel didn't know if it was a bout of drug-induced emotionalism, but the next day Vasili came to church and publicly repented. Cory and I happened to be visiting that day. Vasili went to the front, kneeled, and prayed earnestly, asking God to forgive him.

Vasili now lived in a neighboring village. He drove up, his small car filled with an old woman, a younger woman, and four children.

Pavel explained, "We are trying to plant one church for every collective farm. This collective farm has four villages. The villages are dying. Young people leave to study or work. The men go to Moscow or the south coast for jobs."

The building where the young church met had been abandoned and was falling apart. Village leaders figured it was better to have someone fix it up and clean up the grounds, so they let the church use it. It was now whitewashed inside and out. Lace curtains hung over the windows, and pots with geraniums sat on the wide windowsills.

Besides us, eleven adults and seven children gathered. They began with a song. Children recited verses and sang. Instead of giving a sermon, Vasili led a discussion on John 1. It made the next hour and a half pass quickly.

When leaders of the Training Center tried to encourage the church planters to lead discussions instead of lecture, some of the guys had struggled with the idea. "Why should I ask questions? I'm supposed to be the one with the knowledge!"

Vasili, however, now seventeen months into the two-year course, asked good questions. "What titles do you find for Jesus in this chapter?" "What is the best way to talk to someone who is skeptical about Jesus?"

That question led to a long discussion about evangelism. Just because someone seems unreceptive, don't give up on him. Vasili said, "Like Misha, here, and Oleg. They argued a lot before they came to Christ."

Misha spoke up, "Well, we used to drink and smoke pot with you."

Pavel said that sometimes people can get even more negative before they turn to Christ, because they are trying to resist as the Holy Spirit works on them. "Like after my wife became a Christian, I threw her in the trunk of the car and bent the lid when I slammed it on her legs. I told those Christians I would come back with a bottle of kerosene and set fire to their church. They prayed for me, and I came to Christ."

The next weekend, we drove up to see Mikhail, who went through our second course and started a church in the former Mennonite village. As usual, his wife, Yulia, put out an abundant meal that included homegrown, fried chicken. As we ate, he reported that he baptized eight people earlier that month.

He recalled his early attempts to talk to one of them, an old man, about Christ. The man told him, "Go away. I don't want to talk to you." Mikhail tried a few times but got the same response. Then the man sent a message: "Please come and talk to me." His health was bad, and he feared that he would die and go to hell before he could pray with Mikhail. Mikhail told him that he could have prayed on his own, but together they prayed, and the man gave his life to God.

With the man in such poor health, Mikhail suggested a baptism at home, but the old man wanted to be baptized in the canal with everyone else. Mikhail drove him to the canal but wondered if he would have enough strength to walk into the water. He did.

Mikhail lowered him into the water. Afterward, the man stood to his feet and raised his arms in the air with a burst of joy. When he came out of the water, he could walk without his cane or assistance. He kept repeating, "Now I want to serve Jesus."

A woman in their young church was married to an alcoholic. His drinking problem was so severe that he sold household items and food to buy alcohol. She had nothing but the barest essentials in her home because he sold everything else. She could not even keep flour in the home for making bread, or he would sell it. He had a garden, but he sold the produce and used the money for alcohol. They lived on her pension. The only way she could feed herself and her husband was to keep groceries at a neighbor's house and go there when she wanted something. She came to the end of her rope and considered divorce.

Yulia invited the women of the church to listen to the video on the role of a Christian wife. That video gave the wife of the drunk new perspective and ability to cope with her situation. Yulia told us, "Now she doesn't complain anymore, and if someone criticizes her husband, she tells them to keep quiet. One of the other women told her, 'You put up with so much.' She replied, 'Before, I put up with my husband, but now I have God's love for him.'"

They told of another woman in the village, whose husband died at home, and she needed someone to take him to the hospital for an autopsy. No one would help her, so she finally asked Mikhail, an outsider. His caring act opened her heart and mind, and she soon gave her life to Christ. Not long afterward, her daughter also became a Christian.

After lunch and conversation, Yulia loaded us down with produce from their garden. She said, "I wanted to give you a goose or duck, too, but I did not have time to kill something and pluck it for you before you came. But it is quite simple. You just need a pot of boiling water. Dunk the bird in it, and the feathers will come out easily."

I assured her, "You gave us so much already, we don't need anything else." Somehow, we managed to get away without her going to the poultry yard and grabbing the fattened goose for us. With just three weeks remaining before we left for furlough, I knew we would not have time to eat all the produce they gave, so I shared with a needy neighbor.

A new church for a village.

33

More to Life Than Hot Water

July 2005 – March 2006

I always felt the same before any major trip. Whether going to the U.S. or going to Ukraine, I disliked the final week of sorting, packing, and cleaning. I wanted to skip that week and just BE at our destination.

I took a break to look at an issue of *Just Between Us*, a magazine for women in ministry. Some paragraphs by Shelly Esser caught my attention. She told of a survey where 3,000 people were asked, "What have you to live for?" Ninety-four percent lived in anticipation of a future event, simply enduring the present. They looked forward to retirement or a trip, or waited for the kids to grow up.

Shelly pointed out that in all this "waiting" for life to happen, people miss the life going on around them. They did not fully enjoy this experience, this sunset, this friendship, or this baby.

Properly chastised, I realized I would miss this final week of sorting, packing, and cleaning if it were suddenly taken from me. I also realized that long-anticipated events often do not produce the thrill I expect.
God brought a few Bible verses to mind: "The same Spirit that raised Christ Jesus from the dead dwells in you" and "Christ in you, the hope of glory." My joy, my life, and my hope cannot be dependent on some event "out there" but must be based on an overflow of Christ in me.

People meant well, but their kind words became a weight as we prepared to leave Ukraine in August. "You will be gone until April? That's too bad!" "We will miss you!" "That's so long!" We heard regret over and over.

One woman said goodbye with a different slant: "I am so happy you are leaving. You need to get away and relax. Your parents need to see you and the grandchildren. Enjoy it. Breathe deeply the air of home. There's nothing like breathing the air of home."

Her words brought tears to my eyes. No guilt. Just go and be blessed. Since her daughter lived far away, maybe she understood the need to be with family, but how did she know our air was so special?

I breathed deeply as I stepped off the plane in Portland, Oregon. It smelled fresh and clean, like after a rain. Every time I walked the long dirt driveway at my parents' house, my nose feasted on the pungent smells of pine, sage brush, alfalfa hay, and sweet clover.

We soon settled into a missionary house at a Christian camp in Eugene. I felt a little overwhelmed with the countless choices, not only at the grocery store but also with activities. So many possibilities! How much is too much? I felt like someone who is used to eating oatmeal three times a day and suddenly stands before a buffet table. Some restraint is necessary.

Janelle and Alicia signed up for classes in roller-skating, ceramics, and sign language to supplement homeschool lessons. We got a library card and checked out books. We found a violin teacher and started lessons.

In spite of our busy pace, I felt pampered, like Cinderella who found herself wearing silk instead of gunnysacks. Skin toughens to the rough feel of dirt and poverty—to the feeling of "I don't really belong." Silk feels nice, but I kept waiting for the clock to strike midnight, as though aware this was not my place either.

The Apostle Paul said he learned to be content in any condition, in both lack and abundance. I could accept blessings as gifts from God's hand. Bright green lawns made a feast for the eyes. I enjoyed big trees and wildlife. Someone brought us bicycles for family outings.

I like much about life in Oregon but remembered Pavel's report after visiting his daughter in California. When someone asked him, "How do you like it?" he replied, "It's nice to have hot water whenever you want it, but there's more to life than hot water."

During our medical checkups, Alicia tested positive for tuberculosis. After her chest x-ray came back negative, the doctor explained, "She does not have TB and cannot give it to anyone. The positive skin test shows she was exposed, and she could get TB, so she needs to take antibiotics for nine months." With a high rate of tuberculosis in Ukraine, it was fortunate the rest of us did not test positive too.

My maternal instinct wanted to protect my children, to keep them away from any source of danger. It is one thing to put myself at risk, but my children? One missionary couple told us their family doctor had said, "If you love your children, you won't move to Ukraine." They went anyway.

What should my response be? Should I seek the path that appears safest for me and my children? Life in Ukraine included risks, but bad things happen to people in the U.S. too.

The Bible says that he who tries to save his life shall lose it. I cannot let fear drive my choices. Hebrews 11 lists godly men and women who chose difficulty and sacrifice out of obedience to God. Early missionaries to Africa packed their belongings in a coffin, expecting to die on the field. Many lost children and spouses within the first few months or years. Compared with them, my life was easy.

My ultimate goal for my children is not that they have an easy life, but that they love God and live in a way that honors Him. They learn best by watching their parents. A life of faith requires me to trust God with all the "what ifs" that lie down the path of obedience. I would rather walk with Jesus nearby than run the other way and walk alone.

Nevertheless, I did not want Janelle and Alicia to feel we sacrificed them for the sake of missions. Someone told me about a missionary daughter who struggled and felt like her parents put ministry before her. I told Janelle and Alicia about this conversation and added, "We want to follow God, but we don't want you to feel like you aren't important to us."

Alicia said, "I think we are getting a better education this way. We get to see things and do things that other kids don't. Don't worry about it."

While we were in the U.S., Cory called Stefan almost every week. Stefan reported that a group from the ECB church headquarters in Kiev came to Crimea for meetings in various churches. Over and over, they heard how the Training Center had helped bring renewal by their training and challenge to evangelize and plant more churches.

The visitors invited the Training Center leaders to Kiev to talk about their work, but the TC leaders decided it would be more worthwhile if the folks from Kiev came to a seminar to see for themselves what was happening.

Two men accepted the invitation and spent the night with Stefan. Stefan said the one with more clout seemed skeptical when he met with the TC leaders. After all, what good can come from Crimea? What convinced him was when he met with the fifteen church planters attending the sessions. They all told how the Training Center had helped equip them for ministry.

The TC leaders hoped to expand their training into other parts of Ukraine. Perhaps this would open that door.

Stefan also reported on news from villages where Vanya had worked before he died. Two men Vanya discipled now led groups in those villages. His efforts had not been in vain. Beyond that, the pastor who excommunicated Vanya got down on his knees before the congregation and asked them and God for forgiveness. He said he had not acted right as a leader. He had tried to control people instead of letting God be in control and had had a wrong view of evangelism.

While on furlough, I was often asked, "Are you getting any rest?" With all we had to cram into a few months, I didn't think "rest" and "furlough" belonged in the same sentence. I replied, "I've decided I probably won't rest until I'm in the grave or retired."

The next morning my Bible-reading schedule took me to Exodus 20. "Remember the Sabbath day by keeping it holy." God created the world in six days but rested on the seventh. We are supposed to rest too.

I felt like a deer caught in the headlights. I thought of other verses about rest: "Come to me all you who are weary and burdened, and I will give you rest. Take my yoke...learn from me...and you will find rest for your souls" (Matt. 11:28-29).

If God commands rest and gives rest, then rest is important. Inner rest though, comes not from the lack of responsibility or activity but from a sense of dependence on God—trust in Him to accomplish what I cannot.

The girls and I watched a film about the great composer Mozart. When he sat down to write music, before he ever wrote a note, he penned words in Latin, which translate, "Help me, God," and he finished his work with: "To the glory of God."

I thought about that often. Whether preparing a talk or trying to figure out travel arrangements to Texas and Kansas, I prayed, "Help me, God," and "May this bring glory to You." I wanted to respond appropriately to various responsibilities. My strength, wisdom, and resources are limited, but His are not.

I saw God's provision when a woman gave me a whole set of homeschool books I would need for the next year. Instead of going the easiest route of buying new, my frugal nature usually drove me to spend time I didn't have hunting down used books. Through her generous offer, God met our need above and beyond what I hoped for.

All my effort, all my striving cannot accomplish as much as God's little finger. The command to rest helps me remember that He is God and I am not. It is an act of worship to put our concerns in His hand.

Janelle and Alicia adapted to our transient lifestyle. Audio-books from the library made the miles go by faster to our church appointments. I once told them the parents' profession often affects the children. For example, those who grow up on a farm help with farm chores. Missionary kids help put up and take down the display. The girls got public speaking practice talking to children and youth groups about Ukraine.

I often heard people say, "I could never do what you do." I thought the same as I met other Christians who faced different challenges in their areas of service. Fortunately, God provides strength for each path and equips different parts of the body to meet unique needs.

As our furlough drew to a close, people sometimes asked, "Are you looking forward to going home?" In some ways I did not think Ukraine would ever be home. I would never know the language or culture like a native, but life felt more settled there.

Our focus in the U.S. was to prepare for Ukraine. We bought clothes for Ukraine and school books for Ukraine. We requested prayer for Ukraine. With all the talking about Ukraine and shopping for Ukraine, our stay in the U.S. felt temporary. I was ready to go and settle for a while.

Our nomadic life reminded me of a song from my youth: "This world is not my home; I'm just a passin' through..." Our time on earth is temporary. Life is preparation for heaven. There, I will truly be home.

While speaking to a youth group, someone asked Janelle and Alicia, "Do you look forward to going back?" Oh, yes! They looked forward to helping with Vacation Bible School and swimming in the Black Sea. They looked forward to hiking and camping and being translators for summer interns.

I felt mixed emotions as we prepared to leave: gratitude for the kind reception and practical help of many, but also regret. I wished for more time with people I loved and enjoyed. Separation was the downside of our lifestyle, but God hates separation too. Relationship was so important to Him, He sent Jesus to die for us and bridge the gap.

That is why we returned to Ukraine.

Train travel is common in Ukraine.

34
Longer Than the Road I Travel

April – May 2006

We heard that Ukraine had just experienced an unusually cold winter, but spring had come by the time we arrived in mid-April. Out the train window, we saw blossoms covering fruit trees and freshly tilled gardens.

The road to Feodosia was bumpier than I remembered. Windblown plastic sacks decorated trees. Rundown houses needed paint or whitewash. "Look at the flowers," I told myself. Trash surrounded the entryway to our apartment. We entered a dirty stairwell littered with cigarette butts and dark blobs of squished gum. New scars and graffiti marked the walls we had repaired less than two years earlier. The smell said we still had sewer water in the basement.

We stepped inside our apartment. As Janelle and Alicia walked through it, they said, "The house is smaller than I remember. The bathroom is smaller than I remember. The refrigerator is smaller than I remember."

I found a note from June on the table by a vase of daffodils. The script on the stationery read: "How lovely is your dwelling place, oh Lord." Psalm 84:1. The reminder brought tears to my eyes.

Cory turned on the CD player with worship music. "What can separate us from Your love?. . .Your love is longer than the road I travel, wider than the gap You fill." Our small apartment in a dirty town became a place of worship. How lovely is His dwelling place.

June had stocked our refrigerator with groceries and a pot of turkey soup. While traveling, I really wanted soup upon arrival. What a blessing! The plants looked great, thanks to Stefan's daughter's care. It was good to come home to an apartment with everything we needed in its familiar place.

After we got our suitcases unpacked and most of the stuff put away, Janelle said, "It seems either like a dream that we were in the U.S., or a dream that we are in Ukraine."

Friends soon stopped by to welcome us back, neighbors greeted us warmly, and June invited Janelle and Alicia over to sample cherry turnovers. She lived in our neighborhood, a five-minute walk away.

When they finally came home, I asked, "How do you like being back in Ukraine?"

Alicia clapped her hands, while Janelle said, "Cool."

I found my milk woman in her regular place at the regular time. The old woman who sold milk next to her scolded me, saying, "How did you stay with your mama and not gain weight?"

Good Russian mothers prepared big meals and force-fed their children, no matter what the age. A properly appreciative child ate it. I got us both off the hook by saying, "I did not stay with her very long."

June warned Cory not to park his car by our apartment entrance since Stefan and others got their tires slashed. After the tax office moved into the remodeled former kindergarten next door, war erupted in the neighborhood.

The tax office had no parking lot but generated a lot of traffic since taxpayers had to come in person every month. People, therefore, parked in our courtyard where children once played. Old women scolded the drivers at first, but a knife was more effective.

Stefan took Cory and me to see progress on the Efas Center. Much had changed in our eight-month absence. The wiring was done. Plumbers had installed pipes but still worked on a few extra details. Nine men worked with cement; two scooped ingredients into a small cement mixer, which they later dumped out and shoveled into buckets. They sent these buckets to upper floors by electric pulley. Inside, some men covered rough brick walls with concrete, while others filled in floors to make them smooth and even.

Stefan liked the quality of their work and willingness to take pay less than the going rate. The plumber and electrician had trained with us as church planters and put in a low bid, wanting to help the cause. Others agreed to work for less because Stefan paid on time and did not cheat them, which typically happened elsewhere.

Walking around the building, I felt grateful for Stefan's supervision, but saw the heavy responsibility. So many decisions! He tried to do a quality job while keeping the cost down, and asked Cory for advice. Should we put up wallpaper since it's cheaper or paint since it's more durable? What should we put on the floor: linoleum, carpet, or tile?

His role included unexpected challenges. When a backhoe dug out dirt for a basement entrance, it hit and broke a water line. They turned off a valve, which cut water to the whole village. City officials came immediately to find out why the water was off. Stefan showed them the plan. No pipe was supposed to be there. Who laid the pipe?

A neighbor who ran a café, came over and demanded, "Who gave you the right to dig there?" Of course Stefan had the right to dig on his own property. Apparently, the neighbor had secretly laid the pipe some years earlier and tapped into the main line to avoid paying for water.

My respect for Stefan grew more as he talked about his challenges with dishonest businessmen. He ordered cement, measured the delivery, and found it short by twenty percent. He went to the supplier and complained, "When I go to the market and buy a kilogram of meat, I will not be satisfied with 800 grams." The supplier came and measured the delivery himself. The next delivery was complete, but Stefan never got the missing cement.

He tried another supplier, who also tried to cheat him. They told him, "Why are you so worried about how you spend American money?"

Stefan replied, "It's not American money; it's the church's money." Stefan finally found a supplier who not only delivered in full but gave him a thirty-percent discount because of his large orders.

Though Stefan got a salary for his work, he awkwardly asked Cory for a small loan so his wife could do some repairs to their apartment before summer guests came. "Nadia and the girls will sell souvenirs again this summer on the waterfront, so I can repay you then." Knowing that much money had passed through his hands, his integrity shone even brighter. A lesser man would have taken a "bonus" for himself.

The twenty men who took our third course for church planters completed their two-year training about the time we arrived. Some of these, as well as men from the previous courses, gathered on the last Friday of each month to support one another with prayer.

They now met in three locations to make transportation easier for participants. Cory did not get to see everyone this way, but he still liked hearing of their evangelistic efforts and progress. They talked about groups they led, people who responded positively, and those who wavered. They requested prayer for strength and for God to open doors where they faced opposition.

One said, "I am not someone who can plant a church; only God can. I now realize my part is to simply love people, and God will plant a church."

Before long we drove up to see Pavel. For most of the hour-and-a-half drive, Janelle, Alicia, and their friend Masha sang their way through the youth chorus book, trying to decide what to sing for the service. As usual, the converted house was packed, with an overflow crowd in the entryway.

At the end of the service, a man came forward to pray. He thanked God for forgiveness of sin and asked for a new start. The glow on his face showed he had made his peace with God. He blinked back tears as the congregation sang a chorus: "He's forgiven your sins; you are a new person...He's accepted you. You are His child."

Pavel told us about him later, over lunch. He said that the man had been demon possessed and addicted to drugs and alcohol. He told Pavel, "I'm the Apostle Paul." He began coming to church and would say the same thing.

Pavel told him, "If you were the Apostle Paul, you could preach and you'd know what he wrote about." The man admitted he couldn't preach and didn't know what Paul had written. Pavel invited him to study what the real Apostle Paul had to say.

Through prayer, counsel, and the study of God's word, the man changed. He gave up drugs and alcohol. Right before Easter, he showed up to help church members clean and paint. Pavel said, "He wasn't very strong since he had quit drugs not long before, but he worked with us quite a while."

Vera added, "He didn't even stay and eat lunch with us, as payment for working. He just wanted to help the church. This morning he made public the decision he had already made in private."

Remembering that healthy-looking young man with a clear countenance, I could not have guessed he had been so messed up. Christ was still in the business of pulling people from the gutter and making them new.

In spite of this victory, Pavel and Vera still experienced difficulty and conflict. Pavel told about their neighbor who stole from their garden, taking fruits and vegetables while they were away. They sometimes found produce stacked by the far edge of their garden and caught her a few times.

Vera once asked her, "Why don't you plant tomatoes?"

The woman replied, "Why should I, when I can take yours?"

They got tired of coming home to stripped vines and decided to put up a tall fence. The woman complained to the neighbors, asking them to discuss and decide if Pavel could build or not. None of them had a problem with what he did on his own property. The woman kept trying to stir up trouble.

Pavel told her, "Remember when I was in the mafia, and everyone in this neighborhood was afraid of me? Remember when your husband came over to quarrel, and I threw him over the fence? Let's not have any more problems."

"Are you threatening me? Did you hear that?" she said, turning to another woman. "He threatened me!"

The woman said, "I'm deaf; I didn't hear anything."

Vera tried to give her neighbor some strawberries as a friendly gesture, but she refused them, saying, "I'd rather take them myself."

Pavel and Vera understood the real battle was not against flesh and blood but against the enemy of us all. Nevertheless, what do you do when the enemy's agent lives next door? They asked us to pray.

With his interest in outreach to the Tatar, Cory welcomed the chance to attend a gathering of believers of Muslim background. During this first meeting, they planned to get acquainted, but their ultimate goal was to support one another in ministry. Afterward, Cory told me, "In many ways they are no different from the Russians. Their stories are the same—they told how they used to be messed up with alcohol, drugs, and women."

Ramil, for instance, moved to Crimea from Uzbekistan. Although ethnically Muslim, he did not follow the rules of Islam. He drank, smoked, ate pork, and lived immorally. He went to prison four times. The last time, he met a Christian who talked about his faith. After he got out, however, he continued his former lifestyle. Though homeless and unemployed, he spent any money he got on vodka and cigarettes, hanging out at a certain bar.

A Christian who often passed the bar greeted him and invited him to church. Ramil knew he was in bad shape and said, "Looking like this?"

The Christian replied, "You won't be the first, and you won't be the last."

Ramil decided to go with him. He recalled, "When I got there, people were friendly to me, even though I looked bad and smelled of alcohol. The place where they met was so nice and clean, I took off my shoes."

He must have been used to awfully rough conditions since the church met in a warehouse, with cement floors and long sheets of plastic to divide it into rooms. Ramil said, "Someone came and brought my shoes to me and said I didn't need to take them off. The atmosphere was so loving. It was everything I had ever wanted, all I was searching for."

He came back for other church services but continued his worldly lifestyle, smoking and drinking. Finally, he asked God for forgiveness and invited Christ into his life. He spent that night with church members. The next morning, he still felt different but didn't know why. He thought, *I need a shot of vodka. After staying with holy people, I need to calm my nerves.*

He told the hostess he wanted to go to the cafe for a cup of coffee. She offered to get him a cup, but since he really wanted vodka, he told her, "I have money; I'll go and get my own."

He ordered vodka, as usual, drank some, and immediately vomited. He pulled out his cigarettes, thinking they might help, but he got even sicker. He ordered a cup of coffee, as he said he would do, and soon felt better. From that time, he lost all desire to drink and smoke.

Another Tatar, Arman, told how he pursued a life of drugs, alcohol, cigarettes, and women even though he was married and had children. His lifestyle affected his marriage and his health. Heart problems put him in the hospital several times, but that did not change the way he lived. He finally had a serious heart attack. He felt himself leave his body and watched from above as people worked on him. His wife, a non-Christian, prayed God would not let him die. Doctors brought him back around.

While recovering in the hospital, he overheard a Christian patient talk to another about Christ. He listened intently. Before, he had always thought of himself as a Muslim with no need to consider any other faith.

Not long after he got out of the hospital, someone gave him a New Testament. He spent much time reading it and started attending meetings with Christians. His wife also went and later invited a Christian to their house. As they talked, he understood how Jesus' death provided a way to remove the stain of sin. He prayed, asking God for forgiveness. Finally, he felt free, like a heavy burden had been taken away.

For several days, he stayed home, afraid he would lose that joyous feeling if he left. He finally went to see his buddies at the bar where they always gathered to drink, smoke, and swear. He was surprised, but their talk seemed offensive to him, and the swear words he once spoke freely did not come.

As other Tatar heard about his conversion, they told him, "You have left our faith." Some spat at him as they passed.

He said, "At first, I felt as though I had betrayed my people, the Tatar, even though I had never followed Islam. Now, I understand I am finally submitted to God, as a true Muslim should be."

During a break in testimonies, Ramil, Arman, and Nazer sang several Christian songs in Tatar. Cory told me, "I didn't understand the words, but it was fun to watch. They became more animated when they sang in Tatar."

Nazer told how he and Arman sometimes sang Christian songs like this at the mosque. Some Tatar liked their contribution, though some opposed it.

Nazer said the easiest way for him to meet people and talk to them about Christ was to take his huge dog for a walk. Men liked big dogs and many asked him about his pet.

Though he tried to be friendly, some Tatar harassed him for his faith in Christ. He told about a day he went to warm up his food during his lunch break at work. A group of Tatar always sat near the stove during lunch, smoking and drinking. They often taunted him for his faith. He felt uncomfortable and sometimes afraid, but there was no other place he could heat his meal.

One man was especially hostile toward him and said, "Come here. We need to talk." He had been drinking. With many other Tatar present, Nazer felt the situation could be dangerous. They began to insult and criticize him.

Nazer said, "Can I say something?"

"Yes."

"Are you Muslims?"

"Of course."

"Tell me—what does it mean to be a true Muslim?" They all became quiet. He repeated, "What does it mean?" They didn't say anything. He explained, "It means to be submitted to Allah. Are you submitted to Allah?"

The most aggressive drinker said, "Oh, yes."

Nazer told him, "So you think Allah is up there saying 'Good job, you are down there drinking vodka, and that is submission.'"

The man picked up a Muslim prayer book, and another Tatar said, "Don't touch that. You are drinking and that is holy." They started fighting with each other. That gave Nazer a way out, but the incident gave him an opportunity to get the men thinking.

Village mosques.

35
Every Day an Adventure

June – August 2006

W hen temperatures rose into the 90s, I bought several rolls of plastic sheets with metallic coating. Hung in the windows, they reflected the sun and helped keep the house cool. They also blocked out so much light, our apartment looked like a cave.

Hearing an American ship in town had provoked a protest against NATO, I wanted to see it for myself. The girls and I met Anya at her apartment, and we strolled toward the port. We didn't find any Americans or ship but saw perhaps twenty old people sitting under colorful canopies listening to music from a loud-speaker and drinking tea. Translated, their banners read: "Russia is a friend, NATO an enemy" and "No NATO in Crimea."

For several years already, NATO had held brief peacekeeping exercises in Crimea, aimed at improving cooperation between countries during a crisis. This year, however, protesters gathered at Feodosia's port to object. According to rumors, the ship brought weapons and nerve gas, and the Americans wanted to build a military base in Crimea.

According to more official reports, a merchant ship had brought construction materials to upgrade a Ukrainian base in preparation for the exercises. NATO and American authorities said they had no plans to build a military base in Crimea, but the uproar centered on that, nevertheless.

It became a hot topic in town. One old woman told me she didn't get her pension on time and blamed America and NATO. She claimed America had bought the election for the president, so he sold them Crimea to pay them back. I wondered, *if America had bought Crimea, then where was Walmart?*

A few days later, a car drove around town with a loudspeaker, inviting people to join the anti-NATO protest the following day. Political parties opposed to NATO brought in reinforcements from other cities of Eastern

Ukraine. Cory said they were blocking the street when he drove home that night after dark. He had to get home, so he drove toward the crowd, and they peacefully parted.

According to news reports, 1,500 people attended, but their protest was pointless since the ship was no longer there. Furthermore, the ship brought the cargo at Ukraine's invitation, but the cargo would not be released until after the parliament ruled on it.

A street vendor told us, "It's all politics. NATO has held exercises here before. American soldiers walked in town, and there were never any problems." Although Ukraine's pro-Western president had made membership in NATO a priority, other political parties disagreed.

A man who attended the protest told us his perspective: "Under the Soviet Union, daycare and university were free. Coal and food and other things were cheap. People struggle now, especially the older people. They blame America for the breakup of the Soviet Union. They say now America wants to cause division between Ukraine and Russia—divide and conquer. They say if NATO builds a military base in Ukraine, then the rockets that are aimed at America will be aimed at Crimea since Crimea is closer, and our people will suffer. I think Russia is a bear you don't mess with. It's better to have friendly relations with them."

Also in the news, the Russian Duma, or parliament, suggested annexing Crimea to Russia, based on a treaty signed in 1774 between the Russian Empire and the Ottoman Empire. Ukraine dismissed this as provocation, saying that modern countries must work with the realities of current borders.

Although some ethnic Russians welcomed the idea of Russian citizenship, others feared Russia. One woman told June: "You'd have to leave, but they would shoot me or send me to Siberia." Though many talked about how good life was under Communism, she remembered a different side.

Another woman said that her husband, who once served in the Russian army, silenced uptight visitors in their home by saying, "NATO has never brought harm to any nation that belonged to it. We can't say the same thing about Russia." She thought Russia had prompted this uproar and added: "Every year right before tourist season, they promote some scandal so Russians will go to Russian resorts instead of Crimea."

Tourism was down from the usual numbers for that time of year. Someone said she heard on Russian television that a thousand people were demonstrating day and night. Concerned friends and relatives called from Russia saying, "We heard tanks are rolling through the streets of Feodosia, and there is going to be war." In reality, life went on as usual, except for the few pensioners who continued to sit by the port with anti-NATO banners.

We always tried to keep a low profile—avoided speaking English in public—but this controversy felt unsettling. What would happen? How would it be resolved?

I then read in Psalm 131: "I am not concerned with great matters or with subjects too difficult for me. Instead, I am content and at peace. As a child lies quietly in its mother's arms, so my heart is quiet within me" (TEV). A small child does not fret about problems in the world but simply trusts the mother's care. With God in charge, I could relax.

"Our train gets to Feodosia at 7:00 in the morning on June 21," Alina said over the phone. "Will we stay with you, or should we find another place?"

The first thing that popped in my mind was, "How long will you stay?" I didn't say it; to ask that was considered rude when I lived in Kenya. "Sure, you can stay with us," I replied, "if you don't mind sleeping on a lumpy couch."

After I hung up, I wondered what we had gotten ourselves into. We had heard good things about Sasha and Alina but didn't know them. At a recent team meeting, our new teammates, Tim and Heather Miller, recommended this young couple and said they were thinking about moving to Crimea to minister.

They knew Alina better, since she had taught them Ukrainian. Alina met Sasha when they worked together forming a new church in another part of Ukraine. They had been married just one year.

We had prayed a long time for an outsider to come in and start a church in Feodosia. Could they be the answer? We invited them to visit, but were we in for a two-day meeting or long-term guests?

They stayed seven days. Before they left, Alina asked me, "Did it seem like a long week?"

I could honestly answer, "No, it didn't. We enjoyed having you."

It helped that they came looking for ways to serve. They joined two medical outreaches with June: one in a village and another in the Primorski church clinic. While people waited for medical help, Alina sang, and they talked to patients about Christ.

They were easy guests. They asked questions about us, not just the ministry, like, "How are Oregonians different from other Americans?" Since both knew English fluently, I could lean on English when I didn't know the Russian word. After one week, I felt closer to them than many people I'd known for over ten years.

Were they the church planters we wanted? It felt like a blind date. Both sides had an agenda they could not discuss until they got to know each other better. After a few days, Cory finally talked about some ministry needs.

They explained they were looking for some place to serve in the Russian-speaking part of Ukraine since he was Russian and could more easily preach and teach in Russian. He had been invited to teach at a seminary in Moscow, but Alina was Ukrainian. She wanted to use her talent as a musician to serve, and about half her songs were in Ukrainian.

They had come to Christ through a more progressive church, but their core doctrine was similar to the ECB churches in our network. On Sunday, we took them to visit three churches for morning, afternoon, and evening services. Trying to fit in, Alina wore her longest skirt and a head scarf. She sang and Sasha preached.

I thought her music was like a breath of fresh air, more lively than the typical fare. She smiled widely and with one song, did simple hand motions. Janelle and Alicia's friend, Masha, said, "We're not used to that." Smiles in the audience told me many liked it, though, and several asked if she had a CD of her music. When she sang to non-Christians at the clinic, one said, "I would go to church every Sunday if they had music like that."

Cory thought this would probably be the last we saw of them, but a few hours before they left, Sasha said, "We feel God is calling us to come and minister here. I don't look for God to speak in a big voice, but I look at the needs, and I look at the gifts God has given me, and I see I can be of use."

Alina added, "There are other places in Ukraine where there are needs, but it seems as though God has led us here." She repeated the story of how they heard our name from two different missionaries in less than a week and took that as part of God's leading. They had several things to take care of before they could come but were fairly mobile since he could work at his job of designing web pages anywhere he had Internet access.

After they left, I felt like someone who just finished a blind date with good impressions but wondered, "Will I see you again?"

Assertiveness training teaches people to say "no," but good things can come from a "yes." Our "Yes, you can stay with us" had unlocked the answer to a longtime prayer.

Upheaval over NATO died down and visitors from Russia, Ukraine, and other CIS countries packed the beaches. Vacationers staked their claim with a beach towel and baked all day until leather brown or lobster red.

I usually waited until late afternoon for a dip in the sea. Janelle and Alicia's friend Masha usually met us there. While they continued to swim or play in the sand, I often read a short novel from the girls' reading list.

I could identify with Janey, a ten-year-old girl in the book, *Blue Willow*. Janey's father became a migrant farm worker after a Texas drought. They moved into an abandoned shack, but Janey longed for a real home and escaped reality through her books. She read about King Arthur and wished she lived back when life was an adventure. Her father pointed out that an adventure is simply when something unexpected happens, and you don't know how it will turn out. She had been living an adventure all along.

Like her, I wanted to feel settled, but I wanted to do something important too. The sense of "I don't know how this will turn out, but I'll do my best," is the adventure of life. My lack of control over the outcome invited me to trust in God, who eventually makes things work together for good.

Our life contained adventure on several fronts. In the political arena, we wondered which direction the country would take. Success in ministry also lay outside our control. We hoped churches would attract people to Christ, but some Christians seemed to hinder instead.

Summer church services along the coast often included tourists from neighboring countries. Allowing them to participate was part of church hospitality. They usually made a positive contribution.

I cringed, however, when a speaker from Belarus got up and preached against modern trends in Christian music. He said that satanic African rhythms affected western music styles, and those styles had crept into the church. "We heard it even this morning," he said, referring to the visiting youth choir. I felt embarrassed for them. A young man had played the guitar. Their music seemed conservative to me, but the preacher believed piano accompaniment was more sacred.

Pastor Piotr stood up after the sermon and said, "There are two kinds of music: worldly music and music that honors God. It is not a question of whether it's western music or not. I have been in America, and people there also fear God and honor Him with their music." Still, the sermon left me feeling drier than when I went in.

This man usually preached that way. The previous Sunday, he spoke on the evil of earrings. The Israelites used earrings to form the golden calf, so earrings were bad. Furthermore, the Apostle Peter said a woman's beauty should not come from external adornment.

That afternoon, I told Cory, "I'm glad he wasn't here when Alina sang." She and Sasha still planned to return to Crimea and start a church focused on reaching non-Christians using more contemporary music. I wondered what criticism they would attract.

Life is an adventure. Since God is in control, I don't have to be.

Babies are kept warm, even in the summer.

36
Notice God at Work

September – November 2007

W hen we visited Pavel and Vera early in September, I asked, "How is it going with that neighbor who stole from your garden?"

With a big smile, Vera replied, "It has changed, praise God. In fact, this morning she gave me greens from her garden for the borscht we ate for lunch. Our relationship began to improve when I gave her bee propolis for a toothache a few months back.

"Then about two months ago, her husband hung himself. She asked to borrow a table for the funeral dinner. Pavel gave her a table and 100 hryvnia to help with expenses. When we went over later, the other neighbors said she had told them about the gift.

"Whenever I saw her after that, she looked depressed. She told me she was struggling. I reminded her of a time many years earlier. Back then we were friends, and our children played together. Life was hard for me with Pavel drinking so much and in the mafia. I complained to her, and she told me, 'Look at me. I'm strong.'

"I repeated those words back to her: 'Look at me.' I explained how Christ gave me a new life and a changed husband. I told her, 'Even more importantly, look at Christ. He makes the difference.'"

I checked on Janelle and Alicia to see how they were doing. Janelle had brought a book, not sure what she would do. She didn't need it though. The girls played with the cat, the puppy, and Pavel and Vera's nine-year-old daughter. I found them in a game of ping-pong with a ball that was flat on one side.

As I helped Vera in the kitchen, she recalled the first time we met, soon after her daughter was born. She was almost nine months pregnant when Pavel told her an American wanted to visit. That made her so nervous, she got girls

225

from the church to help her clean house, put up new wallpaper, and whitewash the ceiling. She lay on the couch while they did most of the work. The day we were supposed to visit, however, she was in the hospital. She laughed, telling the story.

I laughed too. "At least you got a clean house out of it," I said. "We went to see someone else that day, and I met you later. I don't remember your house though. I remember your love and your joy." Her bubbly personality had not changed, and she still punctuated her conversation with Christian songs. I took note—visitors to my house probably also notice my attitude more than my décor.

Cory kept in touch with other men who went through our church planters' training program when they gathered to pray together and talk about their work. Some of them lent Christian books as a way to build relationships and spark discussion. Some invited neighbors to view Christian films. Some visited orphanages. One was starting a rehabilitation center for recovering alcoholics and drug addicts. Many worked with children and youth. One took young people hiking every Saturday during good weather. Some taught in schools about social problems like drugs, alcohol, and AIDS. Christian doctors and nurses occasionally helped these men by providing free medical care as a way to attract people.

Vladim had moved from the city of Simferopol to a village for ministry. He told Cory, "Many people think I'm crazy to move to the village, but I feel called to be there. There's more to life than material comforts." Though city apartments came with indoor plumbing, central heating, and constant electricity, houses in most villages did not. Christian friends told him he was needed for ministry in Simferopol, but Simferopol already had churches—this village had none.

Cory visited Mikhail and heard how God had blessed the Harvest Day Celebration at his young church. He had invited important people in the village to attend the event. The school director, collective farm boss, and others came, filling their meeting place. That morning several women of the congregation cooked and set the tables outside so everyone could eat right after the church service. When they sat down for the meal, however, it began to rain.

They quickly moved the food and tables inside. It rained hard for the next three hours, giving Mikhail a captive audience. He explained the foundation of their faith. Church members sang and recited poetry. Some visitors asked questions. When the rain finally stopped, several guests said, "I don't think I've had a better time in my whole life."

At the end of September, over forty men gathered for a three-day seminar. Perhaps the teaching strengthened these church planters for their work, but many valued the fellowship the most. They were involved in a difficult task and felt refreshed through contact with others who shared the same vision.

I needed the support of fellowship occasionally too, and looked forward to a women's retreat in Kiev. While toiling in the kitchen, I thought, *It will be good for me to go away so my family will appreciate me more.* Even before I left home, however, the three-day outing had an additional effect: I gained extra appreciation for family and my role. My daughters sent me off with big hugs and assurances that "we'll be fine." Cory carried my bags to the bus. I had a good family.

Fellowship started when I met up with missionaries living in Simferopol and we boarded the train together for Kiev. I didn't sleep well that night, with another traveler holding a crying baby outside our compartment. I thought of the monks we recently read about in our homeschool study of Christian history. They had deprived themselves of sleep as an act of worship. My sleep deprivation was not on purpose, but I could still worship God in it.

The retreat was held at a forest location in a somewhat run-down building. Though the showers lacked hot water, the building had heat. About one hundred women gathered from various parts of Ukraine for fellowship and encouragement.

I enjoyed worship in English. In honoring God's greatness, I remembered I could leave my concerns in His competent hands. I loved the forest setting and walked on dirt roads and breathed deeply of pine-scented air before breakfast and during free time.

The guest speaker, Sarah Lanier, focused on the theme of "finishing well" and wove many stories into her talk. "From a distance," she said, "sailboats appear to be all sail. But a sailboat is only as good as its keel, the hidden part." Like a boat, we need to take time for "dry dock" to evaluate and strengthen our keel, or character. Little things can hinder our walk with Christ. The desire for a "normal" lifestyle, for instance, can become an idol and keep us from following God to the end.

Cory met my train early Monday morning. I was looking forward to a hot shower when I got home but walked in and learned that the water had been off since Sunday morning. A stack of dirty dishes filled the sink, and some yogurt smoothie spilled on the floor could not be cleaned up. Hours passed. The water stayed off.

Workers from the housing department finally came and asked if our walls and floor were dry. They said water had been pouring into a store on the first floor, so they turned off water to the whole building. They thought the water came from the apartment below us, but no one was home.

Our sense of urgency for returned water service grew when we heard that the city would turn off the water that night all over town for the three-day, semiannual cleaning. Cory walked to June's apartment to fetch some so I could wash dishes. Before he returned home, the faucets began to gurgle and spurt.

I felt *so* grateful. I successfully washed dishes, did three loads of laundry, flushed the toilet, mopped the floor, took a shower, and saved water for our three-day outage. In spite of it all, it was good to be home again. A more "normal" lifestyle sometimes seemed appealing, but God gave strength and the ability to cope.

The three-day water outage every spring and fall was inconvenient but manageable. Stepping around various buckets and tubs of water on the floor was much easier than walking two miles to fetch water, as I might do if I had been born in Africa. Still, when water service returned, the sound of a flushing toilet was sweet music.

Life became more interesting for Janelle and Alicia after they joined the youth group in Primorski. They were the youngest, just fourteen and thirteen, but felt accepted by others who were well into their twenties. Their leader did not lecture but sparked discussion by asking, "What did you read this week in the Bible? What stood out to you, or what questions did it raise? Where have you seen God at work, either in your life or around you?"

The youth choir and adult choir also invited them to join. Practice took another two evenings out of their week, but they came home with happy faces and lots of news. The youth would be in charge of a service that month, so they put in extra practice for that.

While parents in the U.S. went to their kids' sporting events, we attended concerts at the music school. One violin concert started with a first-grade girl who sawed away on her tiny violin while Mother nodded her head in time to each stroke of "Twinkle, Twinkle, Little Star." Father videoed their precious doll until Mom jabbed him in the ribs for taking too much video. She lost a beat with her head nodding but soon continued. Janelle and Alicia played more advanced music toward the end.

The choir director at church wrote down notes for Janelle and Alicia, so they could accompany the choir on their violins for one song. I thought they did a good job but remembered what one pastor said of his own two girls, who were learning the violin: "They might sound like they are pulling a cat's tail, but parents always think their children sound good."

The youth group discussed ways to serve and decided to start by visiting the elderly and others with disabilities. The girls later reported on their visit to a blind man and his frail, elderly mother who was almost blind. Their one-room apartment contained two beds and a couch.

"Is it clean?" the blind man asked. "I vacuumed this morning." The room was so dimly lit, they could not see well, but he finally remembered to turn on a light for his guests. He did all the cooking and housework, though a church member brought him groceries.

The youth leader asked, "Is there some way we can help you?"

"I would like to hear you sing," he said. After a few numbers, he recited chapters of the Bible by memory. He had learned them by listening to the Bible on tape.

After their visit in June, Sasha and Alina had hoped to move to Feodosia in August. With their arrival delayed until November, we continued to pray for them, knowing they would need God's blessing for the difficult task ahead.

Cory recruited five guys to help unload the minivan that brought their belongings. They would initially live in June's apartment while she was on furlough. June considered it an answer to prayer to have reliable people staying there in her absence.

We wondered who might help Sasha and Alina with evangelism—perhaps Tolik? He often handed out New Testaments near the market and talked to people about Christ. Though he lived in Feodosia, he rode with Stefan out to church services in Batalnaya, where his wife had grown up and became a Christian.

We took Sasha and Alina to Batalnaya on Sunday so they could meet. Stefan knew how to handle introductions. He told Tolik, "Sasha is here to start a church." He turned to Sasha and asked, "Sasha, do you need any help?"

"Yes."

"Tolik, do you want to help him?"

"Yes." And so they got acquainted.

Tolik once sought meaning in life through various philosophies and religious systems including Buddhism. He finally found what he sought through the Bible. He had a tender heart for those without Christ and said, "People are dying all around us." He had also been praying for a new church where the seekers he met could be nurtured.

Tolik, his wife, and another couple invited non-Christian friends to meet Sasha and Alina. A group of seven gathered at June's apartment the following Saturday. With pieces falling in place so nicely, we rejoiced.

Knowing how hard it is to work independently in Ukraine, Cory tried to get foundation stones in place. He talked to other leaders at the Training Center. He met with the overseer of the ECB churches in Crimea, who seemed positive but stressed the importance of obtaining the support of Igor, the current pastor in Feodosia.

"I doubt he'll go for it," Cory told me.

Sasha met with Igor and others on the church council. Igor told Sasha that even though he also hoped to see a new church started in Feodosia, he wanted to make sure it kept the same high regard for the traditions and worship style practiced in the existing church.

Since Sasha and Alina had belonged to a different denomination, he believed they should first sit for a year without doing any ministry. If they could properly conform and show themselves trustworthy, they would be allowed to start a new church. If they decided to simply start a church on their own, then no one connected to the existing church should have any fellowship with them.

Sasha and Alina decided to work independently. They had not moved to Feodosia for the Christians, but for non-Christians. "For us," Sasha said, "the most important question is: 'What is the best way to help people come to Christ?'" Although they had hoped to work cooperatively with the existing church, that route looked like a dead-end.

Tolik had been eager to help Sasha with evangelism, but when he talked to Igor about it, Igor said he could not. He could not even attend Sasha and Alina's Bible study.

The practice of shunning seemed so childish to us: "If you don't join my group and do what I say, I will tell my friends not to play with you." It may not work well on independent Americans, but it was widely practiced in Ukraine. Scriptures encourage avoidance of Christians walking in sin, but with no sin in this situation, we had a hard time accepting it.

A friend of Tolik, a seeker named Boris, continued to study the Bible with Sasha and Alina. He got so excited by the things he learned, he stayed several hours each time they met.

When they read from the book of Romans that we are justified by faith, Sasha explained that justification is when we stand clean before God, just as though we had not sinned. Boris liked this idea of a clean slate and said, "I want this justification." Before he left, he asked if they could meet twice a week.

The next time he brought his girlfriend, Luda. He said right away, "She isn't interested in this Bible stuff, but I brought her anyway."

On the contrary, she seemed very interested. Though shy at first, she liked everything: the food, the singing, the fellowship, the discussion, and she even asked at the end, "Can I pray too?"

37

Something Better

December 2006 – February 2007

We received an email from a mother who said her eighteen-year-old daughter had requested no Christmas presents that year. Instead, the girl wanted the money normally spent on her to help children in need. "May I send the money to you?" the mother asked.

I thought we might buy oranges, candy, and small gifts and put on a program at the local orphanage, but I asked Alina what she thought.

She said, "Children in orphanages already get a lot compared with children in really poor families. It would be better to help them, and it would be better to buy basic food items instead of sweets. They need that more." She described a project they did in the last place they lived, where they bought groceries for needy families. Visiting those homes made her feel wealthy.

The next day, Sasha and Alina went to the social services office, explained their plan, and asked for the names and addresses of the neediest families in Feodosia. The woman readily gave them the information and told a bit about each family: "These parents are alcoholics and beat the girl, who is sixteen; the girl also drinks. The mother of these five children doesn't drink, but she is very poor. She tries to work, but she has another child almost every year. This child is handicapped and needs an operation, but they can't afford it."

In the end, they got the addresses of fifteen families with the names and ages of thirty-five children. Alina and I looked through humanitarian aid to pick out clothing for each child. Cory helped with the grocery shopping. We also had shoebox Christmas gifts from a church in Kansas. Sasha and Alina decided to make deliveries after the New Year holiday, to attach their outreach to Christmas and God's gift to us.

Boris and Luda continued to come for Bible study and asked many questions, such as, "Don't you get to heaven by being good?"

Sasha pointed out Jesus' words in John 14:6: "I am the way, the truth, and the life; No one comes to the Father except through me." Even good people sin, but Jesus' death made the way for forgiveness.

Boris seemed bothered and said, "What about all those people on the streets of Feodosia? Hundreds, thousands have never heard! If they have heard the name Jesus, it doesn't mean anything to them."

He and Luda decided that they wanted to sing Christmas carols on the street near the market with Sasha and Alina and pass out tracts. Boris said, "You should put a phone number or address in the tracts so people can get more information." They also offered to help deliver Christmas gifts to the needy families.

They walked to the apartments of three families the first day. No one answered the door at the first place. At another, the parents of four teenagers were gone, but they had a good visit with the two teens at home.

At the third house, the thirty-five-year-old mother seemed much older, the result of serious alcoholism. Her face looked worn and unhealthy, and she lacked teeth. A man lay on the couch, passed out. The fifteen-year-old girl, left alone with the visitors, admitted her mom drank a lot. When Sasha and Alina prayed for the mother, tears ran down the girl's face.

Cory drove them around another day, so they covered much more territory and connected with nine families. They came to our apartment for lunch afterward and told about their visits.

Alina described how they sang Christmas carols at each home. "We told them we came with gifts because of God's gift to us: Jesus, whose birth we celebrate. They were surprised and happy to get the food and gifts. We also gave each family a New Testament and prayed for them before we left."

At most stops, people invited them in. Conditions in the homes varied: from simple but tidy to shabby, smelly, and dirty. Some children were cared for by concerned grandparents, while others lived with alcoholic parents in conditions of neglect.

At the edge of town, they found a mother and her sixteen-year-old handicapped daughter, Mika. Mother and daughter came outside, poorly clad for the cold weather. The mother wore a dirty sweater and smelled of alcohol. The girl waved her arms and squealed with delight, first to have visitors and then to receive gifts. Joy filled her face the entire visit.

The mother explained that Mika had been born with problems, but she kept her anyway. She usually pushed Mika in a wheelchair into town and left her to beg for the day. Alina told the mother, "Even as you did not leave your child at the orphanage, God does not leave His children." Tears rolled down the mother's cheeks. She continued to cry as they told her about God's love. They gave her a New Testament and encouraged her to read from it to Mika every day.

The mother of five young children in a remote part of town looked tired, but the children hopped with excitement to have color crayons and coloring books. "We finally have something to do!"

We did not know what long-term results these visits and gifts might have, but Jesus' coming fulfilled an Old Testament prophecy: "The good news is preached to the poor."

Although I usually baked cookies for neighbors for Christmas, I decided to take it a step further and invite them for a Christmas tea, with Alina providing entertainment on the guitar. I did not know if any neighbors had interest in spiritual matters, but if they did, this could be a good way to connect them with Sasha and Alina. Of four families we invited, two came.

I first met Anatoli, the businessman on the fourth floor, not long after we moved in. He rang the doorbell on a cold winter night and asked if he could sit in our kitchen and drink some coffee until his wife came home with a key. He was drunk. "It's my birthday tomorrow and people at work wanted to help me celebrate," he explained. "Oksana will be mad at me if I don't sober up. She hates the smell of alcohol. The neighbors upstairs aren't home, so I can't wait there."

Besides Anatoli and Oksana, the new family living above us came. While Janelle and Alicia helped the children cut out sugar cookies in the kitchen, adults drank tea, ate cake and cookies, and made stilted attempts at conversation in the living room.

Alina noted later, "People are used to parties with alcohol and crude talk, so without that it takes a while to find something in common." She and Sasha helped move the conversation along with questions like, "Where did you grow up?" and "How did you meet?"

I tried to insert something spiritual with, "People often ask why we moved to Ukraine. It relates to this celebration of Christmas. God sent Jesus to the world because people need hope. People in Ukraine also need hope." I thought Alina did a better job of connecting through her music.

She began with some popular Russian songs of their generation. Oksana sang along, while Anatoli mumbled a few lines. We sang some Christmas songs in English and Russian. Oksana blinked back tears during Alina's final song, a touching number with a Christian slant. No, it wasn't the final number—the three-year-old guest asked for more music, fast music, so she could dance.

By then the conversation flowed more freely, and it was after 10:00 p.m. before they left. At the door, we gave shoebox Christmas gifts to the children and New Testaments to the parents.

Christmas seemed like a natural time to try to connect others with Sasha and Alina. Knowing Grisha and Sasha shared an interest in computers and ham radio, we invited both men and their wives for lunch. Cory had met Grisha about ten years earlier when they had neighboring garages. Grisha now wrote computer programs for companies overseas and often asked Cory to proofread his English.

As I set homemade pizza on the table, Cory gave their three-year-old daughter a shoebox Christmas gift. It served as a great icebreaker hearing her laughter and squeals of delight. Those gifts and Alicia kept her occupied for the next four hours while the adults sat around the table and talked.

Since we already knew Grisha, the conversation flowed much more easily than when we invited our neighbors over. They discussed computers, politics, and prices of apartments, since Sasha and Alina wanted to buy one.

"Why did you decide to move here?" Grisha asked.

Alina explained, "We came with the goal of starting a new church. Why a church? Because people need to have a choice. They often go in destructive ways but don't understand they can live a different way."

Sasha added, "We who grew up in the Soviet time were taught some sense of right and wrong, but the new generation doesn't have that."

Grisha said he thought Jesus was a good example and a good teacher. The conversation moved to who Jesus is, why He came, and the nature of sin. The talk shifted to other topics, but I hoped they might meet again.

Boris and Luda continued to meet with Sasha and Alina for Bible study. They decided twice a week was not often enough and asked to come every day. Luda's simple questions revealed ignorance about Christianity, but she loved the fellowship, singing, and discussion of Scripture. Sometimes, they brought others.

When Boris's neighbor, a hairdresser, began coming, she wanted to minimize the time spent chatting over tea and get on with "reading the Word" as soon as possible. With many Jehovah's Witnesses coming to her door, she wanted to understand what the Bible taught.

One evening Luda brought her eighteen-year-old sister to visit Alina. The sister talked freely about her life of discos, boys, and sex. By comparison, Christianity seemed boring to her.

Alina gave a different slant: "If you found something better, those things would not seem fun anymore." Though not convinced, the girl enjoyed the Christian songs Alina sang.

Before they left, Alina offered, "Can I pray for you?"

"Uh, well, okay."

Alina prayed simply, asking for God's help and blessing.

Luda called the next day to say her sister was so impressed by that prayer, she kept repeating, "No one has ever prayed for me before!"

After spending three days on the road, Cory didn't feel like going to church on Sunday. "If I go, I'll have to preach," he said.

We went anyway. Knowing his state of mind, I did not expect such a good sermon. Instead of taking his place behind the pulpit, Cory started out next to the communion table and commented on the words printed there in Russian: "Do this in remembrance of Me."

"We often come to church and think about ourselves or our own struggles, instead of thinking about what Christ has done for us and what is important to Him," he said. "We need to be concerned about things that concern God." He encouraged the audience to share God's love with those who don't know Him, including the Muslim Tatar.

Cory attended the afternoon service at another church and preached there, too. "They need help," he told me. With three sermon slots to fill, those who had something to say were given a place. Some who didn't have anything to say preached as well.

I was ready to stay home and warm up, however, since the church building had been quite cold that morning. Even with long underwear and stretch pants under my long skirt, several layers on top, a heavy coat, boots, and hat, I still got chilled. Cold churches do eliminate the need for a coat rack.

As usual, Janelle and Alicia attended their Sunday evening youth group. When they got home, Janelle said, "I think I like the custom of greeting with a 'holy kiss.'" The kiss was typically a mutual peck on the cheek: women with women and men with men. Teenage boys preferred to shake hands.

Alicia noted, "Masha has learned to close one eye so I don't jab her in the eye with my glasses. And with Olya, we tilt our heads to the side so our glasses don't collide."

"It helps to know which cheek the other person will head for," Janelle added. The Primorski girls were all "right-cheek kissers," but they experienced some confusion when they visited the Feodosia youth group and encountered some who went for the left cheek. You could end up bonking noses if you weren't careful.

The only accepted contact between boys and girls was to shake hands. Janelle and Alicia explained even that gesture had peculiarities to master. Some guys gave hearty handshakes, but others acted like anything more than one-second contact would contaminate them with girl germs. Alicia said, "It's embarrassing for a girl to squeeze a boy's limp hand, so we try to remember which boys give what handshake."

Janelle and Alicia joined the Primorski youth on an outreach to a village one Saturday morning. They sang in the church service and then went to visit people in their homes. Janelle noted, "American teams have to spend a lot of money to come to Ukraine and do this, but we can do it for free."

The Primorski youth became more involved in evangelism under the guidance of their new youth leader. Alicia described his friendly manner when passing out New Testaments on the street: "Would you allow me the opportunity of giving you this Bible?" he'd say. Many accepted it with gratitude. If they replied, "I have one already," he asked, "Do you read it?"

When Janelle and Alicia were small, a two-hour church service was about ninety minutes too long. After they sat through one sermon, we let them go outside for the final hour. When their friend Masha decided she should sit through the whole service, they endured it with her.

Joining the youth choir and adult choir made Sunday mornings more interesting for them, but I couldn't believe my ears when Janelle and Alicia asked to go to church one Thursday in February.

"What for?" I asked.

"It's a church holiday celebrating 'The Meeting,' and the choir is going to sing."

The church in Ukraine held services for religious holidays I had never heard of growing up. "The Meeting" celebrated the time Joseph and Mary brought Jesus to the temple as a baby and met Anna and Simeon. In more secular society, the holiday celebrated the meeting of winter and summer, even if temperatures were dropping, instead of rising.

Orthodox believers took water to the church to be blessed at The Meeting as well as the January holiday of Baptism. Some drank their "blessed" water every morning for health and good fortune. A vial of holy water kept in the home was supposed to protect it from fire, lightning, and sickness.

Janelle and Alicia came home from The Meeting service in good spirits, reporting that more choir members came than people in the audience.

"Was the building cold?" I asked.

"Fifteen degrees." They understood Centigrade better than Fahrenheit, but I had to translate the other direction. It was about 60°F.

"That's cold!"

Janelle said, "Sunday it was ten degrees (or 50°F), so that's warm!"

38

Have You Ever Seen God?

March – July 2007

When the Training Center leaders held seminars on evangelism that spring at the Primorski church, Janelle, Alicia, and many others in the youth group took the course. With the girls going, I had no reason to stay home.

While teaching one lesson, Andre asked the group, "How do you know you are saved?"

"Because I repented," said one person.

"I was baptized," said another.

"I belong to the Church."

"My life has changed."

Andre rejected all answers except: "Because Jesus died for my sins." Our salvation is not based on what we do but on what Christ did.

I thought of the Bible verse: 'To all who received Him...He gave the right to become children of God.'" I asked Andre afterward, "Isn't 'receiving' something we do?"

Andre replied, "If a cook made a big dinner and served it, the person who receives it lifts the food to his mouth, but he can never claim credit for the meal or say, 'Look what I did.' Nevertheless, people often say, "I'm saved because I did such and such," instead of, "I'm saved because Jesus died on the cross for my sins."

He later addressed the question, "What does it mean to receive Christ?" He filled in the words I skipped over in 1 John 1:12: "..to all who received Him, to those who believed in His name...." He said, "The first time my wife told me, 'I love you,' I did not say, 'I receive you.' I simply believed her, and it gave me great joy."

He acknowledged that faith affects one's actions. "If you heard that your grandpa left you an inheritance, you could say, 'I don't believe it,' and stay home. If you believed and traveled across Ukraine to get it, your faith prompted action. That still doesn't mean you did anything to earn the inheritance. It was a gift."

The youth group supported one another in their attempts to share this hope with other teens. Janelle and Alicia told me about Deanna's conversation with a classmate who cut herself with knives. Janelle made slicing motions on her forearm to demonstrate and said, "She learned her ideas from songs and from her friends."

The girl brought a book to school about Satan worship, downloaded from the Internet. Deanna told the youth group, "She showed it to me, and I started to read it, but the first two lines were so creepy I quickly gave it back."

The girl bragged, "I have seen Satan. Have you ever seen God?"

Deanna replied, "No, but God lives in my heart."

"Satan gives me everything I want. Does your God do that?"

"No, He gives me what I need."

The girl claimed Satan was superior to God, and said that following Satan was better than following God.

Deanna asked her, "Have you ever felt alone?"

"Yes."

"I have never been alone, because God is always with me."

Alicia showed Deanna the passage in Revelation that reveals the ultimate end of Satan—cast into the lake of fire. Satan was not more powerful.

The Efas Center no longer looked like a limestone skeleton but now had doors, windows, and a nice finish on the outside. Late one afternoon, several hefty men in fancy, black cars drove up. They said they hoped to sell artwork to summer guests and asked, "Will you sign an agreement allowing us to display paintings in your building? We will pay you, of course."

Stefan had heard of a similar proposal where the crooks changed the document, bribed the judges, and took possession of the building. He made it clear that the building was not ready for summer guests. Furthermore, he was not the owner but a Christian organization was.

The man in expensive clothes claimed, "I'm a priest," while waving the bottle of beer in his hand.

Stefan asked, "Do you even believe in God?" The man's chauffeur laughed. Stefan did not sign anything, but invited them to leave their card. They left nothing and drove off.

Stefan hired an excavator to come and bury a huge water tank, since the village had chronic water problems during the summer. The excavator did not get far before he uncovered the corner of an underground bunker.

Some workers hopped inside to investigate. With several rooms, it was as large as our apartment but completely empty. Who built it and when? Was it from World War II, from an earlier period, or from the Cold War? Stefan talked to an elderly neighbor who had no answers. Knowing it would take too much work to remove the bunker, Stefan moved the burial site for the water tank instead.

When the fabric shop in Simferopol called to say the curtains we ordered for the Efas Center were ready, Cory invited me to go along and choose bedspreads. I welcomed the outing and a chance to help with the project.

While Cory packed our car with bedspreads, pillows, curtains, and curtain rods, a Tatar gal who worked at the shop asked me, "How are people in America different from people here?"

"There are good people and bad people everywhere, but people in Ukraine are very hospitable."

"Especially Tatar," she said.

As if to prove her point, while Cory settled the bill, another Tatar set a plate of cookies and sweets on a small table, slightly hidden by the curtain display. She brought out two small cups of strong coffee and invited us to sit down. Stifling the impulse to rush off to the next task, we obeyed. She brought a third cup and the Tatar owner joined us. This man, in his late fifties with salt and pepper hair and a friendly face, introduced himself as Isa, which is Tatar for "Jesus."

Isa asked, "What are you doing in Ukraine?" Cory explained that we wanted to help the country through improved morals, and we worked with the church.

Isa nodded and told how he had moved back to Crimea in the early 1990s. He was just a small boy when Stalin deported his family and other Tatar after World War II. He came back to Crimea without his wife and children to work on a house for the first year. "A group from America came to my village, and they helped me build," he said. "I could not have done it by myself. They worked on my house for two months and did not accept any pay."

Cory replied, "I remember hearing about some American Christians who helped the Tatar build about that time." When Isa named the village, Cory affirmed, "I'm sure it was the same group."

"I will never forget that as long as I live," Isa said.

We also got a short-term work crew. Seven men came from Oregon for a week in May to help transform the rocky, weedy grounds around the Efas Center. They buried pipe, spread soil, laid sidewalk bricks, and made benches.

Right after they arrived, the city turned off the water for three days for the spring cleaning of the system. Stefan and Cory rigged up an outdoor shower and tapped into water stored in the recently-buried underground tank.

The team painted a small holding tank over the shower black to take advantage of solar heating. "We take so much for granted back home," one said. The rest of the team agreed.

Soon after they left, Alicia looked at her calendar, puzzled. "Why do I have June 6 circled?" she said aloud. "Oh, I know...that's when our inmates arrive. Oops, I mean interns."

Two Bible college students, Kyla and Katlyn, came for a two-month internship to help with summer camps and experience a different culture. To ease their adjustment, we invited them to stay with us at first, though they soon moved in with Stefan's family.

Kyla and Katlyn came home from their first Russian lesson with aching heads. "Alina wouldn't talk to us in English," they complained. "She would talk to us only in Russian." Despite their pleas for mercy, she pushed them until their brains turned to mush.

Besides torturing them with Russian, Sasha and Alina included them in some outreaches. One day they went on a day hike and picnic with four teens Sasha and Alina had met while delivering groceries at Christmas and Easter. The arrival of two American girls gave another reason to make contact with them. Some members of their Bible study also went along.

Kyla and Katlyn marveled at Alina's stamina, saying, "She is seven months pregnant, and she still hiked up that hill. After the hike, we took a nap, but she took one of the teenage girls shopping for several hours, looking for a graduation dress."

The Russian lessons soon paid off, and they felt as if they could at least communicate and understand a little. One said, "When you live in the United States and hear English all the time, you forget that not everyone in the world speaks English. Of course we knew that, but you don't really realize it until you're in another country."

They began helping Sasha and Alina with outdoor evangelism and learned how to say, "Take one please," so they could pass out tracts. Some people wanted to stop and talk, at which point Alina took over. A few knew English and wanted to talk to an American. With several good conversations, the interns could even say, "It was fun."

Sasha and Alina already had many years of experience doing street evangelism and believed most people will not seek out a church just because it exists. Alina became a Christian after meeting a missionary who stopped her on the street and asked where he could get a haircut. She had studied English, but this was the first native speaker she had ever met. She started attending his church, liked the loving atmosphere, and found peace with God.

Sasha began his Christian journey in 1992 as a university student when someone gave him a Bible. Before this, the Bible was forbidden and unknown. Recalling this period, he said, "I heard of a church many students attended.

When I went to it, it was like drinking water when you are thirsty. It was joyful and interesting, and I learned about God."

Whether or not the interns joined them, Sasha and Alina continued to pass out New Testaments every Saturday near the market. Many people ignored them. Some responded rudely or cursed at them. Others, however, took a New Testament with thanks or showed interest in other ways.

One Saturday, a teenage boy asked Alina, "Where is the justice of God?" His friend had recently been stabbed and killed by a drunk. "Why do innocent people die, and evil people go on living?"

Sasha joined the conversation and said, "God lets evil people go on living because He wants to give them a chance to know Him." They talked a long time before the teen parted with a tract and their phone number.

When Alina heard about the catcalls a Christian girl got when she visited a university for entrance exams, she said, "Lilya is a beautiful girl. I should tell her how to handle those guys. She needs to go up to them and say, 'I'm glad you called me over. I have some good news to tell you about Jesus.' That's how I handled it. I would remember: 'Greater is He who is in you than he who is in the world,' and I knew I didn't have to feel intimidated."

When the interns and another visitor finished with day camp on the Fourth of July, I invited them over for hamburgers and red, white, and blue dessert. Cory, Janelle, and Alicia had an even more memorable celebration on their hiking camp with youth from Sudak and two guys from Colorado. Cory reported that after dinner, the Sudak youth trooped past the Americans. Some held hands in a large rectangle around others who waved branches or threw candy. Cory had told someone about Fourth of July parades with floats, so they became a parade float to help the Americans celebrate.

In spite of the difficult hike, Janelle and Alicia sounded chipper on the cell phone and reported, "It's going great!" Janelle and Alicia jumped about twenty times from a high ledge into a deep, cold pool called the "Pool of Youth." With that many dips, I expected to see toddlers when they came home.

Fortunately, they did not turn into toddlers since they were needed at camp the following week. While Alicia was in charge of crafts, Janelle served as interpreter for the interns. Alicia thought crafts went well, except paint day was messy. Janelle said that interpreting wasn't hard, just hot, since they stayed in the sun during sports and games.

One day the four American girls acted as survivors of a plane crash for a scavenger hunt. Children got points for finding gold, pieces of wrecked plane, and the four survivors. Leaders held up painted rocks and pieces of cardboard, so the children knew what to seek.

They explained, "The survivors are scared, and they don't understand Russian, so they might run away." The children eventually forcibly rescued three but never did find Katlyn, who hid on the roof. When Stefan came for the interns after camp, he was shocked to see big bruises and black eyes. They had not removed their make-up.

With the girls occupied at camp, I felt free to join Cory on his next trip to see Salim. Seeing deep ruts in the dirt road to his village, I understood why Cory said it was difficult to get there in the winter, the rainy season.

As we drove up, Salim and Alma came out to meet us, along with their suntanned and shirtless boys, ages fourteen, twelve, and four. Cory stayed outside with Salim, who tended a fire for barbecue, but I joined Alma in the house. While she cut up cucumbers and tomatoes for salad, I asked about her family. I already knew that her father was an Islamic religious leader, and her parents opposed her Christian faith, but I wanted to hear the story from her perspective.

Her father was ten years old when Stalin deported the Tatar from Crimea after World War II. Forced from their homes, stuffed into cattle cars, and shipped to Central Asia, many Tatar died on the way or soon afterward. Because of this, he and other Tatar hated Russians and could not understand why Alma would leave Islam, the religion of the Tatar, for Christianity, the religion of the Russians.

We heard a visitor with a loud voice arrive outside. "It's my father," she said. Noting his almost one-sided conversation with Cory, she added apologetically, "He likes to talk."

Alma poured water into a small pot with a wide base and narrow top and set it on the stove for coffee. "I was twenty-five years old when we moved to Crimea," she said. "Even though my parents thought of Crimea as their home, I grew up in Uzbekistan, and that was home to me. I had a job and was used to the city. I thought the quiet life of a village might be nice, but it was hard for me to adjust when we moved here."

She met Salim, who was ten years older and played in a band at a nightclub. She knew his sister in Uzbekistan. They soon got married, but before long it seemed like a mistake. He drank heavily and treated her badly. She tried to think of ways to escape, to take the children and start over somewhere else. Then Salim met some Christians and became one. She saw a dramatic change in him, went to church too, and gave her life to Christ.

She poured strong coffee into small cups and took a tray out to the men, with sugar cubes and candies. The four-year-old with mischievous eyes unwrapped his second piece of candy before she returned. She wiped the faded plastic tablecloth, set a cup and candies before me, and continued her story. She nibbled on a sugar cube between sips of coffee.

"My parents were very upset when I became a Christian," she said. "Other Tatar asked them, 'How can you allow your daughter to abandon the faith?' My parents told us it would be better if I moved, since I was an embarrassment to them. My father will at least talk to us now, but my mother is still ashamed of me. I tell them, 'You know how Salim was. Do you think that was better?' They say he didn't have to become a Christian to change, but I know that only the power of God helped him change."

The barbecued chicken was soon done. Though just 10:30 a.m., their sense of hospitality required a meal. I greeted Alma's father with "Salaam Alakum." He switched from Russian to Tatar until I explained, "That was the only Tatar I know."

Seeing them lined up at the table, Cory said, "The grandsons look like grandpa." I tried to imagine the boys with sagging wrinkles, scruffy gray whiskers, and missing teeth. This man did not look like the revered Muslim leader I had heard about. Granted, he did not know Salim and Alma had guests and arrived unshaven, in his old clothes. He claimed to be seventy-six years old and had never been to school, with the upheaval of his family's deportation coming on the heels of World War II.

Soon after Alma served dessert and tea, the cell phone rang. "Mama wants you to go home," she told her father.

He left, and Cory reviewed their conversation. "He asked if I bow down to icons, like the Orthodox, or drink. 'Not even 100 grams (a shot of vodka)?' He was trying to figure out who I was and what I stood for."

Salim told the children to go outside and play, and then spoke of frustrations with his home church. If he preached with any emotion, the pastor accused him of being an actor. He felt as if he did not have even one person he could talk to openly, believing that if he shared from the heart, people would use it against him.

He found some villages not far away where no Christian work had taken place. "People there have never heard about Christ. I took a bag of New Testaments, and I was surprised how open people were. They took the Gospels gladly and often asked if they could have an extra one, to give to a neighbor or a brother."

The pastor of his home church, however, said they should focus on areas where they had an existing work. "But why should I hand out Bibles here when everyone in my village already has one? And why should bundles of Scriptures simply sit around at the church for mice to eat?" He showed a map and pointed out six or seven villages where no outreach had yet taken place. Lacking a car, he could take only a few Bibles in a bag as he traveled by bus or a bicycle.

The three hours we planned to stay at their house passed quickly. It felt as if we had just started talking but needed to leave, since we had promised the girls and interns we would attend the closing program at their camp, a two-hour drive away.

Cory and I arrived in time and noted a good turnout from the parents. An attractive girl in the oldest group signed a song her group sang. I loved watching sign language put to music, but the group leader told me later that the girl's grandmother went outside and wept. "She was afraid people would judge her granddaughter for her handicap," she said. "The girl is mostly deaf and speaks Russian poorly."

"I'm handicapped too," I said, "since I also speak Russian poorly."

The leader laughed and added, "Did you notice the man who stood up and videotaped her? He is deaf. At first, he refused to let his daughter come to camp, but she cried and we talked to him, so he finally gave in. He came to the program to videotape his daughter even though he could not understand anything. When that girl signed the song, he heard the Gospel too. He will show the tape to his wife who is also deaf, and she will also hear the Gospel."

Have I ever seen God? The wind is invisible, but I witness its effect. Likewise, God's power is evident all around. He changes people for the better and uses them to make the world a better place.

Village children learn about Jesus at day camp.

244

39
Big Plants Grow From Little Seeds

August - November 2007

As our summer interns, Kyla and Katlyn, reflected on their two months in Ukraine, one said, "We learned that being a missionary is hard work." The other nodded. When missionaries visited their college, it seemed like a glamorous profession. In Ukraine they saw it takes much effort just to live and learn the language, and even more to make any progress toward spiritual goals.

Kyla asked me, "Do you resent it that churches send out so many people on short-term trips—people like me?"

"No, I got started in missions by going on a short-term outreach. Many long-term missionaries do. Of course, not all visitors return, but they still go home with a better understanding of needs in the world and are more apt to support missions. Some people might have an unrealistic idea about what can be accomplished in one week, but many come with expertise and put it to good use."

She admitted, "I feel as if we've barely scratched the surface when it comes to understanding the culture and making an impact, and we stayed for two months."

Sometimes I felt as if we had barely scratched the surface too, but big plants can grow from little seeds.

With Janelle and Alicia working in yet another camp, I joined Cory on his next trip to Simferopol. Our 8:00 a.m. breakfast appointment with missionaries lasted four hours. I enjoyed the fellowship and laughter amid the exchange of ideas and information. Cory usually told me the highlights of his outings, but a five-minute summary could never cover all I soaked in by being there.

As we drove away, Cory said, "I'm going to stop by the church for a bit." There he unexpectedly saw the women in charge of a Bible correspondence course. He had questions for them, and they wanted to see him also. They remembered his comment about Muslim Tatar at an evangelism seminar and wanted Tatar literature. He had some in the car.

He also saw Hasad and offered him a ride home. This former Muslim had moved to Crimea to work with Tatar. As we drove, Hasad said his wife and four children struggled to adjust to life in Crimea and cried a lot. Even though his wife spoke Russian fluently, it took time to make new friends.

We pulled up to a two-story house in a Tatar neighborhood on the outskirts of town. His wife, Elena, gave us a brief tour of the house. Though the second floor was not complete, the first floor came fully furnished. "God is good," she said.

I acknowledged, "It's still hard to move to a new place, far from family, and find new friends. Our first few years here were difficult, but God was with us."

"I'm not used to this heat," she complained.

"It will get cold!" I said with a smile. "Be patient." Encouraged or not, she laughed.

Cory answered questions about visas and suggested some good churches to visit. We prayed together, and they urged us to come again and bring the girls.

It was a good day. "Thanks for taking me along," I told Cory as we headed home.

"I'm glad you went," he replied. "It makes it easier for me when I don't have to carry the whole conversation. And you can see that I'm not just running around when I'm running around."

At all three stops—with the missionaries, with the women at the church, and with Hasad—Cory told them of people he knows who could help them meet their goals. He mused, "It's like my role is to tie different threads together. When I meet different people, I don't know if this thread will be short or long or how it will fit into the picture, but it often does."

After we got home, Janelle and Alicia described their time at camp. Village officials had welcomed the church and let them use the kindergarten for their Vacation Bible School. They got one room for classes and lunch and also held lessons under a tree outside. The only bathroom facility was an outhouse about five minutes away.

That morning the village head warned them that the health inspectors were coming. Alicia said, "Probably someone who didn't like us holding the camp called and told them we were there. The building was condemned, so they could have fined us and the village for using it. We had to send the children home and leave quickly. Everybody at the daycare left too."

With broken windows and shattered glass on the sidewalk, Alicia didn't think the building looked very safe for children but reflected, "To me, the conditions seem terrible, but to them, it seems normal to keep using a condemned building. I live comfortably and have many things they don't. I really don't have much reason to complain."

The next day, they returned to their condemned building for a final day of camp with no further incident. When parents came for the closing program, they expressed gratitude for the time and attention the leaders gave their children. Several said, "It gives them something interesting to do."

One woman added, "My son's behavior improved, so I wanted to see what was going on here."

I knew better than to expect Janelle and Alicia to come home right after camp ended that afternoon. They had already told us they had choir practice that evening and meanwhile, they would hang out with the other youth who had helped with camp.

With regular buses between Feodosia and Primorski, we knew they had a way to get home. If they came home after dark, one of the guys in the youth group escorted them to our door. With a cell phone and inexpensive cell-phone service, they could let us know their whereabouts.

They came home that night full of tales about their day. After camp, the woman who lived at the church as caretaker cooked rice for them and some other youth. Then they headed to the beach and jumped off the pier until it was time for choir practice. Jumping off was the easy part—they hey showed me bruises obtained while climbing back up.

We did take Janelle and Alicia for an afternoon with Hasad, Elena, and their four children. Knowing Hasad was a Tatar from Kazakhstan, and Elena was a Russian from the north, I asked her, "How did you two meet?"

Elena began with Hasad's story. Hasad grew up in a large Muslim family. When he was seven, a Christian couple with five children moved in next door. At first they seemed so kind to one another and to him, he thought it was a show they put on for outsiders. Over the years, however, he spent much time at their house. He played with their kids, ate at their table, and even spent the night. He saw they were genuinely good people, and he wanted to be like them.

At the age of twenty-eight, he moved to the northwest part of the Soviet Union to work. He remembered his good Christian neighbors and needed friends in this new place. Away from the watchful eye of Muslim parents and relatives, he visited a church and met Elena there. Over time, they got to know each other and fell in love.

Hasad's mother came to visit and was upset to learn her son attended a Christian church. She calmed down when he promised not to get baptized.

Soon afterward, Hasad asked Elena to be his wife. Elena loved him but told him, "I could never marry someone who is not equally committed to Christ." Because of his promise to his mother, Elena saw no future together and told him, "Do not call or come around until you are ready to make a total commitment to the Lord."

She told me, "It hurt to tell him that. Every time the phone rang or every time someone knocked on the door, I hoped it was him."

Hasad married someone else. A year later, his wife and baby died during childbirth. When Hasad's mother came to the funeral, she gave him permission to follow the Christian faith as he wished.

For several years, Hasad attended a neighboring church but stayed away from Elena. One day he showed up at a baptismal service and asked to be baptized. Some of Elena's friends saw him and told her afterward, "Hasad was baptized too!"

Seven years had passed since Elena told him not to call her anymore. She still had not married. At that moment she decided that if he asked her to marry him, she would say yes. He did.

In the years that followed, Hasad often prayed, "Make us a missionary family." Elena added, "Amen," not thinking about what it meant. Hasad joined a short-term mission to Tatarstan, a republic east of Moscow, as a translator. Several Tatar turned to Christ. Hasad volunteered to return and lead the new group of believers.

Elena interrupted her story to explain that Hasad was not someone who could speak in front of people back then. He did fine one-on-one but usually felt shy with a group. With his glasses and quiet manner, I thought he still looked more like an accountant than an evangelist.

Arriving back home, he got off the train and told Elena, "We are moving to Tatarstan!"

Elena surprised herself by replying, "Okay!" She usually liked to have everything figured out in advance.

She told how God met their needs and used them in Tatarstan. They stayed over three years until forced to leave. They returned home, but Hasad's desire to minister among Muslims never left, so they moved to Crimea.

She said she now felt a little more settled than the first time I saw her. They met friendly neighbors, and she enrolled the children in school.

For an end-of-the-summer outing, the Primorski youth group took a bus down the coast for an overnight campout. We lived on the edge of the flat steppe, and they headed into the Crimean Mountains with rugged volcanic cliffs. At fourteen and fifteen, Alicia and Janelle were still the youngest in the youth group, but we trusted the older ones to watch out for them.

"We had *so much* fun!" the girls exclaimed when they returned home. They took turns telling how they jumped off a rock face into the Black Sea, played games late at night, and slept under the stars. They showed me their scrapes and sunburns. Jagged volcanic rock makes beautiful landscape but grates on those who play tag around it.

Janelle explained, "The ledge we jumped from was about thirty feet above the water. As long as you jump off without thinking about it, it's not too bad, but the second you jump off, you realize you weren't ready."

Alicia added, "If you scream all the way down, it's not quite as scary."

It sounds a bit like stepping into missions, except screaming doesn't help.

It had been four years since Dave and Annette Dryden came to Ukraine as Bible college interns and spent six months with us. They had already experienced the difficulties of mission life, but they returned anyway. They now came with a small son and hopes of ministry among the Tatar.

Two-year-old David loved our parakeets. "Fly, birdie, fly!" he chirped. "Come here, birdie!"

Annette said, "At the park, he tries to make friends with the other little kids. He doesn't understand that they don't know English."

Dave and Annette thought a lot had changed in Ukraine since their internship. For us, the changes came more gradually. Feodosia now had a grocery store with scanners at check-out. The store offered no better selection than we found with various vendors at the market, but we could now get most groceries at one place. Small boutiques with boutique prices replaced the open-air clothing market in our neighborhood. Parks in town now included playground equipment, causing Janelle and Alicia to wish they were younger.

A couple weeks later, a team of eighteen from Oregon brought enthusiasm and strength to help with the Efas Center building. They arrived just in time to get it ready for the first seminar we planned to hold there. Builders had completed just two of the four floors, but these needed cleaning, curtains, and beds. While some worked inside, others did landscaping, hauled bricks, and laid the foundation for an outbuilding.

The next week, fifty men attended the seminar. Most of them had gone through the two-year church planting course. We hoped the teaching and fellowship would give them a boost of encouragement and more tools for ministry.

I went out one morning that week and talked to a few men I knew. Timon, the former collective farm manager, now helped Pavel with new churches in his region. "This training is just what we need here in Crimea," he said. "And to stay at the Center last night, to stand on the balcony and remember what the building was like just three years ago when we cleaned out the trash and began working on it, it seems like a miracle."

Workers still needed to finish two floors and the basement, but for the building to be even partly usable was a miracle indeed.

When Janelle and Alicia offered to sweep the stairwell of our apartment, I felt like I was sending them into the Chernobyl zone. Sure, it needed it. A recent visitor asked if we had bums living there. I sometimes swept it myself, but it did not stay clean long since a teenage neighbor and his friends often gathered there to smoke.

Though pleased by their offer, I knew it would be a dusty, dirty job and urged them to wear damp bandanas over their nose and mouth. I was not afraid of normal dust, but had heard TB cultures in spit could survive heat, cold, and dry conditions until it found a new home. Looking like cowboys or bandits, the girls tackled the task.

A few days later, they looked at the trash around our apartment entrance and exclaimed, "We just cleaned there!"

I also found in the stairwell a small pile of—well it wasn't doggie droppings. I inwardly grumbled, "Why do we even have a security door downstairs if people leave it open?" Not expecting anyone else to clean up the mess, I did and poured bleach all around.

The house never stayed clean either. I popped in a new sermon tape to keep me company while I washed a stack of dishes in the sink. The topic grabbed my attention.

While the Israelites camped in the wilderness, Moses met with God on the mountain. God gave His version of what had taken place during the previous three months: "I carried you on eagle's wings" (Exodus 19:4). The Israelites likely had a different version.

I could easily imagine how the Israelites might have described those three months since leaving Egypt: the traumatic border crossing, water shortages, the long and difficult journey, bland food, and hostile natives. It would make a good missionary newsletter.

God said, "I carried you on eagle's wings."

Reading how the Israelites complained and reacted with fear, I found them foolish. Almighty God Himself led them! He miraculously met their needs, but they could not even see beyond themselves. Nevertheless, my take on life was typically closer to the Israelites' shortsighted view instead of God's big picture. I judged situations by how they affected my comfort level or how they might tax my limited resources.

God's perspective? He displays His power through those who are weak and know it, with those who can't take credit for the results, and in those who don't mind depending on strength beyond their own. When carried on eagle's wings, we can go further and higher than humanly possible.

Through the rest of the week, I tried to look at life from God's perspective. Riding in the car, I inwardly complained about crazy drivers and bad roads until the thought came: *I carried you.* Sometimes I still felt like an outsider looking in, even after twelve years in Ukraine. *I carried you.* The stairwell was dirty again! *I carried you.* Could we expect long-term results? That was God's department also.

May His power be seen in my weakness.

W ith Janelle and Alicia both needing braces, we visited an orthodontist in Simferopol. It took two hours to drive there, but someone told us she was the best in Crimea. We followed directions into a dingy, run-down building. My heart sank as I climbed the dirty steps. I felt more hopeful in the clean waiting room. Good impressions continued as I saw modern dental equipment, watched the orthodontist put on latex gloves for the exam, and heard her treatment plan. She invited questions and showed me their sterilizing equipment. We felt good about proceeding with treatment and liked the price tag.

Janelle said, "People write articles about how to not eat too much over the holidays, but I have the best idea—get braces." I scheduled their appointment for Thanksgiving Day. That way we could join a potluck with other American missionaries and avoid an extra trip.

When Janelle and Alicia showed up at youth group with braces, reactions varied. One boy joked, "You could open cans with those!"

Another added, "Now you don't need to be afraid of walking in the dark. If anyone bothers you, show them your teeth, and they will run away."

An older woman in the choir said, "They look cute, better than the metal bands they used to put around each tooth."

The choir director agreed. "I like them. When I was in school, many kids wrapped wire around their teeth to try to look like they had braces. I did it too. Yours look a lot better."

Dave and Annette Dryden returned to Ukraine as missionaries.

Janelle and Alicia joined the youth choir.

40

A God-Sized Project

June planned to come back to Ukraine after seven months in the U.S., but had to postpone her return twice because of unexpected medical problems requiring surgery. She wrote, "This furlough took me to the wilderness in a difficult journey through an unkind desert called Unknown. I didn't like it. Fear, pain, anger, depression, guilt, and grief met me there. But I'm grateful because I came to the end of myself and was willing to be governed by God. By His grace, I experienced peace that doesn't make sense and the joy of being lost in His love."

Sasha and Alina continued to live in her apartment while they fixed up one they bought. They moved out when Dave and Annette arrived. This gave the new missionaries a comfortable home for three months and time to find a furnished rental before June returned to Ukraine in December.

Before Christmas, Sasha and Alina again got the names and addresses of Feodosia's poorest families in order to take them gift bags for Christmas. June provided toys, hats, and gloves. Sasha and Alina bought groceries and vitamins and added a New Testament to each bag.

I joined them for deliveries one day while June watched their daughter, Dasha, now four months old. Cory drove—a big help with distant deliveries, a heavy load, piercing wind, and falling snow.

At one stop, we found a grandmother caring for two small children in a dimly-lit basement apartment. She led us past a stove in the hall to a room with a fold-out couch and a single bed. Carpets and big posters of half-naked women adorned the wall.

The children exclaimed over each toy. Alina explained, "We are believers, and we brought you these gifts for Christmas, which is a celebration of Jesus' birth."

The woman said, "I'm a believer too." She reached over to the two-year-old boy and pulled out a necklace from under his shirt. "See, I put crosses on the children. I have icons, and I go to church to light candles on holidays, if I can get there."

Alina told the story of Christ's birth to the children and explained that He came so we can have our sins forgiven.

"I'm a believer too," the woman repeated. "I have icons and crosses." She snapped at the children for interrupting and told about her difficult life. She complained that the children's mother ran around during the day and came home only at night to eat and sleep.

Sasha and Alina did not criticize her shallow understanding of Christianity, but gave her a copy of the New Testament and urged her to read it to the children.

At the next house, Alina checked her paper for the names at that address and called through the door, asking if they were home. "Yes, but Mama isn't."

"I have gifts for them," Alina called again. A small twelve-year-old girl named Vika opened the door and let us in. This house seemed the most pitiful of all. With the rough wooden floor and very basic furniture, it seemed more like a small shed than a house. It was so cold, the snow we tracked in stayed frozen for a long time.

Besides Vika and her small brother, two neighbor children sat in the room and blew occasionally on their fingers to warm them. Alina explained the purpose of the visit and gave them gifts. "But the most important gift is Jesus," she said and told them the Christmas story.

Vika seemed mature beyond her years, yet showed childlike enthusiasm for the gifts. Her eyes glowed as she tried on the hat and gloves. Her little brother coughed a lot. Vika turned on a small electric burner in the middle of the floor, and they gathered around to warm their fingers over it, as though it were a campfire.

Alina said, "We will come again at Easter. Do you know why Easter is special?"

"Yes, that's when we color eggs!"

She started to tell how Jesus rose from the dead but said, "I will tell you that story later." She prayed for them and added, "You can talk to God like this any time."

As we went out, a rough-looking man with a skinned-up nose came to the door. He told Vika, "I've come for a little money."

Alina asked her, "Do you know this man?" Vika nodded slightly, but her eyes looked guarded. Alina asked, "Will you be okay?" Vika nodded again. Sasha and Alina got two pairs of gloves from the car to give to the neighbor children. Returning, they said that the man was still there. I hoped he wouldn't take their gifts to sell them.

Alina told me later, "It always makes me want to cry, seeing how children suffer from the sins of adults."

We returned to June's apartment for baby Dasha. Over tea and brownies, I described to June the homes we visited—modern scenes out of a Charles Dickens novel. She saw much poverty during medical home visits and said, "I'm glad you could go."

I was glad too. I didn't do much, other than pray silently, but the visits renewed my sense of purpose for living in Ukraine. My role kept me home much of the time, so it helped to see these who needed hope. It also renewed my sense of appreciation for blessings I took for granted.

When I delivered cookies to my neighbors before Christmas, I included an invitation to the January 7 Christmas concert at Sasha and Alina's young church. Their small group now met in a room they rented at a nearby guesthouse. None of my neighbors came.

In his opening comments at the concert, Sasha told how he had invited a friend who made artificial flower arrangements for graves. The man said, "So many people died over New Year, we can't keep up. We've had one funeral after another." Many had died from alcohol poisoning or froze to death while drunk. Sasha continued, "That holiday brought death, but this holiday, Christmas, celebrates life."

Alina sang and played her guitar. A man who had met Sasha and Alina on the street accompanied some songs on his harmonica. Sasha gave a short message, and the concert ended with a light meal, tea, and pastries.

Only nine came to the concert, including baby Dasha. Watching Sasha and Alina in their efforts to form a new church, I gained greater appreciation for the difficulties other church planters faced. Boris and his girlfriend, who attended early Bible studies, broke up and no longer came around. The hours Sasha and Alina spent passing out tracts resulted in few new members, in spite of some good conversations.

None of the families they gave gift bags to came to the Christmas program. The next week, however, Alina told me, "Remember the children who gathered around the electric burner to get warm? Their mother came to church Sunday with the children. She found the tract inside the New Testament. It had the address of where we meet, and she wanted to thank us. I guess it shows that those who want to come will find us. We plan to visit them again since I promised them a copy of the photo I took."

Cory continued to meet occasionally with church planters who went through our training. One of them told of his recent trip to a large city to the north: "While waiting in the church foyer for someone, I noticed information about a rehabilitation center on the bulletin board and wrote down the phone number. After my meeting, I went to the train station and sat to drink tea while waiting for my train. Many people passed by, but one young man stopped, looked at me, and asked, 'Are you a Christian?' I told him I was.

"He said he needed to talk to a believer. The Lord allowed me to talk to this eighteen-year-old about eternity and God's desires for him. He said he once went to church but got involved with people who drank and used drugs. He said he was now dying from that lifestyle and asked what he could do.

"My train had come, and I didn't know what to tell him. The Lord reminded me I had the phone number of a Christian rehabilitation center in that city. I was able to direct him to Christ and to the rehab center. We continue to write, and he is now walking with the Lord again."

Another evangelist, Nicholi, reported, "Three years ago our church plant decided to evangelize in a neighboring village. We noticed many children in the village and looked for ways to start a children's ministry. We started holding Sunday school, and around twenty-five to thirty children now attend regularly. A Crimean Tatar woman comes with her two daughters and listens intently to the Bible lesson."

Yasha, another church planter, told of a woman who interrupted their meeting one day, looking for someone in the group. She left but returned the next week, saying, "I want to know more about your faith, but I'm afraid people will call me a traitor for leaving the Orthodox faith."

Yasha asked her, "How often do you attend the Orthodox church, and do you know the priest?"

"I never go to the church and I don't know the priest," she replied.

He assured her, "Don't worry; you have not betrayed anything since you did not believe anything."

Stefan came to our apartment one evening to see Cory. While Cory went to another room to get money for him, Stefan grabbed his chest.

I had seen him do that before. "Your heart?" I asked. He nodded. "Stress?"

He nodded again and said, "What a day. I won't tell Cory about it now, so he can sleep tonight." Stefan told him anyway about another unexpected expense for the Efas Center.

Before starting the building project, we had tried to count the cost. The leaders prayed and believed God was in it. They estimated how much money it would take. It was more than we had—a God-sized project.

Money came in. Construction began. Inflation hit. The cost of many building materials doubled or tripled. The price of cement quadrupled. God continued to provide, often from unexpected sources. Four floors were now done. We still hoped to put a kitchen, dining room, and lecture hall in the basement. We had purchased a gas boiler and installed radiators throughout the building, but continued to use small electric heaters. We had not hooked up gas since the gas company wanted $15,000 for their hook-up fee.

Cory grew tired of the administrative details. He preferred to visit church planters and work with people. He felt sorry for the stresses on Stefan that went with his role as manager, so we often prayed God would give him extra strength and wisdom. Even after the building was finished, the project would still need God's provision and guidance.

Watching a video of *Lord of the Rings* on family night, I noted some parallels with the Christian life and service. We did not experience the same hazards as Frodo, but we faced similar choices. Frodo did not want the responsibility that came with the ring. Gandalf told him that since the ring had come to him, he was meant to have it, and he should make the best of it. While trying to fulfill the mission that fell to him, Frodo met hostile creatures and other dangers.

As I watched their narrow path crumble into the abyss, I thought, *Like him, we never know what will happen next. We can only do what we can to keep going.* A higher power seemed to protect Frodo—and us.

With the lecture room not yet complete, Training Center leaders used the church building next door for lectures. Without a proper kitchen ready, they put a stove and table in one of the bedrooms, and cooks served meals in the large foyer.

I caught a ride with Cory to the Efas Center one morning to see for myself how the weekend's seminar was going. I wanted to see who had come and take an informal survey of their impressions. We arrived in time for breakfast.

One participant, Kostya, told me the seminars had transformed his ministry, and he passed on what he learned to the new church he led. "We need this teaching in all our churches," he said. "What often happens is that people end up focusing on traditions. They get away from the Gospel and what Christ has done for us. Even the Old Testament points to Christ. I have learned to focus on Christ when I teach."

His wife had joined him for this session. She said, "When Kostya came home from other seminars, he said they were good. He'd tell me the topics, and I'd say, 'But you already know about that.' He told me, 'Yes, but they take truths from the Scripture and give insights I never thought of before. The teaching is simple and clear but deep.'

"This week, I left the children with their grandparents and came with him. I have gone to church since I was a child. I thought I knew the Bible, but I learned things here that I never understood before. I see now why he likes it so much. I am so glad I came."

Since Stefan was heading back to town for groceries, I caught a ride home with him. As we drove, I asked for his impressions. He said that four people came to the seminar from Batalnaya, where he led a young church. "For me, the best part is to see their enthusiasm. Sergei says he has never heard such good teaching, even at the Bible college he attended. The other three also like it."

"It was good to see for myself how it's going," I said. "Cory comes home and tells me about the problems."

"Wherever you have people, you have problems," he replied, "and Cory hears all the problems. I have questions about money. Food is expensive. We pay transportation costs and the price of gas went up again. But the ministry itself—the results are very good."

As Cory introduced his sermon the next Sunday, he said, "I don't know about you, but I have a problem of wanting to be in control. Only God is all-powerful. When I feel burdened, it is usually because I am trying to take on something God does not intend for me to carry."

He drew principles from the story of Peter getting money for taxes from a fish. Jesus knew Peter's need before Peter said anything. Provision came when Peter obeyed. Likewise, we can expect God to provide all we need when we obey Him.

The completed Efas Center.

41

The Lord Gives Strength

April - June 2008

On another Sunday, I rode with Cory one hour east to visit a church in Kerch. While Cory met with church leaders before the service, I found a pew. An old woman with a cane soon joined me. "Have you attended here long?" I asked.

"Twenty-two years," she replied, and soon she launched into her life's story. She grew up with Christian parents in Siberia, back when they met in secret and sang in whispers. When she was sixteen, at the end of World War II, her mother went to the hospital for some months, leaving her alone to tend the animals. She lived off milk, eggs, and grain. "Later, I had a bad husband, but he died, praise God....My daughter never comes to see me...I'm all alone." She began to cry. "I'm not important to anyone."

I felt a little uncomfortable and thought she must surely have something good in her life, other than her husband dying. "God is with you," I said.

"Of course, but when I was sick, no one came to visit me for days." She dabbed her tears with a handkerchief and said with a trembling voice, "I am ready to leave this life and go to heaven."

After the service an older man greeted me with a firm handshake and inquired about my life and family. I gave a brief report and asked, "How about you?"

He replied with a twinkle in his eye: "The Bible says we can expect to live seventy years or eighty, due to strength. Praise God, I have reached the milestone of eighty years!"

The old woman joined us for lunch in the caretaker's quarters. I had a feeling she ate there often, but she felt she had nothing good in life. The man looked for reasons to praise God, even for the simple gift of old age. I made a mental note: I want to be like that man.

That week I listened to a tape stressing how children learn from their mother's attitude toward life: "Do you complain often? A mother who complains regularly about her lot in life teaches her children that God is inadequate to meet her needs. A mother who usually has a positive outlook teaches her children that God is real and powerful and meets her needs."

Maybe one reason few people want to be missionaries is because we tend to talk more about the hardships than God's provision. If I am to glorify God with my life, I must give Him the honor He deserves. I heard one thought-provoking definition: To glorify God is to make Him look good, to brag about Him.

I could brag about God. I did not know what the future held but had already seen fulfillment of Ephesians 3:20. God had done immeasurably more than we could ask or imagine.

We saw one example of God's power to change lives in the village of Krasni Zorye. After we got a report from Vitya, the church planter working there, we wanted to meet the people he described.

While still enrolled in the church planters' course, Vitya passed out Christian literature and talked to people in ten villages in his region. Five villages seemed receptive, and he started small groups in each. After he completed his training in 2002, he went to work as an electrician. He also got married and began a family. His new responsibilities left less time for making new contacts. Three groups dwindled to nothing as people moved or quit coming. Vitya and his wife continued to minister in two villages.

Outreach to children opened doors to parents and other relatives. Vitya described the village of Krasni Zorye as "drowning in alcohol and drug addiction." Nevertheless, he knew all the residents and made friends with many of them.

He said, "All the children know me since I go there every week. Most of them live with alcoholic parents, so they need special attention. They are the future of this village and the church." The children helped him with outreach by putting on programs for their parents.

One new believer, Nina, opened her home for Bible study and Sunday school. Cory and I drove to Krasni Zorye to meet her, with Vitya and his wife leading the way.

Nina greeted us warmly and gave a brief tour, showing us her garden plot, chickens, and rabbits. Though just fifty-nine years old, deep lines creased her face, giving evidence of a hard life. Beds, the most prevalent piece of furniture in her small house, revealed her big heart. She had taken in two grown daughters, three grandchildren, the mentally-ill daughter of her last husband, and a friend of her son who was in jail.

Nina pulled out her photo album with black and white pictures glued to worn paper. She pointed out her children and three of her husbands. The book contained no photos of herself as a child. "I don't even know what nationality I am," she said. "Since I have dark skin, I'm probably not Russian—maybe Gypsy or Muslim."

Someone took her from her parents when she was five years old. "I barely remember the face of my mother as she ran to catch the car that carried me away," she said. Flipping through the album, she showed the picture of a stiff-faced woman who adopted her and added, "All she did was use me to get money for her drinking."

Nina was a wild child in school, neglected and hungry. She stole lunch food from others and beat them up to keep them quiet. Authorities eventually took her from her adopted mother and placed her in an orphanage in Crimea. "After the eighth grade, I went to work. I always felt on the edge of society and sought to protect myself. I didn't need anybody, including God."

She married four times and each time became a widow. Her first husband died when she was just twenty, leaving her with an eighteen-month-old son. Her second husband died in a car accident, leaving a second son. She moved around and worked in various places. "That was how my life went," she said, "being blown from place to place with no roots and no purpose. The third time I married, I wasn't in love, and there was always fighting and other problems. My third child, Valya, was three when that husband drowned.

"Again a widow, I moved to Crimea. I was thirty when I married a drunk to support my children. My fourth husband brought two children into the marriage; one of them was mentally ill. I bore two more children. I leaned on my own strength, but without the Lord, what strength does anyone really have? I started to drink, and my life turned into hell."

Nina pointed to the picture of her first son, Victor, as a child. He went to jail when he was seventeen and died there fourteen years later from tuberculosis. He came to Christ before he died and wrote to her about it, but she wasn't ready then.

She pointed out Valya, her third child. At the age of twelve, she began running away from home. When eighteen and unmarried, she gave birth to a girl with cerebral palsy. She drank heavily and spent more time with different boyfriends than with her daughter. That girl, now eleven, had greeted us with a big smile when we arrived.

Valya brought in a bowl of steaming *vareniki*, pasta with mashed potato filling. She set it on the table, with various salads. Barely thirty, Valya looked much older—thin and worn out from an alcoholic lifestyle.

As we began to eat, Nina continued with her story. Another daughter got pregnant at age sixteen. Another son went to jail. Nina said, "I couldn't figure out what was going on. I had tried to be a good mother and give them a home and comfort so they wouldn't have to experience what I went through, but they saw how I lived and followed me.

"I spent all my money on alcohol. Of course, all sorts of friends were eager to help me drink up my money. At least half the people in our village are drunks. I started to smoke, too. I tried to leave that lifestyle and went to work, but there I found other people just as ready to suck all the money and life out of me.

"No one could pull me out of that pit, except the Lord. My fourth husband died of cancer, leaving me a widow again. After I lost everything, only then did I find the Lord. Rather, I heard His call."

Vitya held a Christian day camp at the village and invited Marina, the granddaughter with cerebral palsy. She could not walk well, but she loved the camp. Before this she had no friends, because she did not attend school. She soaked up lessons about God's love for her.

Vitya explained, "At home, Marina lived with constant drinking and fighting. She started going to Sunday school, made friends, and learned about her Heavenly Father. Even with her deformed legs, she got down on her knees to pray for her mother, grandmother, and for her uncle in jail."

Vitya took an evangelistic art exhibit with religious paintings to the village. Nina went to it and asked him many questions. She started attending a Bible study he led. She recalled, "I learned that God loves weak and suffering people, sinners like me. I asked God for forgiveness, and He completely changed my life.

"It is difficult to explain the miracle the Lord has done. It is like a new person lives in me. I see everything with new eyes. I quit drinking and smoking. Before, I drank up all my money—but now, I have had new teeth put in. Before, all I could think about was getting drunk. Now, other believers come to my house for Bible study and prayer, and we hold Sunday school in my home. The people in the village don't know what to think about me. They don't understand that God does miracles."

After Grandma Nina became a Christian, Marina continued to pray for her mother. God heard her prayers. Valya agreed to go to a Christian rehabilitation center, where she gave her life to Christ and stopped drinking. "God did this miracle," Vitya emphasized. "Marina prayed for her mother every day when she was at the rehab center—for six months. Valya came home completely different. Marina now has the love of a mother and a Heavenly Father."

Nina also rejoiced in God's love. "As a child, no one cared for me," she said. "For many years I was bitter about my life, but I didn't know God then. The Lord has become the father and the mother I never had. He will never throw away His children."

Cory and I rejoiced to hear how God had worked. Our purpose in going to Ukraine was not simply to start a training program, but that people's lives might be changed for the better. The Training Center had become a tool in this goal.

During our early years in Ukraine, we had tried to work with Igor, the pastor in Feodosia. When we saw he did not share our goals, we decided to focus our efforts elsewhere. Nevertheless, we cringed to hear of ways he misused power and undermined those who showed initiative or potential for ministry. We wondered why the church council did not take steps to remove him.

We finally accepted that church government often reflects the values of a culture. Americans, who believe in equality and democracy, can quickly discard a pastor based on trifles. The culture of Ukraine had more respect for a position of authority, whether that person was a good leader or not.

One council member told Cory, "Even though Saul was a bad king, David did nothing to bring down the Lord's anointed." Like David, they simply learned to dodge spears.

We could do nothing but pray for repentance or for fulfillment of the proverb: "If a man digs a pit, he will fall into it; if a man rolls a stone, it will roll back on him" (Proverbs 26:27).

In spite of what we thought was bad leadership, some people continued to come to Christ in that church. It showed how God's Word is powerful, and God can work even through imperfect institutions.

Some instances of financial misappropriation came to light. When urged to repent, Igor resigned instead. He tried to take as many people as he could with him and start a new church, claiming to be the innocent victim of spiteful council members.

Many in the church urged Stefan to take on the role as pastor, but he claimed he was not qualified. He said he had other responsibilities with the Training Center and as pastor of a village church. A man who went through our training program agreed to step in as the primary preacher.

When I visited Stefan's wife, Nadia, she fussed, "And this happened right before Easter, when we should be celebrating."

I reminded her, "At Easter we remember that Jesus came to a sinful world to give us hope."

Stefan came home briefly during my visit, looking exhausted. He and another council member had been searching for church documents, many of which were missing. As a deacon, it fell on him to sort out the mess.

Like they did at Christmas, Sasha and Alina visited Feodosia's neediest families around Easter. With a baby now, Alina asked if I might take her place one day. "Sasha will do all the talking," she said. "Dave offered to drive, but it would be good to have a woman along since people might be afraid to open the door for two men they don't know."

As we visited homes with bags of food, Bibles, and gifts for children, Sasha asked the residents, "Do you celebrate Easter?"

One man replied, "Like everyone," and flicked the side of his throat with the back of his finger, the sign for drinking alcohol or getting drunk. A woman said she took eggs to the church to get them blessed.

Sasha explained how Jesus came, died, and rose again so we can have hope of eternal life.

At one run-down home, an old woman in smelly, ragged clothes worked in her trashy yard. Her small grandson looked eager to get gifts for Easter, but Grandma wanted more information first: "Who are you, and what is this about?" When she learned that Sasha came from the church and did not expect anything in return, she became friendlier.

"Oh, yes," she said. "I believe in God. I go to the church to light candles." She told stories of God's protection during World War II. Bombs exploded all around, but she remained safe. When the Germans took over Feodosia, they rounded up the Jews for execution. They tried to take her as well, but she agreed to be baptized again to show she was not a Jew.

We took time off from homeschool for Victory Day, which marked Nazi surrender on May 9 and the end of the Great Patriotic War, as they called it in Ukraine. The music school had asked Janelle, Alicia, and the other students to play in a concert honoring veterans of World War II.

I invited Anya to go along. Since she no longer came to our house to give Russian lessons, I saw her less often. She clapped enthusiastically when Janelle and Alicia played, and she wiped her eyes during a song that compared wild poppies to drops of blood on the battlefield. The music school director gave a patriotic speech, telling how the Russian troops preserved Russian music for Russian people to enjoy today. She did not mention that two Americans played in her concert.

As I walked Anya home afterward, she reported, "Everything is better now at the Feodosia church since Igor left." I knew the church council had extra problems to solve, but she thought the atmosphere had improved—not so repressive. She said that different young men had begun to preach, and some members who left with Igor had returned.

In preparation for summer outreaches to children, June visited churches she had previously helped with craft supplies, funds, and sports equipment. Besides hearing their plans, she wanted to see if or how she could assist them further.

She worked with many of the same leaders who had gone through our training program, so I enjoyed hearing her perspective on their ministries.

Sergei led the church in Nizhnigorski, which had started more daughter churches than any other congregation in Crimea. Over lunch, Sergei told June about their ministry to children and youth. They now held groups for children in eight villages. He had a list with the names of 300 children and youth who had attended Sunday school, day camps, hikes, or outreaches for youth. With 3,000 kids living in that region, it meant they had ministered to ten percent of them.

His biggest prayer request was for workers for the harvest field. Many youth moved away from the village to the city for college or work and never came back. In that way, the church lost their investment in those who could help as leaders. Instead of fretting over the loss, Sergei said, "These youth can spread Christianity elsewhere. Our responsibility is to continue to do what we can here."

God partially answered his prayer for workers through Dave and Annette Dryden. Nine months had passed since they moved to Ukraine. They settled first in Feodosia to work on learning Russian while exploring options for long-term ministry.

The owner of the apartment they rented in Feodosia said they had to be out by May 31, since he could make more money from summer tourists. Where would they move next?

Dave and Annette had already met with leaders of the Nizhnigorski church and felt good about possibilities in that region. They had found a house and bought it, but could not move in until after major repairs.

With the May 31 deadline looming, they began packing their belongings. A family in the Nizhnigorski church offered to let them stay with them. It would be crowded, but Dave and Annette hoped something more suitable would soon become available.

Arriving in Nizhnigorski, they learned that a young family in the church planned to relocate to Simferopol. Three days later, Dave and Annette moved into the apartment they vacated. God provided.

One Sunday morning a Ukrainian friend told me of some challenging events in her life. I expressed sympathy, but she replied without a hint of self-pity, "The Lord gives strength."

I heard this expression often in Ukraine. Instead of saying, "Where there's a will, there's a way," Ukrainian Christians often acknowledged their dependence on God. I soaked in the good reminder. When I lean on my own strength, I fear or resent that which drains it.

Another two years in Ukraine had passed, and I began packing for another furlough in the U.S. I thought of her words often that week. Would I get everything done before time to leave? The Lord gives strength. I dreaded the long trip, but the Lord gives strength. When I woke up too early before getting a full night's sleep, the Lord gave strength.

I reviewed our summer plans with Janelle and Alicia. This time, we would not have our own place until early September. Alicia asked, "You mean we are going to live like leeches for the next two months?"

Umm. Something like that. Or else it was a fulfillment of Jesus' promise: When you leave house and family, He gives back to you many more.

Needy families received gifts for Easter.

42

When Is it Time to Leave?

July 2008 – March 2009

Instead of living like leeches, Alicia and Janelle found ways to contribute. They helped cousins pluck chickens and buck hay. They helped grandparents re-roof their house. They attended a music camp and hung out with other missionary kids at a furlough retreat. They learned to drive and took classes at the local community college, getting dual credit toward high school and college.

A good friend, pastor at a large supporting church, asked Cory, "How will you know when it's time to leave Ukraine?"

We had never planned to live there forever. From the beginning Cory had said, "Our goal is to work ourselves out of a job."

When does that happen? Not everyone knew Christ, and many towns and villages still had no church. Jesus did not solve all earth's problems before He returned to heaven, but He could still say, "I have finished the work you gave me to do."

Cory had wanted to train leaders for ministry. He worked as part of a team, not holding veto power or claiming right to the last word. Instead of recruiting them to help him reach his goals, he tried to help them reach theirs. As a result, it was their ministry, not his. By this time, Cory taught fewer hours as they carried most of the load. He hoped the Efas Center's use as a hotel during the summer would provide a local source of income for ministry.

We talked to other missionaries who wished they could have been near enough to help their kids with the transition from life overseas to college. With Janelle soon to finish high school, we put that into the timeline.

As we discussed this with friends, one of them prayed afterward, "Thank You, Lord, that You don't need the Lemkes in Ukraine." Yes, it was God's ministry, not ours. We returned to Ukraine in February, wanting to use the next year well in preparing the Training Center leaders for our departure.

We had lived in Ukraine long enough to know that few people talked about major moves in advance. Many waited until one or two weeks prior to moving before they told anyone.

Someone explained this was rooted in the superstition that if you talked about hopes, plans, or expectations in advance, bad spirits would hinder, and it would not turn out well. Under Soviet rule, an atmosphere of suspicion and jealousy reinforced this notion. Those who thought you were getting ahead pulled you back down, so your final state was even worse than before.

Cory believed, however, it was important to help the Training Center leaders work through issues related to our departure. Soon after we returned to Ukraine, he told Andre and Stefan of our plan. He waited a little longer to tell the others on the leadership team.

Even though the team believed in the vision and already carried much of the ministry load, our presence and the financial support of churches provided a safety net. What would happen when this was taken away?

The recent economic crisis in the U.S. and other countries severely affected Ukraine. Foreign investors pulled their funds, factories cut production as demand for exports fell, and most building projects came to a halt, with workers sent away unpaid. During Ukraine's economic boom, many people bought apartments and cars on credit and now could not pay off loans. With higher unemployment throughout the region, could the Efas Center still provide a local source of income? We could only move forward with ministry and trust God to provide.

Training Center leaders had hoped to expand their influence beyond Crimea. Little came of their offer to teach in other parts of Ukraine, but church leaders in Belarus, a country north of Ukraine, asked them to come.

The invitation came about through a surprising source—the legalistic pastor who preached against modern music and earrings during his summer visit to Primorski. Right before we left on furlough, he met with Cory to quiz him on the Training Center. Someone had told him they taught heresy.

We had heard this accusation before. It typically came from those who believed any focus on God's grace would lead to increased sin. Cory gave him a booklet put together by the Training Center leaders, which outlined who Jesus is and why He came. Our salvation is based on what Jesus did for us, not on what we do to try to please God.

He read it and asked Cory, "This is what you teach?"

"Yes."

"There is nothing heretical here at all. It's based on Scripture." He thought the church in Belarus needed to hear it and invited the Training Center leaders to come and lead a seminar. They went twice while we were gone.

Two of our parakeets died while we were gone. Maggie survived. She had once been June's parakeet, but we adopted her. When I went to get Maggie to bring her home, Anya spoke so fondly of her, I said she could keep her.

Soon afterward, Anya told me she gave Maggie away. "This family really wanted a parakeet," she said. I regretted the huge misunderstanding. Anya did not want her after all.

Our apartment seemed too quiet. We missed hearing the patter of tappy-toes and a chirped greeting when we came home. I tried to be happy for the new family but felt sad for my own. For that matter, I felt badly for Maggie. She was not used to noisy little kids poking fingers in her cage.

I decided to buy the family another parakeet and go rescue Maggie. I told Anya, "It would be better for the family and the bird if they had a young parakeet, so they could get used to each other from the beginning."

She called the family to explain the misunderstanding, and I went to get Maggie. When I delivered the new bird, the mother said, "That's just what my son wanted, a blue male." Since they could not afford one, they had been willing to settle for a green female.

I replied, "See how God loves you and answers prayers!"

Maggie seemed thrilled to be home again. She sang and sang and sat on Janelle's shoulder, grooming her neck. She perched on each of us and then flew to the windowsill, where she remembered her cage should be. The girls did not get much schoolwork done that afternoon, as Maggie chirped her "Come back!" call if left alone. She wanted to sit on someone, like a clingy child who had been left with strangers.

Rescued and redeemed, she was grateful. Her affection lasted a while, anyway. After a couple weeks, she again grew aloof. Christians can be like that too. Another paid the price for our ransom. Forgetting that early joy, we take our rescue for granted.

Cory took me to visit Salim and Alma, the Christian Tatar couple. They had moved to a different village, which provided nearby schooling for the children and got them out of the mud.

When we arrived around 11:00 a.m., Salim had just returned home after his 24-hour shift as a watchman at a plant nursery. He walked to work—one and a half hours each way—but said, "It is pleasant to hike through the forest." He looked tired but glad to see us.

I gave Alma the cake and cheese I brought and joined Salim's tour of the yard. He showed us their rabbits, goats, and garden plot. They had built a new outhouse and put a new roof on their house, but much more work remained.

Salim talked about the young church he led in the village. During the summer he held services outside in his yard. One neighbor would not come but lay on a mattress on the other side of the fence listening to the service. The neighbor kids stood, peeking over the fence.

Salim ushered us inside their home. It was not much warmer inside than out, so I left my coat on. While helping Alma set food on the table, I saw no sink in the kitchen, just buckets of water. Alma later told me, "I can't imagine how anyone could have lived in this house. It was in terrible condition. But we can always fix a house—we can't create a forest."

The children liked living near the woods, and Salim's health had improved there. Alma said that her Muslim parents used to tell her they wished she would leave since she had shamed the family by becoming a Christian. Now that she had moved, her mother complained she had no one nearby to talk to.

After we prayed and sat down, Alma hurried back to the kitchen. Salim said, "I heard Americans like to serve themselves. Is that true?" Cory and I agreed. We tore off chunks of fried bread, took cabbage salad, and dipped into the mashed potatoes, garnished with meat, fried carrots, and onions.

Alma came back with a plate of bread and scolded Salim: "What are you doing sitting there like a guest? Serve them!"

Looking a little sheepish, Salim said, "They told me Americans like to serve themselves." Alma looked at us with raised eyebrows. We nodded.

"What if they are shy?" she asked.

"Americans are never shy about food," I said. Unlike those who grow up where food is scarce, it doesn't occur to them that a polite guest eats less than he really wants, which requires a good host to heap on the food.

Cory told of a Ukrainian visitor to America. When food was passed, he declined. They did not offer him food again, so he went hungry. He learned the hard way to take what he wanted since no one would put food on his plate. Alma shook her head, amazed.

We ate our fill and then some. She urged us to take more. We declined. Twenty minutes later, she urged us again. We refused. She hopped up, "Oh, the potatoes are almost gone." She grabbed the half-full platter and came back with more. She offered a couple more times and finally suggested tea. We were ready for tea. From the time we began eating until the final cup of tea, over three hours passed. It passed quickly, though, with lively conversation.

Salim said that at work the other employees swore a lot, even the women—but they stopped cussing when he was around. Though he never said anything against it, they knew he was a Christian, and he did not talk that way. Once when he started to speak about his faith to a coworker, the fellow cut him off, saying, "You have your religion; I have mine."

Salim replied, "What is your faith? Communism? No matter what you believe in—Communism, Buddhism, Islam, or anything else—everyone will die one day and will have to stand before God's judgment seat. Will you be ready?"

"What do I need to do to get ready?"

"The fact is, everyone has sinned. Have you sinned too?"

The man nodded. Salim explained how Jesus died on the cross to take our punishment and provide a way for forgiveness of sin. The man kept asking questions. "So what do I need to do?"

"Believe in Him. Give your life to Him."

Tears came to the man's eyes as he listened, but he was not ready to make any decision. He finally said, "This conversation has made me tired. I want to go and rest."

Salim told of a recent visit to a relative who drank, smoked, and treated his wife badly. The relative rebuked Salim for leaving Islam. Salim replied, "A true Muslim submits to God. Are you submitted? I follow God's will more than you do."

Another man listening agreed with Salim's verdict. He said he had read the Old Testament and wanted to learn more.

As we prepared to leave, Salim and Alma urged us to come again when it was warmer, to gather mushrooms, hike in the forest, or swim in the lake. "Come and spend the night," Alma said. "The only time we rest is when we have guests, so come and give us a vacation."

The visit gave me renewed appreciation for our warm apartment, running water, an indoor toilet, a washing machine, hot water, and other conveniences Alma lived without. Their house was so cold, it took me a long time to warm up after I got home. Since Cory had installed our own heating system, I forgot how to dress properly for the cold.

Internet service usually cooperated for the distance-education classes Janelle and Alicia now took. We had cable service, a big improvement over the dial-up connection we once used. Still, it occasionally went out for several hours at a time. Fortunately, their teachers forgave a few missed deadlines due to no service.

Their friend Masha now attended college in Simferopol. She sometimes came home on weekends and often called to chat and get help with her English lessons. "What does it mean to 'shoot baskets?'" she asked. She found "shoot" in the dictionary, but why would you shoot a basket?

Janelle and Alicia did not go to church every day, but sometimes it seemed like it. With choir practice for adults and youth, prayer meeting, youth group, and visits to the elderly, they kept busy.

One Saturday they joined a work party at the church with the other youth. When a woman brought groceries for lunch, she handed a bag to Janelle and Alicia with frozen chicken legs and dry noodles in it. Alicia called me to ask, "What are we supposed to do with them? There aren't any other girls here, and we can't ask the guys, because they think girls should know how to cook."

I gave instructions with a grin since they resisted touching raw meat at home. The meal turned out fine, they told me later, even if some impatient boys kept checking to see when lunch would be ready.

Girls in the youth group threw a party for the boys for Men's Day, and the guys returned the favor on the day honoring women. The boys prepared a three-course dinner followed by skits and funny original songs. I liked the way the boys as a group gave attention to the girls as a group, instead of trying to pair off. In that way, Ukraine had been a good place to raise teenage girls—at least we had a positive experience.

Janelle and Alicia used to complain that there weren't any sports in Ukraine for girls other than swimming in the summer. Boys, on the other hand, played soccer almost from the time they learned to walk.

After another Saturday work party, the guys got out a soccer ball and invited Janelle, Alicia, and Masha to play. Masha, who grew up as the only girl with four brothers, had soccer experience. Janelle and Alicia had not played much before, but the boys were patient.

Janelle said, "At first they put me as the goalie, and I stopped the ball a few times. But when one of the guys took my place, the other team scored right away."

The girls did have a little advantage: the guys roughly crashed into each other but avoided getting too close to the girls. They apologized profusely if they accidentally bumped into a girl or hit her with the ball.

Janelle said, "It's fun when I can steal the ball or block it, but it's embarrassing when guys on the other team cheer when I do something wrong, like pass the ball to them by mistake."

43

Live with Purpose

April – June 2009

Sasha and Alina's young congregation grew slowly. Besides holding services in Feodosia, Sasha led a Bible study in a neighboring village. That meeting sometimes lasted four hours with tea and fellowship after their discussion.

A leader with the ECB church in that village told Cory, "I visited Sasha's group and it seems fine, but what should I tell people when they say, 'How can one town have two churches?'"

Cory replied, "The town has more than one bread store. People like different kinds of bread. Sasha is reaching people who wouldn't otherwise go to church, so how can anyone forbid him or condemn him?"

Not long before Easter, I stopped by Sasha and Alina's young church toward the end of their meeting. We had children's books in our garage, and I wondered if they wanted them for their Easter outreach.

Sasha introduced me to the group and urged me to join them for tea and cookies. They finished their discussion and moved on to prayer requests. Alina told of a poor family they took groceries to that week. Their Easter outreach had already begun.

Sasha urged the congregation to use the season to share hope with others. "People are more open to talking about faith in God around Christmas and Easter," he said. Three women agreed to deliver bags with food and gifts to a few addresses in their region.

Sasha added, "If anyone wants to start a Bible study in your home, I am willing to lead it, or you can lead it. Some people will come to Christ because of what you say, not because of what I say." I was impressed by his humility and desire to equip others for service, instead of trying to do it all himself.

With no car and an eighteen-month-old child, it took time and dedication for Sasha and Alina to deliver food packets all over town. A non-Christian who wanted to help their cause occasionally drove them. When Cory played chauffeur, I went along to watch and pray.

They went to some homes they had visited before, but they had new addresses also. While Cory sat in the car with little Dasha, we hunted down one of these. Knocking on the window and door didn't raise anyone, so Sasha asked neighbors, an old man and his son. Both looked unsteady and smelled of alcohol. The son asked, "Who are you? And what do you want?"

"We're nobody special," Sasha replied. "We are bringing Easter greetings and produce to your neighbors." Before long he began explaining the background of Easter.

The fellow said, "I don't believe in God."

Sasha asked, "Did someone make your sweater?"

"Of course."

"Likewise, someone made this earth and everything in it."

The old man finally got someone to come to the door. The woman's voice sounded suspicious at first, but after Alina spoke, she opened it a crack and peeked out. She looked amazed but grateful for the bag of food. Her young son came up, and Alina directed her explanation of Easter to him.

"God made this world," she began. "He made the sun and the trees and the sky and all the animals. What else did God make?"

The little boy added to her list. "Dogs. People. Cats. Rocks."

"That's right," Alina said, "God made everything." She told how Adam and Eve sinned and asked him, "Have you ever done anything wrong?" He nodded. She told how Jesus died on the cross for our sins and rose again.

The mother said, "We saw a film about that on television this morning!"

"Do you know how to pray?" Alina asked the boy. The boy made the sign of the cross over his chest, as Orthodox believers do. Alina explained, "Prayer is when we talk to God with what's on our mind, the same way we talk to a good friend." She prayed, thanking God for His love and asked for His blessing on the family.

Sasha, meanwhile, had continued to talk with the men from next door. Before we left, the younger one said, "You have an interesting perspective. Maybe we can talk again."

One morning soon after Easter, we got up to no running water. It was inconvenient but not too unusual. I waited until 11:00 before calling the water department to report the outage. The woman sneered, "You don't have water? The whole city doesn't have water for three days."

She hung up, leaving me wondering if I had understood her correctly. I called Anya, who confirmed we would have no water for three days for the spring cleaning of the system. My heart sank. If I had known, I would have stored water. She apologized for not telling us beforehand.

Everyone who listened to the radio knew, but we did not listen to the radio. I tried to be grateful that in thirteen years, this was the first time no one warned us. I suppose it meant our friends now considered us locals, no longer needing a babysitter.

If we prepared ahead, we could easily weather the three-day shutoff, but we had not saved any water. "I guess I'll have to go get some," Cory said.

We had canisters with drinking water. On every trip to Simferopol, he stopped at a spring in the hills, about an hour away, and hauled the water up to our third-floor apartment. He could go to a nearby spring, where water was not as clean, but it still seemed like a lot of work.

"What about the water heater?" I asked. Cory successfully drained water from it. That, along with our drinking water, adequately met our need.

I saw a parallel to the Christian life. Some say, "Leave people alone and let them live how they want and believe what they want." I imagined that many will get to the end of life and wonder, *Why didn't anyone tell me? I would have done something different.* We had other options for water, but for them it will be too late.

For almost six months already, the Training Center had held a series of seminars for men and women in ministry. With as many as 170 coming, they divided into two groups. People from eastern Crimea came one weekend, and those from western Crimea the next.

The teachers recorded the lectures, put them on CDs, and gave them out. Church members had copied and recopied CDs from an earlier course, passing them around Crimea and into other parts of Ukraine. Some Christians said, "Why haven't I heard this before—that we are saved by God's grace? Our brothers say we must work for God's favor."

Not everyone approved of the Training Center's ministry. At one regional council meeting, a pastor tried to put Andre down while flipping through a booklet that outlined his teaching on the Gospel.

"You aren't teaching the full truth," the pastor said. "For example, you don't teach on repentance. You teach....oh, I guess you do teach on repentance. Well, whatever you teach, you say one thing and write another."

In April, Child Evangelism Fellowship began using the Efas Center for a three-month course for men and women from various countries of the former Soviet Union. A woman from the far eastern side of Russia rode the train for seven days to get to Crimea.

Their course fit well with the building's purpose—training for Christian workers—and the rent they paid helped Stefan buy extra furniture.

Although they brought in their own teachers most of time, they asked our leaders to teach some sessions. When Romon lectured on expositional Bible study and used Ephesians as his text—we were dead in our sins, but made alive through Jesus—someone commented later, "This emphasis on Jesus is lacking in our churches. We talk about many things, but not about Jesus. We don't preach the Gospel."

Andre believed the Training Center's most important role was to help believers know Christ better, not simply teach programs or methods of evangelism. He said, "Even the Apostle Paul said his chief desire was to know Christ. One might say, 'Didn't Paul already know Him?' Of course he did, but he wanted to know Jesus more. It is hard for Christians to tell other people what is so important or wonderful about Jesus if they don't know themselves."

Sunday was Janelle and Alicia's favorite day of the week; they stayed at the church from morning until evening. They usually rode the bus to Primorski, even if we drove, wanting to get there early to practice with the choir. The youth who taught afternoon Bible lessons for children stayed after the service and made something for lunch in the church kitchen. Janelle and Alicia learned to like buckwheat, as well as zucchini paste on bread or noodles.

At one Sunday evening youth meeting, Alicia got a turn to sit in the "hot seat." Some kids asked her innocent questions like, "What did you learn from your Bible reading this week?" and "What would you do if you were stuck in the middle of nowhere?" A few got more personal. "Have you ever been in love?" "What characteristics do you want in a husband?"

Alicia told me, "The hardest question was, 'If you could change one thing in each person, what would it be?' It's hard to tell everyone their faults tactfully, especially in front of others."

"She did a good job," Janelle said, "but some of the guys twisted her words. She told one boy, 'You should be less shy,' and another guy said, 'Yeah, she shouldn't have to make the first move!'"

They explained that the person in the hot seat often got questions inviting criticism, such as, "How do you think the youth group should be different?" Or "What would you change about me?" The youth believed constructive criticism was more useful than flattery.

Perhaps Ukrainians and Russians developed thicker skins since they often heard criticism by teachers and bossy old women. Complete strangers felt free to bring unsolicited correction.

Even Cory got an extreme makeover after he wore a denim shirt to get passport photos taken for our registration. When we picked up the photos an hour later, we were surprised to see Cory's head attached to the frame of someone wearing a white shirt and black tie. The bony shoulders did not fill out the shirt the way Cory does, but he now looked properly dressed.

We learned early not to sit on cement steps or walls. To do so brought immediate reproof. People believed the cement would cause one's internal organs to "catch a cold," resulting in sterility.

An old woman at church scolded Alicia for ten minutes for not dressing warmly enough. She said she was not careful when she was young, so she never had any children, and if Alicia wasn't careful, she would also end up lonely and alone. Alicia stood there and nodded, listening politely.

When Janelle told Masha she went swimming in May and stayed in the water twenty minutes, the phone went quiet. Janelle knew Masha thought the water was still too cold. Masha finally replied with great concern in her voice, "Why can't you understand? You must not do that! You won't be able to have children!"

Janelle insisted, "I don't believe it, and my parents don't either, and they don't care if I swim."

Masha tried to convince her and finally said, "Fine. Then I won't let my children play with your children."

Janelle and Alicia developed a close bond with the youth group from all the time they spent together serving, praying, and playing. This made it hard for them to consider leaving their friends and moving to America.

It helped to know that their cousin, Gary, planned to come for two months that summer to work in day camps. Janelle explained, "If he comes, we will have someone in America who understands what our life is like here." Kayla, a Bible college intern, also planned to come. The girls looked forward to serving as translators and guides.

Janelle and Alicia helped June sort craft supplies, which June gave to church planters for their summer outreaches to children. Since Cory wanted to visit the furthest recipients, Vadim and Sveta, he offered to take the box of supplies, June, and me.

After the church service and lunch, June showed Sveta and another woman her craft ideas. Meanwhile, Cory gave Vadim books to aid his outreach to adults. Sveta's mother showed me young geese in the yard and two newly hatched goslings, which slept in a shoebox with a heating pad.

Before we left, Vadim gave Cory several jars of preserves, a frozen chicken, and a large sack of fresh dill. Russians often added dill to salads and soups, but my family could never eat that much. The Efas Center could use it though.

We returned home late that afternoon, but we still wanted to wish Stefan "Happy Birthday." Most people gave a box of chocolates or a bouquet of flowers and said, "To your health."

Sometimes I baked him a carrot cake or zucchini bread. It was about the only way he would eat his vegetables. Other than potatoes, he avoided other garden produce, calling it all "grass." This time I had an even better gift.

Cory called Stefan. Since he was headed to the Efas Center to meet a new group coming, we caught a ride with him. As we neared the building, I asked, "How many years have you lived?"

"Fifty-three."

"We want you to live fifty more." I gave him the large bag of dill and added, "To your health!"

He laughed but not as hard as his wife and daughters, who were preparing dinner at the Center. Stefan chuckled again and said, "What have I done to you, that you want me to live in this trouble-filled world another fifty years?"

I also gave him a jar of cold milk and a bag of homemade chocolate-chip cookies, which he decided must be his real gift.

When our intern, Kayla, arrived, we enjoyed her spunky spirit and cheerful attitude. Before camps began, she studied Russian, worked at the Efas Center, and attended youth activities with Janelle and Alicia. She stayed with Stefan and Nadia's family.

To ease Nadia's mind about their guest, I told her, "Kayla is satisfied with everything. She's happy with her room, with the food, and with you."

Nadia thought this showed more about Kayla than about them. "Praise God," she said. "Some people find any reason to be dissatisfied."

Not long after she arrived, Cory left for France for a week of training in coaching for cross-cultural workers. He hoped to use it in helping leaders become more effective. I was glad he could go, but wondered when I would get an outing.

I once joked, or half-joked, "One thing that keeps me going back to Ukraine is that there are so many interesting countries nearby." We visited a few, but I still had a long list of places I wanted to go. We saw no good time to get away, and Cory thought we should save our money for expenses related to our return to the U.S.

I've heard it said that the husband is to lead, and so the wife should let him. Nevertheless, that did not stop me from searching for deals and studying interesting vacation spots using the Internet.

Then I heard a recorded sermon referring to a restless discontent that even Christians get. I had heard of a "God-shaped void" in non-Christians, which they try to fill with other things, but the preacher applied it to believers. They may try to satisfy the void with new experiences or stuff. They spend money, time, and emotional energy on things that bring temporary pleasure and sometimes have negative consequences. When walking in step with God, He fills that vacuum.

I read in 2 Corinthians: "We have as our ambition to be pleasing to Him." I realized most ambitions are tainted with the desire to please self. When Jesus came to earth, He came with a purpose. Maybe He saw the pyramids of Egypt when He was a child, but He did not come here to go sightseeing. As the time of His death drew near, He could say, "I have finished the work You gave me to do."

I wanted to live with purpose also. The Apostle Paul encouraged believers in 1 Corinthians 9:24 to run like they intended to win. If I am self-serving with my priorities, I become like a runner who has lost sight of the goal.

With Cory off doing something new, I decided to break my routine too. Without my morning walking partner, I went swimming instead. The summer's heat had already warmed the water to a comfortable seventy degrees. Ripples on the surface reflected colors of the sunrise. That early in the morning, the beaches were almost empty.

It was peaceful—except for the time two playful, stray dogs stole my skirt with house keys in the pocket. I was too far out to do anything about it. Maybe God sent them to add excitement to my life. A man on the beach rescued my skirt and chased the dogs away. I found my keys still in the pocket.

Cory came home pleased by his training in coaching, or the art of asking questions. Questions help others define and work toward goals. They can assist in conflict resolution and evangelism. Jesus asked many questions. Cory wanted to put into practice what he learned, starting with the leadership team, and planned to teach it to church planters.

Training at the Efas Center.

Puppet drama attracts children and their parents.

Outdoor Christian concert in a village.

44
Walk and Not Faint

June 2009

Janelle and Alicia came home later than usual one Sunday evening after youth group. They had finished early, but Slavik, a new-comer, had many questions afterward. "Is dancing a sin?" he asked.

"It depends on the effect," someone said.

He loved to break-dance and gave a demonstration.

"Was I sinning?" he asked.

"No," several replied.

Questions continued in rapid succession: "Why is drinking bad? If God is good, why is there so much suffering in the world, like all those children who got sick from Chernobyl? Why do people die before their time? What is the difference between your church and the Orthodox Church?"

Sometimes Slavik didn't even wait for a complete answer before throwing out another question. "I don't fully understand it," he said, "but I see that you do." He admitted his main motivation to seek God was fear of hell and said, "I don't have your kind of faith, but I want to."

Before they quit for the evening, the youth gave him a full explanation of who Jesus was, why He came, and how one could be saved. Alicia told me, "Those seminars with the Training Center really helped. The exciting thing was that even though he expressed doubt, he really wants answers. He didn't have a Bible, so the guys gave him one and told him to start with the New Testament."

Before our summer visitors, Kayla and Gary, began day camp for a week at the Feodosia church, I told them, "The first day is always hectic." That was an understatement. Seventy children showed up. Janelle and Alicia said it was the hardest camp they had ever worked in.

A five-year-old boy in Alicia's group bit other kids to get his own way. The woman who brought him said he didn't get good care or much food at home, and his dad was in prison. Others, especially some from the orphanage, also caused problems. Still, when I went on Friday for the closing program for parents, it looked like the kids had learned something. They sang songs with gusto and each age group presented part of the program.

At a village camp the next week, one little boy said a curse word when asked for his name, since that was what he was called at home. His frequent beatings left him addled in the brain. Few of those who came to camp wore clean clothes or showed any evidence of a caring home. Kayla said, "Even with several problem kids, I liked the camp anyway. It helped to understand a little about their backgrounds, to see why they act that way. Life is hell for many of the children, but they got a small taste of God's goodness."

We arranged for Kayla, Gary, Janelle, and Alicia to stay with Pavel and Vera and help with camp in their village. When we took them up, Vera kept mentioning a dear friend who lived next door.

I finally realized this was the same neighbor who once stole from their garden and tried to cause problems. Vera and the neighbor now talked so often and helped each other so much that Pavel installed a door in the wall. Kindness overcame animosity.

As we ate lunch, a man I had seen at church that morning sat silently at one end of the table. Vera told me later he lived with them now. He had needed a place to stay, but he loved to work and was a big help with the garden.

They had taken in other homeless men over the years. She and Pavel still mourned for Ruslan, a young man who became a Christian in prison and lived with them for over a year after he got out. Pavel thought of him as a son. He grew rapidly in his faith and became an effective evangelist.

I knew Ruslan. He went through our second course for church planters and married a sweet Christian gal. Then his twin brother got out of prison. Ruslan stopped coming to church and started drinking again. One day he and his brother rode with a drunk driver, and the car hit a woman. They all ran from the scene, never knowing if the woman lived or died. The brother feared being sent back to prison, and Ruslan disappeared too. After many months, he came to Pavel's church. He arrived late and left early but cried the whole time.

Weeks later he returned to the church and went forward to pray. When he bragged about how much money he had made dishonestly, Vera doubted his repentance was genuine. He stopped coming around, but reappeared now that he was running for office as the village head and wanted their votes.

"I am afraid for him," Vera said. "He says he wants to help the village, but there's a great temptation to use the position to pad his pockets, like all the others do. I hate this talk of politics. I would rather that he come and tell us what he is learning from reading the Bible."

She mentioned others who had lived with them. "No one who stayed with us is walking with the Lord now. I wonder if it's our fault." She blinked back tears, and her voice cracked. "And then there's our church—some people turn to Christ but later go back to the world. Is there something wrong with us?"

Their church had grown, but the losses still hurt. "God is perfect," I said, "but even Adam and Eve went their own way. People make choices."

As we peeled potatoes for supper, another man came by. Vera quickly heated some leftover borscht and set a bowl before him. She looked happy to see him, glad to feed him. She told me he was another who had lived with them and added, "I worry about him and his soul."

I asked, "You have let many people live with you, and you hurt for each one. Why do you continue to love, continue to receive people?"

"Because Jesus loves me, and He receives me even though I fall," she replied with tears. "It hurts when people go the way of the world, but I have to lean on God's Word. It says, 'As the rain comes down from heaven and doesn't return without watering the earth, so My word shall not return to Me empty without accomplishing what I desire.'"

At the end of the week, we returned to the village to get Janelle, Alicia, Kayla, and Gary. Pavel and Vera expressed appreciation for the team and their help. During their free time, they looked for ways to serve. They weeded the garden, sorted potatoes, and helped spin out honey from the bee hives.

"At first Vera wouldn't let us help," Kayla said. "I got bored, so I followed her around, asking for something to do until she finally gave in. I think she finally realized it made us happy to work. I woke up very early every morning because of that awful rooster. We ate him for lunch on the last day—it was the best meal of my life."

At camp, they helped with crafts, games, and skits. Several youth from the church led Bible lessons and songs. Janelle and Alicia said that almost every child in the village attended, about forty. Gary thought they were better behaved than city kids, more respectful. When they walked through the village in the evening, little girls joined them, holding their hands, while boys circled on their bicycles.

I usually went with Cory to church services in Primorski or wherever he was going, but I occasionally attended Sasha and Alina's young church plant in Feodosia. I liked the worship, led by Alina, and Sasha's simple-to-follow, but substance-filled sermons.

I visited again that Sunday. I enjoyed the friendly atmosphere, but wondered if Sasha and Alina felt disappointed that more people didn't come. I recalled my conversation with Vera just one week before. Instead of feeling proud of those who stayed, she and Pavel mourned for those who left. I prayed God would help Sasha and Alina persevere.

I remembered what David Giles, our supervisor with CMF, once told us. "Most of mission work is not mounting up on wings as eagles," he said, referring to Isaiah 40. "Nor is it running and not being weary. If you can walk and not faint, even that is a great accomplishment."

After a one-hour service, they broke for tea and discussion, and the children left for Sunday school. Alina set little Dasha in her stroller and began pushing her up and down the hall to help her fall asleep. I joined them and passed on David's words.

"Thank you," she said, "I needed to hear that. I'd like to see more growth in numbers, but we are growing in maturity."

When a team came several weeks later to help Sasha with evangelism in a park, they seemed disappointed so few people attended the follow-up meeting. One team member said, "I expected to see more results."

Sasha said, "If you are obedient to God, there will always be results, even if you don't see them."

I joined Cory on his next road trip to visit several people. First, we went to see Hasad and Elena, the former Muslim with a Russian wife. By now they had lived in Crimea for two years. While Cory talked to Hasad in the living room, I sat with Elena in the kitchen.

"The kids love it here now," she said, "and they don't want to leave."

"Are you seeing any progress with your Muslim neighbors?" I asked.

"They are friendly toward us," she replied. "We visit in their homes, and they come to ours. They like our children. Many agree with what we say about Jesus, but they aren't ready to follow Him. It took many years before Hasad was ready, and it was the same for his mother. What they saw in the lives of Christians, over time, made a difference."

"How did his mother come to Christ?" I asked.

Elena reviewed parts of the story I had heard before. Hasad's Muslim mother at first disapproved of his church attendance, but after his first wife died in childbirth, she gave him permission to pursue Christianity. When her friends in Kazakhstan told her, "Hasad needs to come back here to find a good Muslim girl," she told them, "Elena is the one for him."

After Hasad and Elena married, his mother lived with them for several years. She saw the difference Christ made in their home, began attending church with them, and eventually got baptized, sealing her decision to follow Christ.

Elena said, "Now she is more supportive of us being missionaries than my own mother, who has been a Christian many years. His mother understands commitment must follow faith, even if it requires separation and sacrifice."

Hasad was starting to see response to his efforts. A young Tatar couple he often met with had recently accepted Christ. The wife's sister also became a Christian.

Next, we stopped to see Salim and Alma in their village near the forest. After we pulled up, Salim urged us to stay long enough to eat with them. Since they were holding a day camp that week, boards set on blocks made crude benches in a covered area in their driveway. Their two teenage sons helped with games, and the six-year-old proudly passed out candy. Two young women from another village led the lessons.

Over dinner I heard about Salim's conversation with the Muslim leader in the village. The leader said that by leading a holy life, he could look forward to having many women in paradise. Salim asked him, "Are there not enough women on earth? If Allah wants you to live a holy life, why would he give that kind of temptation as a reward?" Salim explained Jesus' version of Paradise: no marriage or giving in marriage, for we will be like the angels.

We thanked God for Salim's witness and prayed for his neighbors. We never expected the news we received two weeks later: Salim had broken his arm in three places, simply by throwing a rock. Doctors at the hospital said they could not set it since the bone was too soft. One test showed cancer cells, so they began giving him radiation treatments.

When Cory went to visit him, Salim said, "I told the family that if God is done with me on earth, I am ready to go. God will take care of them, day by day, just as He always has."

I could not imagine his family was ready to release him, especially now that his wife was expecting. One doctor suggested operating on the arm to set the bone, but another advised against it, saying the operation may not help and the risk of infection was too high. They put his arm in a sling and gave him pain pills. Cory gave him calcium tablets, hoping that would help.

With summer camps now over, Janelle and Alicia turned their attention to preparing for two weddings. Not only would the youth group sing for the ceremony, they were in charge of entertainment during the lengthy banquet. They practiced songs and funny skits.

I looked forward to Katya's wedding in Batalnaya. She had waited a long time for her fiancé to set a date. Part of the problem was they wanted to live separate from family but didn't know where. The groom's mother did not even attend the wedding; she was home, drunk. Katya's parents came, but her home life was not much better, other than a brief period after God healed her mother's leg.

They had been sweethearts for many years, even in high school ten years earlier. When Pastor Piotr stood to congratulate them at the wedding dinner, he joked, "I have just one thing to say: 'It is finished.'"

They still had not found a place to live, but with the summer tourist season winding down, they hoped to soon find an apartment to rent in

Feodosia. Until then, they planned to simply return to their own homes—their parents' homes—after the wedding.

Stefan invited them to spend a week at the Efas Center instead. "I hope that was okay," he told Cory and Andre. Of course it was okay. Katya faithfully served in the church and had worked at the Efas Center, cleaning rooms. News of the gift made her cry. The groom blinked back tears too.

When I saw them two weeks later, Katya happily reported that they had found an apartment and had a wonderful honeymoon. God provides, even for those who don't have everything figured out in advance.

Our family experienced God's faithfulness.

45
Answered Prayers

September - October 2009

Earlier that summer, Cory and Stefan had wondered if the Efas Center would get enough business during the tourist season to help the ministry budget much. It looked as if it would be a bad year for tourism. Most who vacationed in Crimea came during July and August, but few had made reservations to stay at the Efas Center, and others were canceling reservations they had made. They said other places were cheaper. In the wake of the economic crisis, people had less money to spend.

Still, Cory did not think Stefan should lower their rates, saying, "We have better conditions than most of those other places." That became obvious when water rationing began for the village. The Efas Center had a huge water tank and a well. People began moving out of other guest houses to stay at the Efas Center. Before long all the rooms were full.

This income would help toward ministry expenses, but it still would not cover typical costs for the year. Since we planned to leave in the spring, Cory tried to prepare the Training Center leaders for independence. When he discussed financial decisions with them, one of them said, "This is a lot more complicated than a family budget."

Another added, "We have taken Cory's role for granted. We'd say, 'Cory, we need money for this,' and somehow he would find it."

One leader pointed out that the ministry had already showed it could adapt to change. With the increased cost of living, they no longer gave stipends. To work around the schedules of those with jobs, the Training Center now held shorter courses on weekends. They held some courses for people in ministry and some to strengthen believers in their faith and ability to share the Gospel. Instead of focusing on men exclusively, they now included women.

Although many churches now sent their members for training, not everyone liked the program. One pastor sent a letter to church leaders throughout Crimea and other parts of Ukraine saying Andre was teaching heresy. Some saw the accusation as a power play without basis in fact. Others didn't know what to think.

The Crimean church council met with Andre and the pastor. Andre said, "If you show me my error, based on Scripture, I will repent." The pastor could not do that but continued to spread his claim.

During one of the training sessions at the Efas Center, I got the chance to talk to Romon, one of the teachers. With no more lectures to give that day, he had time to reflect on his ministry.

Romon had become the primary leader of the small Sudak church when he was only twenty. After Andre left him in charge, he began to hear criticism from someone in the church. He never expected it, and it shook him to the core.

"I was idealistic," he said. "I was still a new Christian myself. I realized the perfection I looked for in the church was not there. Through this I learned I must stay in God's love and seek approval from Him. Only then can I love others the way He does. By abiding in Him we produce fruit."

He compared the Christian to a fruit-bearing tree. "The tree does not bear fruit for itself to enjoy. It bears fruit for others. People with walnut trees hit the branches; so not only is the tree producing fruit for others, it gets beat on. The fruit falls off and breaks. You learn to be longsuffering when you have reason to practice it."

He spent time with young men in the church, mentoring them and preparing them for service. They evangelized in several villages and began Bible study groups there. The young men began well, but three of them left the church. Romon said, "It is one thing to strategize and plan, and another to have the strength to accomplish it."

He compared it to a board game: "You try to make it to the end and occasionally get sent back three steps. You get almost to the finish line and draw a card that sends you back to Start. So you start again, only to draw the same card before you get to the end. Sometimes I wonder if it's something I am doing wrong. I spent many hours with these guys. They ate with us. Some of them lived with us."

I recalled Vera's similar words and asked him, "How does God encourage you? What advice would you give someone else in this situation?"

"All you can do is raise the flag again and keep moving forward. The story isn't over yet. Keep going and pray, so you don't lose heart. Not long ago we celebrated the eighth anniversary of the church, and I put together a slide show showing some of our history. I saw how some had left and others died, but new people came. The church continues to grow. We invest in the youth, and sometimes I think it is all in vain, but they mature and start to take on responsibility."

The church now had 73 members, down from the peak of 81, but a significant increase over the 15 when he first joined. It didn't seem to me as though they had gone back to start in this board game at all.

"No," he said, "but it seems like it sometimes. One man told me: 'It's your fault I left. You never gave me the attention I needed.' I know I'm not perfect and told him, 'I am ready to change and become better. Are you also willing?' He didn't respond. I need to keep loving him like Christ does and not let bitterness grow in my heart."

His struggles reminded me of our experience. "The Training Center has also had its ups and downs," I said. "How do you see this ministry?"

Romon shook his head. "Oh, I don't see it that way at all. I think it keeps going and growing the way it should. Sure, there have been problems, like this recent accusation of heresy, but it never bothered me. To me, it is like a little dog yapping at the feet of an elephant. The dog might even try to bite the elephant, but the elephant pays no attention and keeps on going. I'm not saying the Training Center is the elephant, but this vision, this ministry is from God, and it will keep going. We have this accusation of heresy, but God can use that for good too. Before, people in other parts of Ukraine didn't pay any attention to us, but now they are reading our material."

I wasn't convinced. "I used to hear a lot of talk about trying to start a group in each of the 1,000 towns and villages in Crimea that don't have a church. I don't hear that anymore. Maybe it's because I'm not around much, or it isn't a new goal."

"The goal has not changed," he replied. "The goal is the same, but we see we need to go about it in a different way. It does no good to start churches if the people starting them don't understand the basics of the Gospel, if they don't understand God's grace but simply promote traditions."

I nodded. That made sense to me.

Romon continued, "The Training Center fills an important role. It gives spiritual food and prepares Christians for ministry. The methods we once used for evangelism don't work anymore. Nonbelievers aren't interested in coming to big meetings or a lending library. We need believers who understand the Gospel and live it and share it with others. Our goal has not changed. It's like when you are hiking and expect to reach your goal around the next bend but discover you have another hill to climb. The path may be longer than we thought, but we continue toward the goal."

When Cory learned that seventy planned to come from Belarus for a ten-day seminar, he protested. He had imagined a much smaller number, like fifteen. He understood the stress on the kitchen crew, not to mention our finances. He wondered how many of them were coming for the teaching, or if they simply wanted a free vacation by the Black Sea.

Andre had already told them there would be no charge, and he didn't think he could change that now. "Besides," he said, "God might touch and use someone who comes, who might otherwise be left out if we set a limit or charged for the seminar." He first became interested in church planting through a similar conference.

The course put a dent in our budget, but not more than if we trained a similar number of people from Crimea, using many shorter sessions. It also fulfilled a goal of providing training for other countries of the former Soviet Union.

I visited the Efas Center one morning to see how it was going. During a break, I talked to a pastor with a congregation of 400 members. He said, "When I heard about the conference, I didn't know what to expect, other than it was near the Black Sea, and I had never been to the sea before. I thought my wife could come for vacation while I attended classes. The sessions are better than I expected. I really liked Andre's series on life in the Spirit. It answered questions I had about what it means to abide in Christ to produce fruit. I want to teach this material when I go back. My church needs to hear this."

As the lecture began again, I watched him take detailed notes. Others in the room also looked attentive, even into the fourth hour of teaching that morning. Cory announced right before lunch that they would give out copies of the whole seminar on CD. I heard a clamor, "Can I have one? Can I have one?" Cory said they would give one copy to each of the fifteen churches represented.

Over half of those who went through the two-year church planters' course continued in ministry. Cory and I visited one of them, Iosif, who became pastor of his home church when the former pastor retired. He used his position to develop leaders and encourage outreach. He told me, "I blame Cory and the Training Center for that. I caught the virus." His church worked in five villages in that region.

Iosif spent much time with children and youth and often held hikes for them in the hills nearby. He drove an old Lada, a small, boxy Russian car, and said he once got twenty kids in it for a short drive to an ancient cave town for a hike. Not all of them actually fit in the car, since three rode on the roof and several filled the trunk.

We saw Vitya again. He continued to hold Bible studies for adults and lessons for children in the home of Nina, the former alcoholic. He began a computer club as a way to develop relationships with youth. Town officials liked the idea and let him use the village hall, even though he tacked on a Bible lesson at the end.

They would not allow him to show Christian movies inside the hall, but they let him use the electric outlet and project films on the wall outside. His movie nights became a popular event, held every Saturday evening. After several men started asking him spiritual questions, he began holding a separate meeting for men, hoping to counteract the idea that religion was for old women and children.

He told me, "The Training Center expanded my vision. I was interested in evangelism, but they said it is not good enough to bring someone to Christ if that person had no place for fellowship. We must plant churches." He lifted his hands up and formed a small circle with his fingers. "My vision used to be like this, but the Training Center made it like this." He swept his arms wide. "Suddenly, I wanted to know everything, and they taught us all we needed to know. How to evangelize. How to start a small group and lead it. How to overcome discouragement. They helped us understand the Gospel and grow spiritually. Whenever I can, I teach these things to others."

He supported his family as an electrician and struggled to give enough attention to them, to new Christians and to nonbelievers, also. Still, he said, "The Training Center gave me a push in the right direction. It was such a good push, I will keep serving God until the day I die."

Some weeks later we learned that Nina, a key convert in the village, had stomach cancer. Three operations did not help. She prayed her funeral would be a witness for others in her village. She wanted those trapped in alcohol and drug addiction to find the same freedom she had.

Vitya wrote to Cory, "The whole village watched as believers came to visit and help this suffering sister. Nina died, and many people in the village came to the funeral. They heard they could also turn to the God of love who had changed Nina's life into something good. After the funeral, several people came to the next Bible study. They asked, 'How do I believe in Jesus Christ?' 'How do I follow Him?' The Lord is answering Nina's prayers even now."

While looking through old photos of camp, Alicia recognized a much younger version of Slavik, the break-dancing rapper who occasionally came to youth group and peppered them with questions. Janelle and Alicia sometimes saw him around town wearing hip-hop clothes and flanked by girls or guys.

He always called out cheerfully to the Christian youth and sometimes stopped to talk, even if his friends kept walking. Janelle commented, "He doesn't seem to be ashamed of his interest in church, even when he is around his friends."

One Sunday evening Slavik asked, "What is heaven like?"

Several gave their view, and Janelle added, "When you combine all the happiness you feel on earth, that's what heaven is like."

"Will there be discos and drinking in heaven? Those are the things that make me happy."

"No, heaven is even better."

"Well," he said, "I cannot imagine being happy without those things."

Masha replied, "Look at us—we don't do those things, and we are happy."

"Yes, but I don't understand you. Don't take this wrong, but you are strange."

One of the guys asked, "What is it about discos and drinking that makes you happy? In heaven, there will be the sense of camaraderie found at discos and the carefree feeling alcohol gives but without any negative side effects."

"But I love to dance. Is that wrong?"

"The problem with discos is not the dancing, but the lusting that takes place."

"Well, that's another topic. I like girls. What's wrong with sex before marriage...no, that's too heavy...is kissing a sin?"

The youth explained that if something was dangerous or harmful, instead of seeing how close to the edge you could get, it was better to try to stay far away. They believed it was better to save kissing for marriage.

Janelle and Alicia said that Slavik respected their youth leader, who used to be a lot like him. As a Christian, the leader was still smart, friendly, and enthusiastic. He liked to joke.

Knowing Janelle and Alicia planned to return to the U.S. to attend college, their leader told the youth group, "We don't have much time to get them married off, so they won't have to leave!" He occasionally embarrassed them and the boys by suggesting matches. He told Janelle and Alicia, "Make a list of all the boys you like, and we will get one of them for you. That way you can marry for love; it doesn't have to be a forced marriage."

Slavik did not come every Sunday, but he often brought more questions when he did. One evening he asked, "I believe God exists, but how do you know Christianity is the right way?"

In the discussion that followed, the youth gave reasonable support for Christianity. One said, "If God created us and gave us the Bible to reveal Himself and show us how to live, then we should listen and obey."

Another added, "If you don't believe what we say, ask God. God wants a relationship with you. The Bible says, 'You will find Me when you seek Me with all your heart.'"

Slavik listened and looked thoughtful. During the prayer time at the end of the meeting, he also prayed: "Thank You for showing me the truth. Help me believe it. Bless these youth and keep their faith in You strong."

Janelle and Alicia did not want to get their hopes up too much. They had seen others who seemed interested at first, but never followed through.

46

The Story Is Not Over Yet

November 2009 – March 2010

Our colleagues with Christian Missionary Fellowship in Ukraine lived in different parts of the country. The seven other missionaries also partnered with national Christians, but we got together once or twice a year for a team meeting. They came to the Efas Center in November for the last gathering we would host.

During our four-day retreat, each one gave an update on their personal lives and ministries. Jonathan and Heather Powell, who lived about five hours north of us, helped their host church with campus ministry, children's programs, church planting, and outreach to the deaf. Their church translated services into sign language and trained people from other congregations for this type of outreach.

June Johnson talked about her medical work and her help with camps for children and youth. She had multiplied herself by training Christian nurses in three places. One of them said she had shared the Gospel with eighty-nine bed-ridden cancer patients, and half of them gave their lives to Christ.

Dave and Annette Dryden had settled into their new house in Nizhnigorski. They were getting to know Tatar neighbors and learning their language. When a Tatar family invited them over for a meal, they took several books as a gift, portions of the Bible translated into Tatar.

Dustin and Karilyn Mullenix moved to Lviv in western Ukraine to work with college students. After learning Ukrainian, they started an English club that included a Bible study. Over thirty students attended, and most of them had never read the Bible before.

While the adults gave updates and discussed ministry issues, their children reveled in the "family reunion" atmosphere. Several local helpers watched seven little ones, mostly of preschool age. Janelle and Alicia occasionally came out in the evening, but stayed home most of the time to focus on their schoolwork.

Although Tim and Heather Miller no longer lived in Ukraine, we appreciated the couple they sent our way. Soon after this meeting, Sasha and Alina invited June, Cory, and me over for dinner. "We are celebrating a special day today," Alina said as we sat around their table. "We moved to Feodosia exactly three years ago today."

Sasha added, "Remember in Acts, how no one trusted Paul in the beginning, but Barnabas smoothed the way for him? You three were like Barnabas for us." June had let them stay at her apartment when she was on furlough. We recruited people to unload their furniture.

"I think Barnabas had an easier job than Paul," I said. "We had prayed a long time for someone to start a church here, and we are happy you came." They were talented and dedicated; people needed the hope they had.

I later asked, "You have worked hard to start a church here. Some of those you met with in the beginning don't come now. How has God encouraged you during the difficult times?"

Sasha replied, "Nothing has been wasted. God gave us the opportunity to minister to these people for a while. It is more important to have a healthy church than a large church. A healthy church will grow, and we have that."

June and Dr. Lidiya wanted to see Salim and his broken arm, so Cory offered to drive them. I wanted to go too and see Alma. When we arrived, it looked like Alma was preparing a banquet. Dr. Lidiya and June went in to meet with Salim. With Alma briefly distracted, I picked up her knife and continued cutting a big yellow squash into small pieces.

"I can do that," she said when she returned.

"And I can help," I insisted. She rolled out big sheets of dough and cut it into squares. She showed me how to wrap the squares around the squash and onion filling. We cut, wrapped, and talked.

With a due date in February, she was still adjusting to the idea. "I'm too old; I'm forty-one. There are so many other women who want children. Why me? I gave away all our baby things after the last one was born. He's six now. I never thought I would have more children. And now, there's Salim's health..."

She told of her recent visit to Pavel and Vera's home. Vera, too, had felt dismayed to be expecting at the age of forty-two. Now, however, her eleven-year-old daughter was a tremendous blessing and help. I was glad Alma could hear Vera's account of God's faithfulness.

I found Alma easy to like and appreciated her openness. Perhaps I was simply a safe outsider. She said, "I sure can't tell my mother any of this."

Her parents' recent visit was more difficult than usual. She did not elaborate, except to say, "They don't like our Christian faith."

Though their new house still needed repairs, it was good they had moved, for the sake of the family's health. Many people in their former village had died of cancer. Salim blamed the old rocket-fuel depot in the area. There he suffered from recurring heart problems, but soon felt better in the forest air of their new location.

During dinner Salim said, "They say I have cancer, but I have peace in my heart. I have never felt this close to God before. I wish I could do more for His kingdom though. I took my strength for granted when I was healthy."

He continued to talk to other Tatar about Christ when he could. He visited relatives who read a magazine published by Islamic radicals promoting hostility toward Israel and the West.

He told them, "We are descendents of Abraham, through Ishmael. He also had a son, Isaac. Do you think a father would want one son to kill the other?"

"Of course not."

"That's right. These other people may not believe like you do now, but if you kill them, they won't have a chance of believing. Do you think that would please God, the Creator of life?"

He read to them passages in the Koran that honored Jesus and promoted respect for "people of the Book." They had never heard these verses before and opened their Koran to see if it said the same. It did. Salim then read further explanation from the Bible.

On our drive home, Dr. Lidiya told us what she had learned by reviewing his medical records—in Ukraine, the patient kept his own file. When comparing his arm x-rays from just after the injury and three months later, it looked like no healing had taken place at all. The bones were not even lined up so they could heal.

I asked, "Can't you manually put the bones in place?"

"His bones are this thin," Lidiya said, holding up her little finger "They are so fragile that doing anything to try to set them could result in even worse breakage. The only thing that can be done is to operate and install a pin, but because of his cancer, that's not a good idea. Operating can make the cancer spread like dandelion seeds."

"They gave him radiation and chemotherapy," I replied. "Did he have any test afterward to see if it helped?"

"The test costs money. They did just enough testing to give him disability status. They believe once someone has cancer, it's terminal." She explained that they had found metastatic cells, cancerous cells that originated in another organ, but they could not find cancer anywhere else. He did not have other cancer symptoms, so she thought the cause might be spiritual. Some local Tatar had cursed him and now said his illness was a curse for leaving Islam.

At Dr. Lidiya's urging, the Feodosia church set aside a day to fast and pray for Salim. We did too. A couple of days later, Cory, Andre, and Stefan drove over to visit him and pray for him. Cory told me Salim now had color back in his fingers, which had been slightly gray, and he could move his fingers and wrist a little.

Three weeks later, we visited Salim and his small village church. I was not surprised when he extended his left arm to shake hands instead of his injured right. I was surprised, however, to see him holding a Bible in his bad arm, turning it over, lifting it up and down, and putting his hand in his pocket. All that movement was new. When I saw him a month earlier, he could barely move his fingers, and he kept his arm in a sling.

We went to their house for tea after the service, and I asked about his arm. "I went to the doctor the day before yesterday and got new x-rays," he said. "Let me show you." He first unrolled the x-ray taken right after he broke it and one taken three months later. They looked almost the same. The bone looked like a broken piece of wood with an obvious jagged splinter and gap. Dr. Lidiya had seen these x-rays. In the newest x-ray, the bone appeared almost solid, with obvious growth and no jagged splinter.

Even more convincing—his arm was stronger. He showed us his increased range of movement. He later said, "On the early x-rays there were black spots on the shoulder where the cancer was. On the new x-rays, those are hardly visible. I feel better, and I have my appetite back." He looked better too.

Cory continued meeting occasionally with others interested in outreach to the Tatar. One day an evangelist joined them who worked in Chechnya, a terrorist hot spot in Russia. This Chechen, a former Muslim, was shot in the back eighteen years earlier. In the hospital, he prayed, "God, if you let me live, I will serve you."

He heard a voice, "You will live, and you will serve."

He became a Christian. Though paralyzed from the waist down, he evangelized among Muslims in Chechnya. When entering a new area, he prayed God would bring to him those open to the Gospel and keep enemies away. He could usually stay just five or six days before word got out, and he had to flee. He owned a car and a wheelchair, and someone traveled with him to help him. He gave examples of narrow escapes, staying just a few steps ahead of those wanting to kill him. He said, "God always provides for my needs, but I don't even know how."

Using the example of Scripture, he looked for "a man of peace" to stay with in each new town. Cory described him as having a deep, booming voice.

"Why are they trying to kill him?" I asked.

"The Muslims call him an infidel. And the terrorists don't like him preaching the Gospel of peace."

Instead of sending shoebox Christmas gifts this year, a large Kansas church sent "blessing bags" and a team to help deliver them. Splitting up, some visited village churches to help with Christmas programs, and some went with Sasha and Alina for their Christmas outreach.

The room was packed for Sasha and Alina's Christmas service later that week. Though fewer came than promised, it was their largest turnout so far. Alina told me afterward, "God knows how much we can handle. He gave us the right number, according to our strength."

A month later the same church sent our friend Larry Wren and another pastor, Todd Carter. It seemed fitting, somehow, for Larry to visit as we prepared to leave Ukraine. When Cory first went to Feodosia on a one-week trip sixteen years earlier, he went with Larry. During our difficult early years, Cory sometimes wrote to Larry daily, and Larry sent back notes of encouragement. He came several times to see us and to teach. We valued his input.

On this visit, Larry and Todd taught a two-day seminar for forty men, mostly church planters. When the Training Center gave a banquet for us on the last day, we liked how Larry used it to honor the local leaders. "We praise God for what has taken place over the last fifteen years," he said, "but we know God will continue to use the Training Center and you as the leaders to equip people for ministry and the extension of His kingdom."

When Larry and Todd came to our house later, Larry told Cory, "You've done a good job here. The best thing you can do now is to get out of the way."

Cory replied, "They don't need me here now. I'm extra."

"The other guys on the leadership team don't think he's extra," I commented. "Stefan told me, 'If Cory doesn't feel needed, he can have my job.' Even Andre told the team, 'I can't imagine ministry here without Cory.'"

"I know that they can use me," Cory said, "but there is a difference between being busy and adding value. Yes, I could find ways to keep busy, but we have completed what we came to do. The vision won't fail when I leave, because the vision was never dependent on me."

"To me, it feels a bit like sending kids off to college," I said. "One needs a good amount of trust to step back from either kids or a ministry. Besides trusting them, we have to trust that God can guide, correct, and provide even better than we can. It helps to have co-workers who want to honor God with their decisions."

We talked about the future. Parents may step back when kids go off to college, but they don't usually drop out of the picture completely. Likewise, Cory planned to maintain contact and return in the fall for several weeks.

Our final month in Ukraine passed quickly. Since Stefan wanted to buy our apartment, we didn't have to move out before our departure, but we still had to sort and pack.

Cory met with the Training Center leaders to discuss budgets and ministry goals. One of the leaders said, "I am not as worried about our financial future as our spiritual future. If we are following God's will, He will meet our needs, just as He always has."

We took some final road trips. I wanted to see Alma's new baby. After three boys, she was thrilled to have a little girl. Salim's arm continued to improve.

He told us of a recent funeral in his village. When he arrived at the home of the deceased, most of the people gathered there were well on their way to getting drunk. He stood to the side and prayed the family would ask him to say something from the Bible. The son gave him that opportunity. Afterward, men picked up the casket and took it to the cemetery.

As they approached the open grave, they met an irate woman. Dirt from the new grave had been tossed on the grave of her sister. She brandished a shovel and told them, "If anyone tries to put that body in this grave, I will cut off your head with this. If you try to cross me, you and I will both be buried in this grave."

They argued with her for thirty minutes, but she would not budge. No one knew what to do. With the sun already down, there was no time to dig another grave. Salim finally approached the woman and asked, "You are a Christian?" She was Orthodox and agreed. Salim said, "You know, then, that the Lord's Prayer says to forgive those who have sinned against you."

Finally, she threw down her shovel. "Do what you want," she said and walked away.

Since Salim had broken the standoff, he now had another opportunity to talk about the hope we can have for forgiveness of sin and eternal life through Jesus. He told us, "The crowd grew even bigger when I started talking—to about sixty people. Many were crying before I finished, even the drunks. When I walk through the village now, people bow their heads and greet me with respect."

Mikhail and Yulia begged us to come one last time for a Sunday service in the former Mennonite village. As soon as we drove up, they gave us a bag with two frozen chickens, carrots, beets, and cabbage. "Put this in your car right now," Yulia commanded.

"We are leaving in two weeks," Cory protested.

They insisted. "You will have to eat during the next two weeks."

Mikhail and Yulia were the kind of people who always had their hands out—not to take, but to give and to serve. Yulia took a picture from the wall and gave it to us. "So you can remember me," she said.

How could I ever forget her?

Next, we attended Pavel's fifty-fifth birthday party. His wife, Vera, and several other women had spent hours preparing for the feast. About forty people came. When I told her, "You are brave," she said, "I'm used to it."

Before we left, she asked, "Will I see you again?"

I replied, "If not here, then in heaven."

I felt a little awkward when Pavel, Vera, and others got teary-eyed and said how much they would miss us. To some extent, I had to turn off my emotions to make it through the final weeks. On the one hand I felt, *we are not so special as to merit this.* On the other, we had prayed God would use us, and their affection affirmed He had answered our prayer.

Instead of thinking we had contributed anything wonderful, we felt honored to know and partner with godly men and women, humbled that we could participate in their ministry. Witnessing answers to prayer, we could not boast of great accomplishments; God worked in ways we could not. We had been given the opportunity to occupy a front-row seat with a grand view of God's work in that country.

As we prepared to leave Ukraine, we still had questions. What would happen to those who began well but stopped living for God? What about the pockets of opposition? Cory reminded me, "The story is not over yet."

For months we had wondered what we should do with Maggie, our parakeet. We hoped for a home where she would be wanted and treated well. We all felt good about leaving her with Leonid's family after Cory visited them and saw how well their children treated their parakeet.

Tamara, his wife, stayed up very late one night making a needlepoint picture of birds to give us in exchange. She said, "When we look at your bird, we will think of you and pray for you. When you look at these birds, you can pray for us."

I valued their prayers and understood why they wanted ours. Our Heavenly Father had sustained us. He would help them also.

Aren't two sparrows sold for only a penny?
But your Father knows when any one of them falls to the ground.
Even the hairs on your head are counted.
So don't be afraid!
You are worth much more than many sparrows.
Matthew 10:29-31 (CEV)

"The Lord Is Your Keeper."

Some of the men who continue on in ministry.

References

Esser, Shelly. "Essentials for the Stages of Life." *Just Between Us.* 2005
<http://www.justbetweenus.org/pages/page.asp?page_id=79157>.

The Fellowship of the Ring, Peter Jackson, Entertainment Films, 2001.

Finding Nemo, Andrew Stanton, Lee Unkrich; Walt Disney Pictures. 2003.

Gates, Doris. *Blue Willow*. New York: Viking Press, 1940.

Jesus (The Jesus Film). Peter Sykes, Warner Brothers, 1979.

Lewis, C.S. *The Lion, the Witch and the Wardrobe*. London: Geoffrey Bles, 1950;
rpt. New York: Collier Books, 1970.

Tennyson, Alfred Lord. "The Charge of the Light Brigade." <http://www.
nationalcenter.org/ChargeoftheLightBrigade.html>.

The Tigger Movie. Jun Falkenstein. Buena Vista (Disney), 2000.

Weil, Ann. *Red Sails to Capri*. New York: Viking Press, 1952.

To order additional copies of
Steppes of Faith

Or other books by Janice Lemke:
Five Loaves and Two Bowls of Borscht
Finding Strength for the Journey: A Bible Study Guide

Use the web: www.purposepress.net

E-mail: purposepress@gmail.com

Mailing Address:
Janice Lemke
8200 Bliss Rd
Bonanza, OR 97623

Ask about a discount rate for bulk orders.

Profits go toward ministry in Ukraine.

LaVergne, TN USA
19 August 2010
193754LV00003B/2/P